Identities in Context

Identities in Context
Individuals and Discourse in Action

Andrew McKinlay
Chris McVittie

WILEY-BLACKWELL

A John Wiley & Sons, Ltd., Publication

Contents

About the Authors

Andy McKinlay is Head of the School of Philosophy, Psychology and Language Sciences at the University of Edinburgh, where he teaches discourse analysis and social psychology. His research interests lie in the areas of identity and discourse. This research has especially focused on the notion of 'problem' identities and on how people strive to develop a positive sense of themselves by taking up or challenging a range of inferences which may be made about them because they are categorized in a particular way. He has published over 50 articles on social psychology and discourse and is co-author (with Chris McVittie) of *Social Psychology and Discourse*, published in 2008 by Wiley-Blackwell. Beyond work he is married, enjoys jazz guitar, and owns three dogs which he enjoys walking if it is not too rainy.

Chris McVittie is Senior Lecturer in Social Psychology and Qualitative Methods at Queen Margaret University, Edinburgh. His research interests focus on issues of discourse and identities, especially in contexts of inclusion and exclusion. He has published widely and presented at numerous national and international conferences on these topics and is co-author (with Andy McKinlay) of *Social Psychology and Discourse*, published in 2008 by Wiley-Blackwell. Outside work, he is married, and enjoys playing golf and having the attention of three cats who share their home with him.

Preface

The topic of 'who we are' is one that has attracted scholars and thinkers through-out the centuries. What we have aimed to provide in this book is an overview of contemporary research on this topic from one particular theoretical standpoint: the view on identity as seen from the perspective of those researchers whose focus is on analysing discourse. Of course, discursive researchers had studied a whole range of topics within the broader domain of social psychology, and in a previous book (McKinlay and McVittie, 2008) we showed how the discursive approach can be applied to a wide range of social psychological topics. However, as was also the case in that text, we do not intend here to offer up a 'defence' of discursive meth-ods. Our view is that discursive research is a mature enough discipline to no longer require pleas for acceptance from other branches of psychology. Hopefully, as the reader moves through the following chapters, he or she will be persuaded that the analysis of discourse is a fruitful means for exploring the topic of identity.

We have chosen to organize this book around what we regard as 'key themes' in the psychology of identity. The earlier chapters focus on nationality, ethnicity, religion and gender because these are important 'dimensions' of identity which have been of long-standing interest to social scientists. The later chapters turn to what might be described as 'contexts' of identity: health, law, organizations, and the virtual world. However, as the reader will discover, we do not view these dimensions and contexts as analytically foundational. The viewpoint of identity set out in this book is that identities are constructed, maintained and challenged through the particularities of social interaction. So, for example, when someone is described in terms of nationality, or when identities are made out within legal contexts, this is a matter of discursive action. In this respect, the dimensions and contexts which provide the chapter headings for this book should be viewed merely as signposts to help the reader move through the text, rather than as analysts' terms whose meanings and consequences can be taken for granted. That said, we hope that by selecting these themes as structuring devices we will allow the reader to easily draw comparisons both within the realm of discursive research presented here and across domains by comparing the discursive researcher's perspective on, say, ethnicity with that of other forms of research such as experimental social psychology or sociology. This marks out one potential advantage for the present text. A number of previous texts have used the analysis of discourse as a means of making sense of identity. However, often these texts have been especially concerned with warranting the discursive approach in contrast with that of other approaches, or in arguing for one particular form of discursive research over another as the 'best' way to analyse identities. While we acknowledge the usefulness of setting out methodological distinctions within social science in general, and within discursive research in particular, our aim here is quite different. We seek to offer the reader an up-to-date account of how discursive researchers have explored major themes in identity irrespective of whether they would describe themselves as 'critical discourse analysts', 'conversation analysts' or in terms of some other discursive brand.

In pursuing this goal, we have tried to develop a text which reaches beyond the narrow interests of one section of social psychology. In the following chapters, we will see people discuss themselves and others in terms of gender, the colour of their skin, which god they worship, and where they come from. And we will discover the positive features of such talk, as well as its darker side. In addition, we will follow people as they construct a sense of themselves and others in a variety of contexts such as health and the law. What all of this means is that the following chapters will, we hope, provide an important resource for a large range of people – in fact anyone who is concerned with who we are (or can be said to be) and what consequences follow for us from that. So anyone who finds themselves dealing with the social realities of everyday life, or who is involved with contexts of health or the law or employment, should be able to make use of this book, precisely because the discursive research approach is one that foregrounds the importance of understanding real people in real interactions from their own perspectives.

We have sought to ensure that this book provides the reader with access to a wide range of contemporary research. We have also tried to ensure that what is on offer here has a genuinely international flavour. Much of the development of discursive research can be traced back to Europe and to the United States. However, the topic of identity is one that has been pursued by discursive researchers around the world. We have tried to give the reader a sense of this in the examples of research that we have selected.

Advantages for the Student

As with our previous book, the design of the present text is intended to aid the student reader in his or her studies. Each chapter is structured around clearly 'signposted' themes that are also presented on the title page of each chapter. At the end of each chapter there is a 'Chapter Summary' box in which the major issues raised within the chapter are briefly reviewed. There is also a 'Connections' box for each chapter in which the reader is offered guidance about the ways in which issues that arise in that chapter are picked up in other chapters. In addition, each chapter concludes by identifying several 'Further Readings' which are accompanied by brief descriptions which allow the reader to see their relevance. In any field, jargon can be a problem. To help with this, each chapter identifies potentially difficult terms which are marked out in bold font. These terms appear alphabetically on the front page of each chapter, under 'Key Terms', and also in the book's 'Glossary' section, where a brief explanation of the term is provided. In each chapter, we have interspersed 'technical' discourse research terms with terms associated with the chapter's main theme, in the hope that this will provide a user-friendly way of coming to grips with discursive research terminology. These terms are usually introduced on their first occurrence in the text, unless they are dealt with substantively later in the book.

Advantages for the Teacher

We have made sure that each chapter of the book is a 'stand-alone' text which could form the basis for one or several lessons in its own right. This is one of the reasons why we have adopted the tactic of focusing each chapter on a particular 'theme' such as 'gender' or on a particular context, such as 'health'. The clearly structured nature of each chapter should allow the teacher to develop lessons of this sort with the minimum of effort. We have also provided 'Connections' boxes for each chapter which describe links between that chapter and other chapters within the book. In this way the teacher can, if he or she wishes, create a series of inter-linked lectures which pursue different topics but which are easily presented as a coherent whole. At the end of each chapter we have also included an 'Activity Box' which provides an idea for how students could practically examine one or more of the themes which arise in the chapter, for example through student projects or student-led seminars.

Acknowledgments

The authors and publisher gratefully acknowledge the permission granted to reproduce the copyright material in this book:

Chapter 3
Lamont, P., Coelho, C. and McKinlay, A. (2009). Explaining the unexplained: Warranting disbelief in the paranormal. *Discourse Studies, 11,* 543–559.

Chapter 4
Seymour-Smith, S. (2008). 'Blokes don't like that sort of thing': Men's negotiation of a 'troubled' self-help group identity. *Journal of Health Psychology, 13,* 785–797.
Richardson, E. (2007). She was workin like foreal': Critical literacy and discourse practices of African American females in the age of hip hop. *Discourse and Society, 18,* 789–809.

Chapter 5
Slade, D., Scheeres, H., Manidis, M., Iedema, R., Dunston, R., Stein-Parbury, J. *et al.* (2008). Emergency communication: The discursive challenges facing emergency clinicians and patients in hospital emergency departments. *Discourse and Communication, 2,* 271–298.
Guise, J., McKinlay, A. and Widdicombe, S. (2010). The impact of early stroke on identity: A discourse analytic study. *Health, 14,* 75–90.

Chapter 6
Tracy, K. (2009). How questioning constructs judge identities: oral argument about same-sex marriage. *Discourse Studies, 11,* 199–221.

Chapter 7
Yamaguchi, T. (2007). Controversy over genetically modified crops in India: Discursive strategies and social identities of farmers. *Discourse Studies, 9,* 87–107.
Holmes, J., Schnurr, S. and Marra, M. (2007). Leadership and communication: Discursive evidence of a workplace culture change. *Discourse and Communication, 1,* 433–451.
Tracy, K. and Durfy, M. (2007). Speaking out in public: Citizen participation in contentious school board meetings. *Discourse and Communication, 1,* 223–249.

Chapter 8
Rellstab, D.H. (2007). Staging gender online: Gender plays in Swiss internet relay chats. *Discourse and Society, 18,* 765–787.

1

Introduction

Topics Covered in this Chapter

Key Terms

Action orientation

Categorization

Conversation analysis

Critical discourse analysis

Discourse analysis

Discourses

Discursive psychology

Face

Flexibility

Foucauldian discourse analysis

Ideology

Interactional context

Interest

Membership categories

Membership categorization analysis

Narrative analysis

Norm

Objective

Orienting

Positioning

Pre-analytic categories

Repertoires

Rhetorical psychology

Self-processes

Social constructionism

Stake

Subject positions

Talk-in-interaction

Variability

Identities in Context: Individuals and Discourse in Action, First Edition. Andrew McKinlay and Chris McVittie.
© 2011 Andrew McKinlay and Chris McVittie. Published 2011 by Blackwell Publishing Ltd.

This book is about identities and discourse. Our aim is to provide the reader with insight into the range of contemporary studies drawn from discursive research literature which have explored how identities are developed, maintained, challenged and resisted within particular domains of interaction. To do this, we will examine certain features of identity such as gender or nationality which have been of abiding interest to social researchers throughout modern history. We will also pursue how identities are folded into specific contexts of interaction such as health

> **Pre-analytic categories**
> Typologies produced by an analyst before the analysis has been performed.

or the law. But we want the reader to be clear from the start that we do not view these features and contexts as **pre-analytic categories** which the researcher draws upon to make sense of research data in the way that a chemist might draw upon the categories of matter in the periodic table. As will be clear from subsequent chapters, our view is that identities and the contexts in which they arise are matters which are constructed, maintained and challenged as people go about their interactional business. In this sense, features such as 'gender' and contexts such as 'health' are elements of interaction which the participants in those interactions produce and reproduce in discourse. And so it is through their descriptions and formulations and reformulations that these features and contexts make their appearance. However, we did want to provide the reader with a text that is easily navigable. So we have chosen to structure the book in this way, around readily recognizable themes, so that the reader will immediately have a 'toehold' on the materials being discussed and also so that he or she will find it easy to compare what is said here with what is said about similar topics in quite different areas of research. Towards the end of this chapter, we will describe what the subsequent chapters will be focusing on. However, before doing that, it is useful to begin by providing a preliminary discussion of the central elements which run throughout those later chapters: identities and discourse.

What Are Identities?

We seldom have difficulty in talking about ourselves and about other people. Indeed, discussing one's friends, one's relatives, celebrities and so on is one of the most natural ways in which we engage with other people. This seems to imply that at an everyday level we all have a very clear grasp on who we are and who other people are. However, throughout the ages, philosophers, scientists, poets, playwrights and other thinkers have challenged our easy acceptance that we know who we are and that we likewise know who others are. In more recent times, social scientists have struggled with the same issue and acknowledge that the term 'identity' and related terms such as 'the self', although prevalent, continue to stand in need of clarification.

The definition of 'identity' provided in the *Oxford English Dictionary* is 'The quality or condition of being the same in substance, composition, nature, properties, or in particular qualities under consideration; absolute or essential sameness; oneness.' This definition helpfully highlights the problem that thinkers have faced throughout the years. On the one hand, the notion of 'being the same in … properties' suggests that we must be considering at least two things, which are the same in respect of their properties. The notion of 'oneness' suggests something quite different: that when we think of identity we think of a single thing. Philosophers sometimes distinguish between these two sorts of notion in terms of qualitative identity and numerical identity. So dogs of a particular breed are qualitatively identical, because they share the same breed characteristics, but AMcK's dog Truffle is numerically identical, and the identity relation here only holds between Truffle and himself. Of course, how this sort of distinction works in practice is a puzzle that modern philosophers, since Leibnitz in the eighteenth century, have argued over.

In the realm of contemporary social science, Weigert, Smith Teitge and Teitge (1986) trace the introduction of the notion of identity back to the work of Erikson (1968), especially to his distinction between 'ego identity' and 'group identity'. Thus we can see right from the start that here too the notion of identity involves a certain sort of ambiguity. It seems to refer both to a person's central being that continues through biographical history and, at the same time, to the fragmentary and temporary social positions and roles which people take up and discard as they interact with others, with the crucial point being that when one of these positions or roles is adopted, the individual concerned can be thought of as identical to others in that position or role. Verkuyten (2005b) captures this dual aspect of identity in saying

> The identity concept is not about individuals as such, nor about society as such, but the relation of the two.
>
> Verkuyten (2005b, p. 42)

In attempting to deal with this sort of dual nature, social psychologists have responded by developing explanatory frameworks such as social identity theory (Turner and Onorato, 1999), in which 'personal identity' deals with the notion of the unique individual, and 'social identity' represents the aspect of the person that reflects membership of different social groups. Thus 'personal identity' can be used to refer to uniquely individual aspects of oneself that persist through time, while 'social identity' (or, more properly, 'social identities' since it is assumed that we may have many different social identities) can refer to those aspects of society which one draws upon in making sense of oneself as being the same as or different from others. And the social identity theorist is concerned with understanding the cognitive processes which underpin our ability to switch from one of these identities to the other.

One obvious thought is that if there are these two different facets to our use of 'identity', perhaps it would be easier if we had two different terms. And a second term is readily to hand: 'the self'. For example, Owens (2006) argues that although 'self' and 'identity' are sometimes used as synonyms, they refer to quite different concepts and, indeed, to different levels of analysis. In Owens's view, 'identity' refers to a narrower notion which is intrinsically relational, in that identities are categories that people use to specify who they are in relation to other people. In this sense, the term 'identity' is subsumed within a broader notion of 'the self'. So perhaps we could use 'identity' to refer to the 'social' part of ourselves, the bit of ourselves that we think about when we are considering whether we are the same as the other members of some social group or other. And we could use 'the self' to refer to the bit that is especially unique just to us. But this suggestion implies that we have, at least, an uncontroversial view of what 'the self' is. Now it is true that in some respects, the notion of 'the self' has a more established lineage in social science research than does 'identity'. However, there has been a longstanding uneasy awareness that while 'the self' appears to point to an individual, self-hood does not seem to be a unitary phenomenon. As long ago as the nineteenth century, William James suggested that:

> This me is an empirical aggregate of things objectively known. The *I* which knows them cannot itself be an aggregate, neither for psychological purposes need it be considered to be an unchanging metaphysical entity like the Soul …
>
> (James, 1890, pp. 400–401)

And not much later, in the early part of the twentieth century, George H. Mead claimed that:

> The observer who accompanies all our self-conscious conduct is then not the actual 'I' who is responsible for the conduct in propria persona – he is rather the response which one makes to his own conduct.
>
> (Mead, 1913, p. 376)

In fact, in the decades that have followed researchers have noted that 'the self' can refer to a bewildering array of different notions: the self as a person, construed as a bodily whole persevering through time with an accompanying mental aspect which is similarly coherent and temporally enduring; the self as a personality; the self as the focal point of phenomenological experiences; the self as the source of self-knowledge that incorporates the way that one 'tracks' information about oneself and experiences self-awareness; the self as actor or agent that incorporates one's capacities for willed actions and decision-making; the self as a social being concerned with issues of self-presentation and social role performance (Bamberg, De Fina and Schiffrin, 2007; Leary, 2004). The situation is made more complex because different areas of social research have, quite understandably, different 'versions' of the self that reflect that domain's core concerns.

For example, according to sociologists, we as individuals act within the societies in which we find ourselves. So in one way society is created out of our actions but, in another way, it is our actions which determine the nature of society (Giddens, 1991; Stets and Burke, 2005). Here the central idea of the self is that of a thinking being who creates or construes meaning from experience, perhaps conditioned by the symbolic world in which he or she lives, and whose actions are guided by the repository of cultural understandings, probably codified in some way or another in language, which are contained within the mind of that thinking being. Thus the self emerges as a somewhat minimal core entity, capable of self-reflection, whose nature in part reflects and in part is constitutive of its cultural context. One of the most influential discussions of the self to arise from within the sociological domain was that produced by Goffman. In her review of this work, Branaman (1997) outlines Goffman's view of the self as being doubly social. On the one hand, the self is merely a product of the social performances in which it is engaged and thus the self in a sense is no more than the sum of the social roles we adopt. On the other hand, we are not completely 'free' to adopt any old version of the self – the social performances we can successfully accomplish may be constrained by societal features such as status and social hierarchy. Much of this theoretical perspective is centrally determined by Goffman's concern with **'face'** – the idea that we have an abiding concern with presenting a positive image of ourselves to others. However, Branaman goes on to

> **Face**   a representation of self that reflects socially approved attributes.

draw attention to potential contradictions in Goffman's view of the self. If the self is no more than the sum of social performances, then it seems contradictory to suggest that the self is also responsible for impelling us into and out of such performances in order to achieve and maintain a positive 'image' in the eyes of others. The worry here is that there does not seem to be an available version of the self which could count as the master manipulator standing behind all of these face-saving social performances. However, Goffman (1959) himself suggests that in fact this 'puts the cart before the horse': the self that is imputed to us by others as they observe our social performances is an effect, not a cause, of those performances. Goffman does suggest that 'the person', considered as a unique individual with a continuing and traceable biography, may well be different from the sum total of his or her social performances, but even this distinction is at root a social one. The outcome of this is that the sort of self that, for example, philosophers are concerned with apparently plays a vanishingly small role in the sociologist's world.

As another example, psychologists provide a kaleidoscope of different versions of the self which range from a concern with whether the self is locatable in the brain (and, if not, whether it is a legitimate construct at all), through analysis of selves in terms of personality constructs such as neuroticism, to the social psychologist's interest in the self as the locus for issues such as self-esteem or interpersonal relationships. If we restrict ourselves to what social psychologists have said about the self, we discover that they are interested in discovering how well we know ourselves – some people seem to be able to describe themselves in a way which others who know them would agree with, while others do not. Another interest here is in knowing whether different types of 'self' play a role in the sorts of people that an individual might select as friends or soul-mates. Like sociologists, social psychologists display a keen interest in the impact of culture or society on the self. Thus some social psychologists claim that different cultures (e.g. 'Eastern' or 'Western' cultures) produce individuals who think of themselves in characteristically different ways. And of course, different cultures provide different social roles for individuals to inhabit, and social psychologists have also been interested in understanding how and to what extent the self can be subsumed within such roles. Social psychologists are also interested in how people vary on a variety of aspects of the self, for example whether they are concerned with what other people think of them and in how this relates to the types of 'self-presentation' activity that someone might engage in.

Self-processes analytically derived descriptions of psychological forms of thought that are directed towards the self.

What is interesting about these different social psychological pursuits is the focus on **self-processes** associated with oneself, rather than on selves or identity *per se*. In discussing these sorts of process-models of self and identity, Simon (2004) suggests that the social scientist must view identity as both something that explains social interaction and as something that arises out of those interactions. Now this might seem to raise paradoxical worries about whether identity is something that causes itself, worries which are similar to those that seemed to face Goffman. However, Simon suggests that this apparent difficulty can be resolved by viewing identities as mediators between the input we receive from the social world and our subsequent interactions with that world. One consequence of this is that we might be required to view identity as an 'analytic fiction': 'At best, the search for the essence of identity as a "thing", say, in the form of a physiological or hard-wired mental structure, would then be a futile effort' (Simon, 2004, p. 3). In place of this 'futile' search, Simon advocates a 'process-oriented' approach in which our everyday conception of self and identity remains for lay-people, but is no longer an object of study for the scientist.

What we discover, then, is that when we look at social scientific accounts of the self or identity it often seems that social scientists are less concerned than other sorts of thinkers (e.g. philosophers) with establishing a single, agreed definition of the phenomenon under study. Instead, when the self or identity plays a role as a social science construct it is often because social researchers seek to provide empirical evidence on a range of aspects of human existence in which our behaviours in, and our engagement with, other people and with the social environment can be explained by viewing individuals as having some sort of reflective awareness of, or understanding of, what they are like as individuals. Of course a shortcoming of this sort of approach is that we lack a grand, unified definition of 'identity' or 'the self' with which all social researchers will agree. However, these researchers would argue that by focusing in a piecemeal fashion on the variety of different ways in which identity and the self enter social life, and by concentrating on providing detailed definitions only within these strictly limited domains, researchers are able to address what seem to be important aspects of our lives without being hung up, right at the very beginning, with problems of terminology and definition of the most general level.

So it looks as though our attempt to define 'identity' is, then, only partially successful. Even if we attempt to make use of ancillary terms such as 'the self', we seem left with an unsatisfying situation where sometimes we seem to be referring to unique individuals, and sometimes to people understood as exemplars of social categories – in terms of 'being the same as' other people. And exploring fields of social research such as sociology and experimental social psychology seem to take us no further forward. Indeed, in some sense self and identity seem to disappear from view. One point of interest here, however, is that many social researchers who take themselves to be studying identity apparently ignore one potentially useful resource. We said at the outset that issues of self and other seem to be matters which the lay person deals with all the time in day-to-day interaction. This is at least suggestive of the fact that there might be a different way to approach the study of identity – to attend closely to the ways in which identity and identity issues appear in people's everyday discourse. Indeed, this opens out the tantalizing possibility that the sorts of definitional issues which we have been wrangling with over the last couple of paragraphs may actually have a quite different sort of resolution. Perhaps some of these problems of definition arise because the notion of identity that people actually experience, in their day-to-day lives, is a quite different sort of thing from that which is captured in the analysts' definitions we have been examining. So perhaps a more fruitful avenue would be to discover how people, from their own perspectives, make sense of their own identities in their own discourse. But before we can see if there is any mileage in this idea, we need, first, to turn to the prior issue of deciding what we mean by 'discourse'.

What Is Discourse?

The appeal of turning to the study of discourse has long been recognized in the social sciences. What makes this sort of research distinctive is that it treats discourse as a topic in its own right. Instead of viewing what people say (or write) as in some sense an inconvenient barrier to what they are 'really' thinking, discourse is viewed as a phenomenon which has its own properties, properties which have an impact on people and their social interaction. One important aspect of this approach is to emphasize the way in which participants themselves have an at least implicit understanding that discourse has these properties. In using discourse, participants often rely on some of its properties to accomplish a specific social action. So understanding social actions and interactions just is understanding the ways in which people use discourse to accomplish these actions and to engage in these

Action orientation
the property of talk which directs it towards accomplishing specific outcomes or goals.
Social constructionism
the view that social phenomena are best understood as the outcome of discursive interaction rather than as extra-discursive phenomena in their own right.
Interactional context
the background or setting within which two or more people engage in social action.

interactions. It is this feature of discursive research which is sometimes referred to as the **action orientation** of discourse. And precisely because of this action orientation, discursive researchers take discourse to be a constitutive affair. What it is for someone to have a particular identity is constituted by the discourse which is produced and the actions which are thereby accomplished. And one of the actions that might be performed in discourse is **socially constructing** for oneself or others a particular identity. Another feature of discursive research is the assumption that constructive actions of this sort do not exist in a vacuum. So if someone takes up or challenges an identity, this particular discursive action is likely to be linked with other actions that are being performed within the **interactional context** in which the identity claim arises.

As with any field of research, discursive research encompasses a variety of different theoretical standpoints. Some discursive researchers view society as a his-

Ideology an organized set of ideas which typifies the thinking of a group or society.
Norm a standard or rule which applies to human behaviour.

torical entity in which particular ways of thinking have become crystallized in the form of an **ideology** or social **norm**. Because of this, they hold the view that some forms of talk are, in a sense, already predetermined for members of that society, and that the range of discursive actions that they can accomplish is limited by such ideological forces. Other discursive researchers draw similar conclusions about discrete parts of society. So, for example, they suggest that within institutions such as health or the law, what we say and do is partly a reflection of the historical development of those particular institutions. This does not just refer to the fact that there may be normative or legal constraints on what we say in these contexts, but that our very ways of thinking about those contexts are 'pre-set' by our own development as members of the particular society in which we find ourselves. Yet other discursive researchers hold a more sanguine view of the potential impact of society upon the individual. From their perspective, discourse is root-and-branch constructive, and this extends not only to unique matters of talk as they might arise in a particular conversation, but applies equally to 'larger scale' forms of thinking or categorization. So for these discursive researchers, for example, what it is to have a particular gender identity or a particular ethnic identity is determined completely by how these notions are worked out in discourse, and the analyst need make no recourse to extra-discursive notions such as ideologies of femininity or race in explaining how such an identity appears and is treated during an interaction. Thus while some discursive researchers feel that large-scale issues such as ideology, power and socio-historical forces are intrinsic to the research programme, others claim that these issues are only amenable to analysis to the extent that their participants can be seen themselves to make reference to such issues.

Associated with these theoretical differences are corresponding debates about methodology. For those with a broader interest in issues of ideology or power, the materials which can be drawn on as data are extensive and can include a wide range of both written and spoken texts, including newspapers, government reports, educational texts, or any other written sources generated within a specific domain such as health or law. On the other hand, those discursive researchers who eschew reference to explanatory concepts lying beyond matters dealt with by participants themselves tend to restrict themselves to a narrower range of data. In many cases, these are verbatim accounts of what people actually said. Even here, dispute may arise over what counts as an 'appropriate' verbatim account. In particular, some forms of discursive research restrict attention to verbatim accounts of what is said by people in 'naturally occurring' talk arising out of real-life social interactions, with the implication that some forms of interaction, notably research interviews, are not 'real-life' enough to produce acceptable data.

So it turns out that if a discursive researcher were to answer our question 'what is discourse', that answer will depend on the particular theoretical and methodological position which he or she inhabits. We mention this here for a very particular reason. In the chapters that follow, we will make little attempt to highlight these sorts of theoretical and methodological debate. Instead, we will be focusing on how discursive researchers, of whatever bent, have sought to throw light on identity. However, we did want the reader to be aware that the findings we discuss in subsequent chapters are drawn from a range of different research perspectives. As an aid to developing this awareness, we provide below some thumbnail sketches of some of the more influential strands in discursive research which have informed identity research as it is developed throughout the rest of this book.

Two approaches to discursive research which lay emphasis on the influence of ideology on discourse are **critical discourse analysis** and **Foucauldian discourse analysis**. Critical discourse analysts (Fairclough, 1995; Meyer, 2001; Van Dijk, 2001; Wodak, 2001a) are concerned with the way in which social and political inequalities are embedded within our discourse. So in considering gender identities, say, a critical discourse analyst will want to understand how ideologies reproduce unequal aspects of masculinity and femininity. Arguably, from this perspective such ideologies can be

> **Critical discourse analysis**
> the analysis of discourse with an emphasis on the way it is affected by power and ideology.
> **Foucauldian discourse analysis**
> a form of discourse analysis which relies on the work of Foucault and emphasizes the historical and ideological aspects of discourse.

thought of as existing within society as a whole and exerting a social force that constrains the ways in which women and men can think about themselves. An important aspect of critical discourse analysis is that research is viewed as having the potential to challenge these sorts of ideological forces.

Foucauldian discourse analysis (Parker, 1992; Burman and Parker, 1993) draws its inspiration from the work of Michel Foucault (Foucault, 1980, 2002). Foucault's view was that the structure of language reflects the historical development of what is being discursively represented. Because of this, language shapes or conditions the way we can think of things. However, language itself arises out of our own social practices. So, over time, this language structure itself develops in response to the activities of societal members as they act upon the social world. One result of this interactive process is that particular ways of thinking about an issue come to be seen as the obvious ways of thinking about that issue and so, like critical discourse analysts, Foucauldian discourse analysts seek to explore how these sorts of ideological forces impact on our own use of discourse. However, from this latter perspective the issue is not so much to grasp how society as a whole is structured into powerful elites whose thinking becomes the ideological norm, but instead to understand how particular domains such as health or the law embed or codify specific sorts of historical-ideological features. In part arising out of this focus on specific social and historical domains,

Subject positions   a social role or standpoint that is made available to the individual as a result of social action being embedded within a large-scale or framing discourse.

Foucauldian discourse analysts have a greater interest than their critical discourse cousins in how identities are represented by the **subject positions** we all inhabit in such discourse domains; what, for example, are the real-life consequences of discovering that when one enters hospital, one acquires an identity of an 'ill person' or a 'doctor' depending both on our own histories and on the socio-historical development of the health domain as a social phenomenon.

Two approaches which are usually associated with a rejection of these sorts of ideological notion are **conversation analysis** and **discursive psychology**. Here, the view is not that ideological discourse does not occur but that ideologies do not represent useful analytic referents which exist outwith the context of discourse itself. Conversation analysis (Sacks, 1992; Hutchby and Wooffitt, 1998; ten Have, 1999) grew out of the work of Harvey Sacks and the theoretical and methodological interests of the ethnomethodology movement, especially the work of Harold Garfinkel (Heritage, 1984) and the work of Erving Goffman on the social structures of everyday life (Goffman, 1959).

Conversation analysis   the collection and analysis of naturally occurring talk emphasizing its sequential properties and the actions performed.
Discursive psychology   the use of discursive techniques to analyse talk of psychological states and the application of those analyses to real world settings.

Conversation analysis focuses on the social actions which people perform in naturally occurring interactions. Its emphasis is on the way that sequences of utterances are organized and it examines how utterances are designed to accomplish specific actions. Here, the action orientation of discourse receives particular emphasis, along with the idea that participants may co-produce such actions, and the contexts of talk which conversation analysts draw upon are sometimes referred to as **talk-in-interaction**. Conversation analysts are concerned with discrete 'action sequences' which arise in discourse. In particular, they examine the ways in which participants in a sequentially unfolding interaction **orient** themselves to the normative expectations which any competent speaker can be expected to display in relation to such sequences. So, for example, a competent user of dis-

> **Talk-in-interaction**   discourse which reflects and is constitutive of the local context of a particular social interaction.
> **Orienting**   interpreting what is said in a specific way and displaying this interpretation in how one responds.

course is likely to display an understanding that when two people meet, one greeting is normally followed by a greeting in response. And the speakers' awareness of this expectation can be publicly displayed, for example, in how the interaction will sequentially unfold if a greeting is followed by a silent response. It is this public aspect of the way participants understand each other's talk which underpins the conversation analyst's analytic claims. The analyst warrants a particular claim by drawing attention to the public display of understanding which the participants provide for each other. In terms of identity, then, the conversation analyst is not, for example, concerned with whether ideologies of nationhood or race are underwater currents around which the participants' talk swirls at any given moment. Instead, the analyst picks out for study those elements of talk in which the participants themselves produce versions of national or ethnic identity and then subsequently accept as unremarkable, or take up and challenge, such identifications.

Discursive psychology (Edwards, 1997, 2005; Edwards and Potter, 2005; Potter, 2003) was developed by Jonathan Potter and Derek Edwards and is closely aligned with the theoretical and methodological approaches represented by conversation analysis. However, discursive psychology is especially concerned with a rejection of the theory and method of cognitive psychology. Instead of viewing phenomena such as memory or perception as interior mental states, the discursive psychologist explores the ways in which such phenomena get to be introduced and dealt with in talk. So this approach focuses on a switch of interest away from cognitions as mental states to how talk makes cognitions or emotions inferable outcomes of what is said. This switch to understanding how inferences of this sort are made available underpins a particular interest in how people display sensitivities about, and manage the potential interactional consequences of, inferences that other people might draw

about themselves in virtue of what they have said. This is sometimes referred to as the management of **stake** and **interest**. Of special interest in the present context is that talk often makes available inferences about what sort of person one is – inferences, in other words, about one's identity. So discursive psychologists view identity talk as the sort of context in which people may display, through what they say, that they have a stake in how

> **Stake**   an interest in or concern with how what is said is interpreted by hearers.
> **Interest**   a concern held by someone that is relevant to the discursive actions that are being produced.

they are perceived and are attempting to manage the sorts of inferences that can be drawn about them, such as inferences about one's currently ascribed identity, or

Membership categorization analysis analysis of discourse that proceeds by examining the ways in which people are characterized as belonging to particular social groups.
Membership categories discursive labels indicating that an individual can be classified as belonging to a particular group.

inferences about how one views other identities (e.g. inferences that one is or is not prejudiced towards those other identities). Allied to this is a focus, shared with conversation analysts, on **membership categorization analysis**. This is a form of analysis that pays particular attention to the way that **membership categories** such as social group labels get introduced into and managed within talk.

Other discursive research perspectives lie somewhere in between these critical and conversation analytic extremes. **Discourse analysis** (Potter and Wetherell, 1987; Potter, 1997; Wetherell and Potter, 1998) has explored the ways in which our 'accounts' of actions and events display interesting properties of **variability** and **flexibility**. 'Variability' means that different sorts of accounts might be generated in order to accomplish different effects. 'Flexibility' means that the same sort of account could be used to perform different social actions on different occasions. Discourse analysts suggest that we can study similarity and variation in the accounts which people produce to understand how language is used to perform a variety of social actions. In particular, discourse analysts attempt to show how such flexibility and variability is deployed in the 'construction' of 'versions' of actions and events. For this reason, discourse analysts often refer to themselves as social constructionists because they

Discourse analysis the collection and analysis of verbal material, spoken or written, which emphasizes properties such as structure and variability and focuses on action.
Variability a property of discourse that allows for different discursive constructions to be employed for similar ends.
Flexibility a property of discourse that allows for similar discursive constructions to be employed for different ends.

wish to examine how people deploy flexible and variable accounts in producing or constructing a particular version of an action or event. Thus, like other discursive researchers, the discourse analyst has an abiding interest in the action-orientation of discourse. Discourse analysts are also interested in categorizing accounts in terms of the **discourses** or **repertoires** to which they belong. So, for example, if the discourse analyst seeks to understand gender identities, he or she might be interested in how repertoires or discourses of masculinity and femininity are reproduced in the accounts that people produce.

Discourses extended elements of talk and/or text that represent routinized ways of formulating a broad topic such as masculinity or oppression (see 'repertoires').
Repertoires extended elements of talk and/or text that represent routinized ways of formulating a broad topic such as masculinity or oppression (see 'discourses').

Rhetorical psychology the application of discursive techniques to the study of persuasive language and, more broadly, the view that talk is inherently argumentative.

Rhetorical psychology arises out of Michael Billig's work, especially his influential book *Arguing and Thinking: A Rhetorical Approach to Social Psychology* (Billig, 1987). In this book, Billig explores the history of persuasive talk and then produces a number of analyses of the

way that everyday argumentation relies on implicit rhetorical skills. For example, he draws attention to the way
that ordinary processes of **categorization** are often produced in talk alongside processes of particularization in
which people provide argumentative counter-examples

> **Categorization** organizing experience by using terms which denote sorts or kinds of phenomena.

to general claims. Billig has also been influential in our understanding of national
identities by applying some of these insights to his work on the everyday ways in
which nationhood is culturally represented to us in acts of 'banal nationalism'.

Narrative analysis (Daiute and Lightfoot, 2003)
stems in part from the work of William Labov (1972).
Narratives can be thought of as extended portions of
talk which have an identifiable, story-like structure
such as a beginning, middle and end. This form of

> **Narrative analysis** the analysis of talk in terms of its story-like elements.

analysis is considered to be important in the study of identity because people
often rely upon biographical narratives in trying to make sense of their own experiences and to report on the important aspects of their lives.

Identities in Discourse

So far we have suggested that the definition of 'identity' is a challenging task and
we offered hints that the study of discourse might provide some help in this area.
Now that we have examined in some detail what discourse is, we can go some way
towards filling out that hint by setting out some of the central features of identities
that discursive researchers consider important:

- Identities are discursive characterizations of someone (either oneself or others) which are not reduc-
  ible to **objective** facts about a person.

> **Objective** pertaining to aspects of the world independently of any individual's view or perspective.

- These categorizations construct a version of that
  person either as a unique individual or as being categorizable in a way that
  establishes commonalities with other people.
- These characterizations are action-oriented, in that they are bound up with
  social actions such as inclusion or exclusion, or blaming or exonerating, or maintaining or challenging established social norms.
- These categorizations are, like all discourse, situational either because they
  draw on discursive features of the local context of their production or because
  they reflect broader issues of ideology.
- Some analysts will go further and argue that these
  categorizations are not 'free creations' but rather
  reflect the **positioning** which ideological structures in society (e.g. ideologies of gender or class)
  provide for us.

> **Positioning** adopting or being placed in a particular role through discursive means with the assumption that what is said will be heard as influenced by this perspective.

So identity discourse, just like all other forms of discourse, should be understood as flexible and varied, and as intrinsically caught up with the action-orientation of language. People will construct identities for themselves and for others as they interact with others through discourse. In part, what this means is that the interactional consequences of a particular identity claim depend in part on what other actions are taking place within the local context in which the identity claim arises. It also means that people will display a sensitivity to the sorts of inferences which such identity talk makes available, and so issues of identity management may well arise as other bits of interactional business are being performed. So this move to discourse as a topic in its own right is accompanied by a shift away from a search for the 'essential core' of the concept of identity to a consideration of how identities are 'performed' just like any other social actions. And this move is accompanied in turn by a switch in emphasis towards the everyday practices that people produce within social interactions. As we follow the rest of the chapters in this book we will, however, discover that on occasion some discursive researchers will also draw on broad notions of social power and ideology in making sense of how such identity 'work' gets accomplished in discourse. We will also see a range of occasions where the notion of membership categorization plays an explicit or implicit role. It is clear that one of the practices that we all engage in when describing ourselves and others is that of categorization. And so we will find that some of the research which is presented in later chapters is precisely directed towards understanding what happens when someone is characterized as being a member of some social category or other.

In summary, it seems as though discursive researchers have in many respects followed the practices of other researchers. As we saw at the start of this chapter, many social scientists forego the attempt to provide a universally acceptable definition of 'identity' or 'self'. Instead, they provide locally relevant definitions which are useful in pursuing other projects such as understanding self-esteem or measuring self-awareness. In an analogous fashion, discursive researchers treat identity discourse as something that is variable, flexible, contextually sensitive and influenced by the action orientations of those who produce that discourse. Of course, unlike the former, in the latter case things could not be otherwise, since this is entirely consistent with the overall theoretical approach to discourse which is the cornerstone of the discursive researcher's work.

About this Book

We said at the beginning that we have drawn upon common themes and contexts in the study of identity because we want to provide the reader with a preliminary 'toehold' on the material being covered in each chapter. Hopefully, the caveat we introduced there, about this being a textual convenience rather that the introduction of pre-analytic categories, now makes more sense to the reader. To the discursive researcher, identities are accomplished through discourse, so a particular religious identity, say, is not a predetermined given from which other conclusions follow, but is instead an interactional outcome of the actions and interactions which set the context in which the relevant identity claim appears.

Chapters 2, 3 and 4 examine gender identities, national identities, ethnic identities and religious identities. We will include in each of these chapters a consideration of how each of these identity terms has been defined within the broader social science arena. These broad discussions can be found under headings such as 'What are national identities?' Our goal here is to help the reader to locate what discursive researchers have said about these identities within a wider framework of social analysis. As we discuss these definitions, we will note the ways in which, for each case, the 'traditional' definitions provided for these identities stand in need of some amendment.

In Chapter 2, we will focus on national identities. We will find that the term 'nation' seems to refer to a variety of different phenomena and seems to involve characterizations not only of oneself but also of 'the other'. As will be the case for all of the other chapters in this book, we will set out the claim that this form of identity is best understood from the perspective of the discursive researcher. Having done this, we will turn to consider discursive research on national identities by first considering issues of time and place. We will note how people such as politicians draw upon national histories to create national identities, but we will also see how features of talk such as 'place identities' play a role. We then move on to a discussion of prejudice in respect of national identities, and conclude with a brief foray into the world of the media.

Chapter 3 moves on to the study of ethnicity and religion and the ways in which ethnic and religious identities are formulated. The chapter begins drawing attention to similarities between ethnic and national identities, and then moves on to provide a definition of 'ethnic identity'. Some examples of discursive research in ethnic identities are then examined, with particular reference to the notion of 'hybrid identities'. The chapter then switches tack to examine religious identities and, once again, we start with the definitional task. The chapter then presents data on how religious leaders and religious followers make out a sense of themselves in relation to their faith. Finally, as in the previous chapter, we turn to the question of prejudice as it applies to ethnic and religious identities.

Chapter 4 turns attention to gender identities. As with previous chapters, we spend some time at the start of this chapter by exploring different definitions of 'gender identity'. The main body of the chapter is given over to a discussion of women's gender identities, focusing on women's constructions of themselves in relation to their interpersonal relationships. Next, the chapter discusses men's gender identities with specific reference to 'macho' identities. We then briefly discuss how gender identities can be interwoven with other forms of identity. Again, this chapter concludes by discussing some of the ways in which these gender identities can leave men and women facing problems of prejudice.

Chapter 5 marks a change in the text. Here, we move away from considering different general 'types' of identity such as nationality, ethnicity, religion and gender and turn instead to a consideration of the sorts of context in which specific identities make their appearance. In this chapter, we examine identities as they appear within the context of health. We begin by looking at the ways in which the identity of 'being ill' is constructed and at the parallel notion of the construction of the health worker's professional identity. Among the contexts which we focus on are the interactional settings of doctor and patient and psychotherapist and client. We then discuss how people weave concerns with 'care' into their talk and then examine how these sorts of discursive features are played out in the hospital setting. Finally, we conclude by examining challenges to health identities by looking at how one's identity as a 'healthy person' can be undermined and at the different ways in which the health professional's identity as a competent practitioner can come under challenge.

Chapter 6 moves us into legal contexts. In this chapter, we are going to begin by looking at how legal contexts offer the lawyer and the judge opportunities to develop a sense of themselves and others. We will note that in this context, discourse is bounded by a set of legal and procedural requirements. And yet, we will find, the lawyer and the judge are able to negotiate these constraints in a way that still allows them to engage in the social construction of identities. We will see that this applies not only to the legal professionals' talk, but also to legal writings. As we follow these discussions, we will see that legal professionals are not only concerned with developing their own legal identities, but also with constructing versions of other people as they pursue their legal projects. But in the next part of the chapter, we will discover that lay-people within the legal system have their own constructive resources at hand. And this will be seen to be the case both within the courtroom, where witnesses rely on techniques such as 'narrative expansion' and outside the courtroom walls, where people construct identities for other people who are, or may be, caught up in the legal system.

Chapter 7 switches to the context of the organization. The chapter begins by noting that occupational identities are complex creations, and that they reflect interactions with the employing organization, with co-workers, and with clients of the services that the organization provides. The creation of such identities is, then, inextricably linked with the practices that occur within such organizations. After discussing the ways in which identities are created both within the organization itself and in interaction with the 'outside' world, this chapter moves on to consider two specific examples: the helpline service and the educational sphere. For example, we will see that when people contact helpline services, one of their identity concerns is to demonstrate that they are responsible people in having justifiably 'bothered' those who provide such services. We will also see that the vexed issue of educational policy and practice is an arena in which schools are required to demonstrate identity concerns that lie far beyond the scope of the three Rs. The chapter concludes by exploring the sorts of identity challenge that can arise in organizational contexts, such as the difficulty of negotiating unemployment status or acquiring a problematic workplace identity.

Finally, Chapter 8 takes us into yet another context: the virtual world. The chapter begins by providing an account of communications technologies and the identities which can be constructed in such contexts. In particular, we look at phenomena of turn-taking in text messaging and at the relevance of social groups to processes of identity formation among computer users. The chapter then moves on to consider the special virtual domain of online communities. Here, we examine how identities can be formulated and renegotiated in such communities and how individuals strive to develop and maintain 'authentic' identities. The chapter continues by considering a further aspect of virtual identities: identities as they are constructed in online support groups. The chapter moves to a close by discussing some of the challenges to identity that can arise in this domain.

A Note on Transcription

Each of the following chapters contains a range of transcription extracts drawn from research articles. Wherever possible, we have tried to retain the original author's format and line-numbering scheme. However, the typographical layout of this text differs from that of many academic journals. For this reason, the reader will note that on some occasions, where an extract uses line numbering, text which spreads across more than one line is denoted by a single line number. In addition, where we have thought it helpful, we have included the original author's foreign language transcription along with the translation into English.

The transcription of talk is a complex affair. Most discursive researchers rely upon a form of notation developed by Gail Jefferson. However, transcription schemes vary, and the reader will find that different researchers have their own transcription preferences. In order to aid the reader in making sense of the transcribed examples presented in this book, Box 1.1 describes the way that special symbols are used in transcribing talk. The box summarizes some of the main features of Jefferson's transcription notation which is described more fully, together with explanatory examples, in Jefferson (2004).

Box 1.1   Transcription Notation

[ ]	Overlapping talk is shown by square brackets, with '[' indicating where the overlap begins and ']' indicating where the overlapped utterance (or part of an utterance) stops.
=	An 'equal to' sign, '=', at the end of one line and another at the end of the succeeding line, indicates that there is no gap between the two lines.

. (dot)	A dot in parentheses, '(.)', indicates a very slight gap.
: (colon)	A colon, ':', indicates that the sound immediately preceding the colon has been elongated, with the lengthening of the sound indicated by the number of colons.
↑	An upwards pointing arrow, '↑', indicates that the speaker is raising pitch.
↓	A downwards pointing arrow, '↓', indicates the speaker is lowering pitch.
Numbers	Numbers in parentheses, e.g. (0.3) indicate time elapsed in tenths of a second.
Underlining	Underlining of letters or words (e.g. 'Doh') indicates that the speaker is stressing that part of the speech by increasing volume or raising or lowering pitch.
Upper case	Upper case (e.g. 'DOH') indicates that the speaker's utterance is produced with a particularly high volume.
Punctuation	Punctuation markers indicate the speaker's intonation. For example, the question mark, '?', indicates a 'questioning' intonation.
° (degree sign)	The superscripted degree sign, '°', indicates unvoiced production.
< (left outward facing arrow)	Placed before a word, a left outward facing arrow, '<' indicates a hurried start. Placed after a word it indicates that the word stopped suddenly.
> < (right/left inward facing arrows)	Right/left inward facing arrows, '> <', surrounding an utterance (or part of an utterance) indicate the speech is speeding up.
< > (left/right outward facing arrows)	Left/right outward facing arrows, < >, surrounding an utterance (or part of an utterance) indicate the speech is slowing down.
– (dash)	A dash, '–', indicates that an utterance is 'cut-off'
hhh	A row of instances of the letter 'h', 'hhh', indicates an out-breath.
.hhh	A row of instances of the letter 'h' prefixed by a dot, '.hhh', indicates an in-breath.
( )	Empty parentheses, ( ), indicate that the transcriber could not make out what was said or, alternatively, who was speaking.
(Doh) (word in parentheses)	Placing parentheses around a word indicates that the transcription is uncertain.
(( ))	Doubled parentheses contain transcriber's descriptions.

Chapter Summary

Two ideas are drawn upon throughout this book – identity and discourse. Thinkers throughout the centuries have tried to produce an acceptable definition of 'identity'. Most of these indicate that identity involves both the idea of unique, individuality and the apparently contrasting notion of two or more people sharing the same qualities because they share the 'same' identity. So identity is sometimes treated as an individualistic thing and sometimes as a social thing grounded in social group categorizations. A suggestion is made that this potentially problematic mix of features may be better understood by examining the discourse of identity as it is actually used by people in everyday life. This leads to a discussion of the nature of discourse. The key suggestion here is that unlike other forms of study, discursive research treats discourse as a topic in its own right. However, it is noted that different approaches to discursive research focus on different aspects of discourse. A description is provided of some of these different approaches and of how they deal with discourse.

A common thread that runs through many of these approaches is that analysing discourse involves treating discourse as context-dependent, action-oriented and as socially constructive. In light of this, the chapter moves on to suggest that 'identity' is a notion that stands in no need of a single, unifying definition. Instead, the discursive researcher should examine how identity discourse is produced and dealt with within the specific particularities of the interactional contexts in which it appears.

Further Reading

McKinlay, A. and McVittie, C. (2008). *Social Psychology and Discourse*. Oxford: Wiley-Blackwell.

The goal of this book is to provide a broader understanding of the relationships between discursive research and central themes in social psychology, beyond the narrow confines of identity research. It therefore represents a 'companion reader' to the present text.

Activity Box

The suggestion in this chapter is that we can understand identity when we understand how identity discourse is produced in everyday talk. Pick two items from a newspaper in which characterizations of people appear. Either might involve what happened on television last night, or a description of the latest political fiasco, or even the love-life of your favourite movie actor or sports-person. Read through the article and decide what sort of identities are in play as the story unfolds. Are there other actions which are being performed at the same time (e.g. is someone being accused, or blamed, or defended)? What do you perceive to be important similarities or differences in the two newspaper accounts? In the context of producing identities, why do you think these similarities or differences appear?

2

National Identities

Topics Covered in this Chapter

Key Terms

Apartheid

Asylum-seekers

Attributions

Banal nationalism

Concessions

Disavowals

Disclaimer

Evaluation

Globalization

Imagined community

Immigrants

Macro-analyses

Metaphors

Narrative

Nationalism

New racism

Place-identities

Prejudice

Supra-national

Temporal discourse

The other

Undermining

Identities in Context: Individuals and Discourse in Action, First Edition. Andrew McKinlay and Chris McVittie.
© 2011 Andrew McKinlay and Chris McVittie. Published 2011 by Blackwell Publishing Ltd.

> *Former US vice-president DAN QUAYLE: 'I was recently on a tour of Latin America, and the only regret I have was that I didn't study Latin harder in school so I could converse with those people.'*
>
>   *Daily Record*, July 2006

At first blush Quayle's suggestion (or at least the suggestion attributed to him by the *Daily Record*) that the people of Latin America all speak the language of the ancient Romans seems farcical. But although inaccurate, the suggestion does draw upon something that most of us believe: it seems natural to assume that people who share a geographical locality also share other similarities. If outsiders think of the citizens of Brazil, then it is the social and cultural similarities of Brazilians, including footballing prowess but also including speaking Portuguese, that probably come to mind. If you imagine what an Argentinean is like, perhaps you think of someone skilled in the tango, but you probably also think of someone who speaks Spanish. So Quayle was attempting to represent something that most people believe: the citizens of a particular nation state all have features and properties that mark them out as different in some way from the citizens of other nation states, and this includes the language they speak. However, appealing though this notion of 'the nation' might be, researchers from fields such as social psychology, sociology, social anthropology and linguistics have spent decades demonstrating that it is over-simplistic. So before we explore the complexities of how national identities are brought into play in discourse, it is useful to start by getting a clearer handle on what exactly we mean when we talk of nations and national identities. Once we have done that, we will turn our consideration to some important aspects of such identities: time and place. Finally, we will spend some time looking at how national identities are sometimes bound up with forms of prejudice.

What Are National Identities?

A short answer to this question is that national identities are those identities which we or others take ourselves to have in virtue of the nation to which we belong. Unfortunately, as a definition this is not worth a great deal. Because although, as a result of the discussions presented in the last chapter, we now have a reasonable working notion of what 'identity' means in the context of discursive research, we have not yet established how to understand 'nation'. But this is an important task. Across the world, the precise nature of what 'the nation' is, and in consequence the precise nature of what 'national identity' means, has become a subject for debate. Taking Europe as an example, it is clear that the fall of the Iron Curtain in 1989 led to major changes in national geography. What had once been two countries, East and West Germany, became one, Germany. What had been one country, Yugoslavia, became several: Bosnia and Herzegovina, Croatia, Macedonia, Montenegro, Serbia, Slovenia, and arguably Kosovo. Changes such as this were matched by large-scale movements of individuals across Europe, especially in terms of people from Eastern Europe seeking to take up residence in Western Europe. There are other influences which also play a role here. For example, Giroux (1995) argues that economic processes of **globalization** represent a major threat to the status of the nation state. Forces such as the increased internationalization of capital and the creation of giant cross-national corporations are reflected in the development of **supra-national** political entities such as the European Union. So history demonstrates that the question of what a nation is, and who its peoples are, is not one that is readily answered. In discussing this complexity, social researchers have sought to take on board the way in which the rigid lines and primary colours of the schoolchild's atlas can be in some sense misleading.

> **Globalization** a reference to international processes in which facets of life such as economic prosperity or legal frameworks are said to have taken on characteristics that transcend national boundaries.
>
> **Supra-national** a term used to refer to elements of interaction or organizational forms which arise at levels beyond that of the nation state, such as international bodies like the European Union.

Discussions of nationality often draw on Anderson's (1983) claim that the nation can be considered to be an **imagined community**. For example, Triandafyllidou (2001) expands upon this notion of the political and communal features of the nation being in some senses conditioned by how the members of a nation conceive their nation to be. She suggests that an adequate definition of 'nation' draws on the idea that, to be a nation, a categorizable group of people must have certain features: a shared territory and history, a common set of shared memories of the nation's history, a common mass culture and economy, and a shared understanding of legal entitlements and responsibilities, all of which is conditioned by what she describes as a 'sense of belonging'. A similar expansion on Anderson's definition is seen in the work of de Cillia, Reisigl and Wodak (1999). They also suggest that the contribution of those who make up the nation is an important aspect of the definitional task. When people consider themselves in terms of national identity, they conceive of cultural similarities and national boundaries. And part of this involves attention to the common national memories, myths, symbols and rituals of everyday life. In this sense, national culture can be thought of as a symbolic repository of what it is to be a member of that particular nation state, a repository from which members draw when they think of themselves in terms of the nation to which they belong.

> **Imagined community** a phrase that highlights the way in which political and social entities are perceived by their members as having an underlying sameness even if such similarities are difficult to establish on an objective level.

National identities and discourse

However, de Cillia and colleagues also suggest that the symbolic processes of national identification are not static but dynamic. And the site through which this dynamic construction of national identity occurs is discourse. Reicher and Hopkins

(2001) argue that a key aspect here is to understand how it is that we construct people in terms of whether they belong to our own nation. In discussing the case of Northern Ireland, which is officially recognized as a part of Britain but which some people claim as being a part of Ireland, they point out: 'given the flexibility and creativity of national definitions, it only provides a dramatic case for abandoning normative uses of nationalism in favour of a more analytic investigation of the ways in which national categories are construed and used' (Reicher and Hopkins, 2001, p. 63). Similar conclusions, they suggest, can be drawn by considering the locus of Scotland within Britain, with some people arguing for a distinctive Scottish identity and others subordinating that identity within a broader British identity. So although the historical and cultural features which macro-analyses identify represent a context in which such negotiations are pursued, they enter into processes of national identity formation not as external causal factors but, rather, as discursive resources which speakers can draw upon in setting out their identity claims. And, Reicher and Hopkins suggest, the analyst

Macro-analyses analyses of analytic terms such as 'nationality' that draw upon large-scale features such as economic histories or socio-political developments.

must recognize first that there is a wide variety of such 'resources' open to individuals in pursuing this task and secondly that these resources are drawn upon within particular contexts of discourse. National identity talk, precisely because it is variable in this sense, allows speakers to develop and pursue other locally relevant goals by deploying national identity talk in particular ways. Thus Reicher and Hopkins point to the ways in which British politicians will selectively draw upon 'British' identity to indicate a national inclusivity that incorporates English, Scottish, Welsh and Northern Irish identities while producing characterizations of this 'British' identity that are hearably related only to English concerns. And so it turns out that characterizations of nation and nationality not only draw upon varied resources, but they are 'flexible' in that one and the same characterization might be employed to achieve different ends.

National identities and 'the other'

So from the discursive perspective, national identity can be understood as a discourse which both enables a nation's members to construct the meaning of their own identities and, at the same time, influences and organizes how they perceive themselves to be. However, those who have studied national identities also point out that what matters here is not just how we construe ourselves, but how we construe other people. Thus Triandafyllidou (2001) has suggested that part of what determines whether people see themselves in these ways is the presence of other people who are categorizable as being different– whom she terms **the other**. And like Triandafyllidou,

The other a term whose usage has grown in the social scientific domain as a catch-all expression denoting one or more sets of individuals who are classified as not belonging to one's own category.

de Cillia, Reisigl and Wodak (1999) not only point to the notion of commonalities underlying a specific culture but also to the way in which such commonalities are often made out by characterizing a given national identity in contrast with different identities. This feature is often associated with **nationalism** – the claim that ethnic and cultural boundaries coincide with political boundaries, and therefore that the world can be divided into different nation states constituting the basis of

> **Nationalism** the view that peoples across the world can be thought of in terms of the nation states to which they belong and that in consequence members of a particular nation state should give due consideration to their own nation's best interests.

political power. Bound up with nationalism is the view that political or social efforts must be made to protect our own national interests and identity in the face of external threats from 'the other'; Indeed, Smith (2008) argues that, in what he calls the 'modernist' movement in sociological analyses of nationality and nationalism, sociological thinkers have focused on the role of the nation-state as a historical actor in inter-state wars and as a context against which rivalries between 'us' and 'the other' were played out. However, Smith also notes that more recently some analysts have begun to reject 'macro-analyses' and historical causality explanations of nationalism in favour of construing its development in terms of 'nationalist practices'. Thus, for example, Billig (1995) has analysed the ways in which **banal nationalism** – practices of nationality such as nationalist talk of 'we' and 'us' – are used to reproduce common-sense understandings of our relationship to 'the nation'. However, like Reicher and Hopkins, Billig also argues that 'an investigation of national identity should aim to dis-

> **Banal nationalism** nationalistic talk which relies upon everyday, commonplace forms of expression and which can be contrasted with extreme or overtly xenophobic forms of nationalism.

perse the concept of "identity" into different elements' (Billig, 1995, p. 60). So from this perspective, it is important to understand the range of different occasions and contexts in which such nationalism is accomplished. And a crucial part of this, says Billig, is that to think of oneself in terms of 'national identity' may involve thinking of others in terms of their different nationalities.

So what we find is that a 'national identity' is a slippery concept: first, because the notion of identities can be tricky to nail down, and secondly, because the same holds true for our idea of the nation. However, drawing on discussion from the previous chapter, we note that identities are representations of ourselves and others which are produced then taken up or challenged in discourse. This allows us to produce a working definition of 'national identity': from the discursive perspective national identities are characterizations of ourselves and others which (a) are produced through discursive processes of identification of the sort summarized in the last chapter, and (b) are formulations of oneself or others that make relevant different features of nationality such as common history, common territory, common values, shared sense of belonging, or exclusion of the other.

It is this idea of national identity which are we are going to pursue in the rest of this chapter. As we do so, we may see other identities flit on and off stage. Identities are multiple, in that we think of ourselves in a variety of different ways. And some-times our different identities overlap or clash. For example, it is a commonplace in talking of national identity to draw upon talk of ethnicity: in his discussion of Brazilian national identity, Lesser (1999) draws attention to this feature in talking of the 'shifting sands of nationality and ethnicity'. So although we will examine these shifting sands in more detail in the next chapter and will there focus more precisely on ethnic identities, it should come as no surprise if they appear here as bit players.

Time and Place

One feature we have already remarked upon is the historical process in which geo-graphical boundaries shift and change. This provides us with two important early clues: constructions of national identity are likely to arise in respect of time and in respect of place. So let us look at each of these in turn.

Nations and time

We saw above that a number of researchers suggest that when we talk of 'the nation', this may invoke the idea that we all share a common sense of a past, present and imagined future. Now this need not suggest that we all share a com-mon understanding of what 'the past' is as it applies to our nation, nor that we all have a shared understanding of what the future holds for us. However, the reason that talk of this sort is important to our national identity is that it provides for us a sense that, whatever the past or future was or will be like, it is something that we as members of a common nation all share in. And in part it is this sense of shared history and fate that underpins our 'imagined community' view of ourselves as being somehow the same and inter-connected with one another.

These themes have been explored in a series of studies of Austrian national identity by de Cillia and Wodak (de Cillia, Reisigl and Wodak, 1999; Wodak, 2001a).

Temporal discourse   talk or text which employs referents to time such as historical accounts or descriptions of the future.

For example, Wodak and de Cillia (2007) note that in 2005 the Austrian Chancellor Wolfgang Schüssel drew upon **temporal discourse** during a commemorative event which celebrated the 'birth' of modern Austria in 1945.

Extract 2.1

perhaps it will be precisely in this year of thoughts, in this year of anniversaries, 2005, on the threshold of a new Europe, that the opportunity opens for us to view Austria and its history, the last century of its history, in its full context, to understand it, to discuss it, and in doing so probably also to discover a new homeland

(Wodak and de Cillia, 2007, p. 349)

Wodak and de Cillia note that Schüssel establishes this historical theme through the use of 'this year of thoughts' which establishes for his audience that in some way the year 2005 represents an important beginning or 'threshold' for international developments. Indeed, it is interesting to note that not only are temporal referents such as 'year' and 'last century' introduced, but the notion of 'anniversaries' allows the hearer to understand that these are to be thought of as inter-related and that they are to be associated with 'history' as an ongoing process in which past events are somehow connected with future events. And Schüssel's argument here is that once this is understood, this will lead to the discovery of a 'new' Austrian home-land, itself a notion that is replete with ideas of commonality and shared life. Wodak and de Cillia also draw attention to the way that Schüssel makes use of other historical referents at other points in his speech. For example, his references to the 'State Treaty', signed in 1955 and leading to the Second Austrian Republic, allow him to establish the historical lineage of the Austrian state and further help to establish that Austrians share a collective history that is uniquely Austrian. So the clever deployment of references to time helps Schüssel to construct a national identity for his audience.

However, we noted earlier that the contemporary development of national identities takes place within a context in which larger, supra-national entities exist. And elsewhere, Wodak has noted that the same sort of temporal appeals drawn on by Schüssel can be used to construct identities in relation to these quite different configurations of national boundaries. In a study of how different politicians make sense of the nature of the European Union, Wodak describes how temporal forces can be seen to play a part.

Extract 2.2

Hu-M1   I think it's a cultural rather cultural and common historical phenomenon which obviously has a very strong, I mean in history. ... You have all this Roman and Christian traditions which is coming bringing it together

(Wodak, 2007, p. 667)

Wodak points out that it would be unconvincing to argue that all of the member national states within the European Union shared a single historical **narrative**. However, this can be dealt with by talking instead of

> **Narrative**   an episode of talk or text that displays recognizably story-like features.

the vaguer notion of a common historical 'culture' or tradition. Thus, for example, in this case we see a politician who is seeking to establish that membership of the European Union should be curtailed. The immediate context here was one in which the entry of Turkey into the Union was under discussion. And what we see here is the politician who is being interviewed creating a particular history for Europe: one in which Catholic and Protestant Christianity have historically been defining characteristics of the European identity. And, of course, such a claim implies that nations such as Turkey whose peoples are perceived to be predominantly Muslim ought to be excluded from Union membership.

So the production of particular versions of national identity is often associated with broader political goals. This is seen especially clearly in Achugar's (2007) study of how the Uruguayan military produced a narrative of events during the military dictatorship in Uruguay which lasted for more than ten years during the 1970s and 1980s. He points out that in narratives of this sort, depictions of the country can be developed to position social actors in particular ways. Achugar notes the way in which the military's descriptions of the dictatorship stress a common national identity grounded in shared history. Against this shared common identity, other individuals are characterized in negative terms such as 'intransigent' or 'fanatic'. This contrast between national identity on the one hand and problematic identities on the other is then used to provide justifications for actions taken by the military against the individuals so described.

Another example of this is a study of children's history books conducted by Oteiza and Pinto (2008). These authors draw our attention to the way that the national histories of Chile are constructed in schoolchildren's textbooks in order to achieve particular effects. In 1973, Augusto Pinochet led a military coup against the Chilean government and set up a military dictatorship that lasted until 1990. But the authors note that the national historical stories that are produced in these texts lay great emphasis on conciliatory discourse that seeks to establish national consensus and political stability. Now given that Pinochet's government was associated in the world press with human rights abuses, this might seem to be a difficult task. However, Oteiza and Pinto show how specific Chilean national historical events are constructed, for example with some of Pinochet's victims being characterized as 'militants' rather than as innocent civilians, and blame being ascribed to economic upheavals caused by the previous civilian government. These sorts of constructions allow the textbook authors to draw relatively benign conclusions about their own country's history:

> Similar to what happens with other milestones of national history, regarding the events that happened with respect to that date; [we] probably will never reach an agreement about the causes that brought about the loss of the democracy in Chile.
>
> (Oteiza and Pinto, 2008, p. 341)

What is happening here, Oteiza and Pinto suggest, is that the events leading up to military dictatorship are constructed as intrinsically debatable and that in consequence it does not make sense to produce a moral or legal argument that offers an explicit view of Pinochet and his effect on the nation's history. And the point of this sort of discourse, they suggest, is that it allows the textbook authors to downplay potential threats to national unity arising out of this turbulent history and thereby to aid in the construction of a unified, patriotic national identity among the country's young.

It is important to remember the guidance offered by Billig (1995) in this respect. The delineation of a national (or supra-national) identity does not just arise in the speech of politicians, who can be expected to have a professional interest in developing and defending particular types of identity. National identities are also established in the everyday aspects of life that involve all members of society. For example, Kjaer and Palsbro (2008) are interested in how the legal community in Denmark responds to the issues surrounding legal integration within Europe arising out of the development of the European Union. An important aspect of such integration is the way in which European human rights law is accepted or challenged within individual EU member states. Kjaer and Palsbro are especially interested in the way in which apparently dry legal debates of this sort can be seen as domains in which issues of national identity are discursively worked through. One finding they report is that legal identities are constructed by drawing on discourses of commonality of past and future. Moreover, some of these discursive constructions turn out to be flexible: they can be used either to develop a sense of national legal identity or, contrastingly, to develop a sense of a Europe-wide legal identity.

Extract 2.3

the incorporation of the Convention on Human Rights in Danish law rests on the explicit presupposition that it must not distort the traditional balance between the Folketing [the Danish parliament] and the judiciary.

(Kjaer and Palsbro, 2008, p. 611)

Extract 2.4

At the court in Strasbourg they don't just pass judgements. They are trying minutely to work out what is shared European heritage.

(Kjaer and Palsbro, 2008, p. 614)

In Extract 2.3 talk of a shared history is drawn upon to warrant the idea that the European Convention on Human Rights might potentially distort Denmark's traditional legal heritage. But, as Extract 2.4 shows, this sort of formulation can equally be drawn on by those who support this Convention. Here, European courts in Strasbourg are presented as dealing with issues which are part of a common heritage across EU nation states, including Denmark.

However, it would be mistaken to assume that this talk of time and history is a 'one-way' process. The discursive production and reproduction of identity is a field of contest. And so just as temporal referents can be drawn upon in making out the national sense of self, so too can such attempts be resisted. For example,

Condor (2000) has examined how English people display a sensitivity towards being identified as English. This sensitivity in part stems from what they seem to regard as problematic aspects of England's national history, such as the period of the British Empire in which it could be argued that many of the country's activities were morally questionable. What Condor found in her participants' talk was that the 'English' identity was imbued with historical connotations implying that 'the English' were a people who were prejudiced against other races and nationalities. And so her interviewees resisted the notion that they had acquired a uniquely 'English' identity in order to avoid problematic associations with prejudice towards others. However, in a later study Condor (2006b) examines a different sort of temporal talk about British identities:

Extract 2.5

1   Kate: Britain's an island and we have our own identity which is just
2   different from the Continent. We have a different history, our own culture
3   and it's just little quirky things but it is things that go back
4   like hundreds of years and I don't like that now we are
5   going to lose that identity just because some bureaucrat
6   in Brussels thinks we should all be the same.

(Condor, 2006b, p. 666)

Here, Kate associates 'our' identity with aspects of time and history which are presented in a relatively more positive fashion. It is in virtue of the fact that 'things' go back over centuries that their loss, as might arise from a greater Europeanization of Britain, is to be resisted.

So what this research shows us, then, is that references to time and historical processes can be used to develop a sense of national identity. In particular, we have seen how particular constructions of historical events can be deployed in the development of particular 'versions' of that identity. And we have also seen that this sort of temporal talk in the creation of identity is itself a flexible notion. Where required, national histories and temporal events can be either disowned or celebrated.

Nations and place

If we were to glance at the schoolchild's atlas of the world, with its carefully cir-cumscribed lines and its colourful shadings, we might be tempted to think that place, at least, is a relatively straightforward aspect of national identity. But we pointed out at the start of this chapter that these lines and primary colours are likely to mislead. The peoples who live within these boundaried areas need much more than a shared colour in a child's atlas in order to see themselves as sharing an identity. Perhaps even more importantly, in order to understand shared identities of this sort we need to begin by understanding what 'place' actually means. And as usual, it turns out that the definition we need is a bit more complex than we might have imagined.

Of course, in some sense we can think of space as the way in which we perceive the external world, and as something that can be divided up and parcelled out through the use of the land-surveyor's measuring tape. But just as contemporary physics tells us that in many respects space is not actually like this, so social scientists report that space, as a social phenomenon, is a much more subtle concept. For example, Dixon and Durrheim (2000, 2004) point out that places can be described and characterized in lots of different ways. What this means is that in social interaction, talk of 'place' does not work by referring to some neutral, mutually agreed 'out-thereness'. Instead, descriptions of particular places are formulated by people for particular reasons at particular times. So one can, they suggest, think of people as developing and maintaining **place-identities** which do of course carry some sort of sense of belonging to the relevant place, but at the same time perform other discursive work such as providing a warrant for a given individual to be (or not to be) in that place. One example of this which they provide is located in the particular point in the history of South Africa in which the politics of **apartheid** gave way to social integration movements. White residents of townships found that the spaces they had once

> **Place-identities** constructions of people in relationship to particular formulations of location.

> **Apartheid** a political and legal system of social separation based on race.

considered to be 'theirs' were being used by black residents as well. Some of the white residents reacted against such developments but, given the political context of the time, were relatively unwilling to produce arguments that relied upon overtly racist sentiments. So instead they could be seen to provide characterizations of place which allowed for inferences about who should, and who should not, inhabit those spaces. Thus some places came to be described as 'rural areas' which were associated with particular sorts of 'rural life'. And what this meant was that certain sorts of people could be depicted as not fitting in with this particular sort of place and life being, for example, more suited to life in other sorts of places such as 'squatter camps'. Elsewhere, Wallwork and Dixon (2004) found similar forms of discourse in the leafy climes of England. In a study of how proponents of fox-hunting defended their points of view, they noted that one argument produced was that British national identity was essentially caught up with the enjoyment of rural spaces and that, since fox-hunting takes place in such spaces, it was an activity that was essential to Englishness.

So it turns out that formulations of national identity which focus on the question of place, just as with those that focus on time, appear in contexts in which those producing the national identity also have other aims and interests. Witteborn (2007) provides a clear example of this in her study of Palestinian national identity. Witteborn notes that in the Palestinian narratives of identity which she examined, specific versions of place appeared in which boundaries and demarcation played an important role.

Extract 2.6

  7   I lived in Bethlehem which is about twenty minutes away
  8   a:nd we had permanent checkpoint between the cities
  9   and it was <very difficult to go to college>
10   <u>unless</u> you have a permit from the Israeli government.
11   and they don't give it to anybody
12   >even if you are student<
13   you don't get permission
14   a:nd I didn't ask for permission because this is my country
15   (.)
16   this is <u>my</u> land
17   I don't need per<u>mission</u> for it

(Witteborn, 2007, p. 152)

In this narrative, Witteborn notes, her participant provides a particular account of the nature of her 'land' which emphasizes the divisive nature of Palestinian experience. The account provided contains detail of spatial movement, but the ways in which this movement is described allows the reader to understand the social and political realities of life as a Palestinian – a life where the individual's everyday movements are controlled by a government which is hearably presented as acting in an illegitimate way, since permits are required and yet not given. Indeed, by stressing that the country and the land belong to her, the participant makes available the inference that for the Israeli government to insist that she gain its permission before moving from one space to another is, itself, illegitimate.

Another example of the discursive nature of apparently objective spatial boundaries is offered by the study of China. Following a civil war throughout the middle decades of the twentieth century, republican elements in China established a political existence on the island of Taiwan while the Chinese communist party took over governance of what is now referred to as 'mainland China'. To date, the precise relationship between mainland China and Taiwan is debated, with some viewing them as two separate nation states, and others viewing them as two parts of a single China. More recently, in 2003, the island of Hong Kong was returned from British control to China. This political change caused unrest among many Hong Kong residents, and this unrest continued in the years that followed as the mainland Chinese government sought to extend its control over the island. These events have meant that discursive researchers find China to be an especially fertile ground for exploring the ways in which debate about national identities can ebb and flow over geographical boundaries.

In one study, Flowerdew and Leong (2007) explored how the political debate between the Chinese government and Hong Kong residents unfolded in the national press. In particular, they were interested in the ways that **metaphors** were used to construct an identity of the 'patriotic Chinese'. For example, they note that those propounding the Chinese government position sometimes relied on a family metaphor in which mainland China was portrayed as the parent and Hong Kong as the (potentially troublesome) child.

> **Metaphors** figures of speech used to refer to something not literally identified by means of similarities between it and the thing which is explicitly mentioned.

However, Flowerdew and Leong also note that characterizations of this sort allow scope for challenge. Thus, in one instance, a newspaper article which sought to challenge the mainland Chinese government position took up this family metaphor but recast the relevant actors, with mainland China being presented not as a concerned parent, but as a grouchy granddad. In relation to Taiwan, Lu and Ahrens (2008) have examined the ways in which 'building' metaphors are used by Taiwanese politicians to effect ideological goals in relation to national identity, either in support of Taiwan as a part of mainland China or as a separate nation state. Of particular interest here is the way in which Taiwan's first president, Chiang Kai-shek, relied upon the use of building metaphors as a means of establishing national continuity with the past. However, later presidents relied less on such metaphors and in the twenty-first century the Taiwanese president Chen Shui-bian rarely employed this metaphor at all. The point of this, suggest Lu and Ahrens, is that Chen's ideological concern is to establish difference between the Taiwanese nation and China, and that this effort could be **undermined** were he to rely on metaphors which emphasized the way in which Taiwan was 'built' out of prior changes in China. Kuo

> **Undermining** weakening or countering an argumentative position.

(2007) has noted similar elements of resistance against a 'mainstream China' identity in which everyday Taiwanese people seek to assert a distinctly Taiwanese national identity through the use of indigenous dialects in place of the 'dominant' Mandarin Chinese language.

Nations, time and place

The construction of national identities in terms of time and space can also be a more complex affair, in which both temporal and spatial issues are drawn upon. Take, for example, the island of Cyprus which although formally a republic is divided along a 'fault line' following the invasion of the island by Turkey in 1974. This 'fault line' separates out 'Greek' Cyprus from 'Turkish' Cyprus. Because of this, Cyprus is a feature of talk of nation and nationality among the citizens of mainland Turkey. In a study of how this sort of talk is reproduced by Turkish students in online discussion forums, Baruh and Popescu (2008) note that the forum contributors regularly relied on metaphorical constructions of Turkish identity. One of these metaphors was built around notions of sacrifice and the shedding of blood for one's country. Here, Turkish national identity is reproduced by reference to those soldiers who, in the past, had given their lives to protect Turkish land. The 'bite' in this particular representation of national identity is that a number of Turkish Cypriots seek to address their problems of living on a divided island by applying for passports issued by the (Greek) Republic of Cyprus. For the Turkish students in Baruh and Popescu's study, however, this represents an abandonment of their Turkishness and a betrayal of those who died to protect 'Turkish lands'. So it turns out that to be a 'good' Cypriot requires not only a historical understanding but a commitment to a particular spatial location. These sorts of issues are also seen in a study by Kuzar (2008), who examines the way in which the term 'return' is deployed in debates about Palestinians who left their homes in 1948 and subsequently were refused re-entry into Israel. Kuzar notes that when people speak of the 'Palestinian right of return', they focus on the notion of these individuals being afforded a 'political identity' in which they are viewed as returning to their own country, with all of the citizens' rights that that notion entails. So the place of residence of any given Palestinian, and what that means in terms of that person's national identity, is linked, through the use of 'return', to a historical past which does (or does not) legitimate that individual's present spatial location.

As a final example of this intertwining of time and space in the construction of identity, we can turn to a study by McKinlay and McVittie (2007). In this study, the focus was on understanding how English **immigrants** into a Scottish island coped with the potential difficulties they faced. We noted earlier, in reference to Reicher and Hopkins' work, that the status of Scotland as a source for a national identity, separate from that of the English identity, is an indeterminate one. This places English people who move into certain areas of Scotland

Immigrants people who have left their place of origin and have settled in another place, such as those who have left one nation state and settled in another.

in a difficult position. As people who view themselves in terms of their British national identity, they might be taken to face a change of location to this Scottish island as identity-preserving. However, if they find themselves in a context in which they are viewed as outsiders or 'incomers', this sense of self may be put at challenge. In order to discover whether this is the case, one of the questions that McKinlay and McVittie asked of these individuals was whether incomers to the island were really different from 'locals'.

Extract 2.7

1 I do you think it is possible to make like a distinction between a local and an incomer
2 Molly Oh ay:ye I think so aye
3 I how would you
4 Molly I don't know (.) just (.) you know the locals are funny that way (.) you know, I mean
5 (.) especially the older ones (.) you know they they think incomers I mean I've been up

6		here fourteen years
7	I	Mm
8	Molly	and they probably still think (.) I'm an incomer (.) it's not so bad right enough because
9		the likes of when we came up because Fraser's Dad came from here he was born here
10	I	Oh did he
11	Molly	em the old house was just across from the eh (our) house and then ( ) was not so bad
12		because his father came from here

(McKinlay and McVittie, 2007, p. 179)

McKinlay and McVittie suggest that while Molly's initial hesitant response reflects some sensitivity towards being labelled as an 'incomer', she goes on to provide warrants for why this is really inappropriate as regards herself. On the one hand, she stresses the longevity of her connection to the island through 'Fraser's Dad' and on the other, she makes particular spatial connections relevant, pointing out her family connections to specific locales on the island. So by subtly combining in her family narrative aspects of both time and place, she is able to indicate that the problematic 'incomer' label is one that is 'not so bad' as might at first seem.

Nationality and the Media

One issue that we have referred to in this chapter, but not explicitly discussed, is the role of the media in the creation of national identities. We noted above, for example, that Billig draws our attention to the way that 'banal nationality' is accomplished in a variety of contexts including the media. In fact, the role of the media has been a major concern for many discursive researchers. For example, Juan (2009) suggests that one important context in which identity construction occurs is in newspaper accounts, and argues that such accounts are important because they show that national identities are not static, but rather emerge within media representations of specific socio-political events. As one example of this, Juan analyses the way in which the *New York Times* newspaper describes Chinese responses to a particular event: the bombing of the Chinese embassy in Yugoslavia by NATO forces during the war in Kosovo in 1999 which caused the deaths of three Chinese journalists. In the *New York Times*, the presentation of Chinese responses is designed to emphasize the irrational nature of these responses. In another study, Amer (2009) argues that discourses of international war are often bound up with discourses of legitimation. He argues that who or what gets to be treated as legitimate is often an outcome of socio-political processes involving the power (or lack of power) of the speaker. As an example, Amer points to the way in which the Palestinian/Israeli conflict known as the 'second intifada' is dealt with in an article which appeared in the *New York Times*. Part of the process of delegitimation which Amer identifies is, he suggests, the way in which Palestinians are identified with violence and confusion while the Israelis are described as peaceable and rational. Amer suggests that an important aspect of why this works as delegitimation is that the article's author is able to establish something about his own identity. As a *New York Times* author, his own identity is in a sense already established as one of being an authoritative source whose opinions should be listened to. A third study is Winter's (2007) examination of a pair of op-ed pieces in Toronto newspapers. Winter discusses the ways in which Canadian identity is formulated both in international terms but also in intra-national terms. This latter is of special interest not only because Canadians struggle with internal debate over national identity between English speakers and French speakers, but because the outcomes of these 'national projects' are often characterizable as resolutions which ignore the quite separate interests of Canada's indigenous peoples.

However, it is important to note that the creation of national identities in the media is a two-way street. Journalists may well seek to pursue an 'agenda' by creating particular sorts of national identity. But those who are interviewed by media representatives are equally alive to the socially constructive possibilities that lie within the newspaper's pages or the radio station's broadcasting booth. For example, in relation to the Middle East conflict, McKinlay, McVittie and Sambaraju (in press) have shown how Palestinian leaders can use the media to respond to the sorts of 'delegitimation' that Amer describes. In the following extract, one of the leaders of the Palestinians responds to an accusation levelled by a media journalist that Palestinian leaders brainwash their followers into committing acts of violence.

Extract 2.8

Meshaal   First of all we do not brainwash anyone. Every Palestinian spontaneously feels that his land is occupied. That Israel is killing children and women, demolishing their homes, taking their land, building the wall, the settlements, that journalism favours Israel, and digging under the al Aqsa mosque. So the Palestinian finds himself going directly to fight for the resistance. This is his duty. As the French fought the Nazis, and in the American revolution, as the Vietnamese people fought, as did the South African. This is ordinary behaviour it doesn't need brainwashing.

(McKinlay, McVittie and Sambaraju, In press)

What McKinlay, McVittie and Sambaraju note is that Meshaal does not merely deny the accusation. He constructs a version of 'the other', in this case the Israelis, that highlights the illegitimacy of their actions. In doing so, Meshaal makes available for the media audience the inference that the Palestinians are justified in their actions. But he does not stop here. He draws upon other national identities in order to identify other points in time and place at which resistance to illegitimate state force has occurred. By aligning the Palestinians with these other national identities, Meshaal is able to indicate not only that the Palestinians' actions are justified but that the Palestinian nation is no different from other nations in carrying out such justified actions in contexts of state oppression.

Nationality and Prejudice

Although the study of national identities is of interest as a social phenomenon in its own right, it is probably fair to say that one of the reasons they draw the attention of the social scientist is because of the relationship between national identifications and **prejudice**. Contemporary theorists argue that prejudice is not always overt and need not involve blatantly prejudiced discourse or actions. For example, Buttny (2004) points out that most of us understand the 'rules' of polite society enough that if we want to express a prejudiced claim, we do it in a way that makes what we are saying sound 'reasoned' and based on evidence, rather than the rantings of a bigot. Now what this means is that it can sometimes be difficult to identify prejudice in discourse precisely because speakers design their utterances to make it difficult. As just one example of this, speakers may use explicit **disavowals** such as 'I am not prejudiced, but …' in order to express a prejudiced point of view while trying to appear to be non-prejudiced. So for discursive researchers, the issue is not just whether some claim or other is explicitly racist but, in addition, whether an individual is managing what is said or written as though it is a sensitive matter that might allow inferences about that individual's prejudiced nature to be made (Edwards, 2005). The issue is made more complex, according to some discursive researchers, by the fact that prejudiced talk or text might work as prejudice not so much in terms of what is said as in terms of the ideological context in which such discourse is produced (Reisigl and Wodak, 2001; Verkuyten, 2001).

For discursive researchers, then, the analyst's interest in prejudice lies in the way that prejudice is attended to, handled and managed in talk and text. This focus on prejudiced talk as being potentially subtle and indirect has come to be called the study of **new racism**. Augoustinos and Every (2007) provide a useful review of a number of studies that have focused on this new racism phenomenon. In addition to the denial or disavowal of racism, they point out that 'new' racist talk can also be accomplished via the provision of warrants or reasons for why what is being said should be taken to be true. So, for example, racists may make

> **Prejudice** dislike of others who are described as different from oneself, for example in terms of category membership.

> **Disavowals** utterances designed to inoculate the speaker against negative inferences.

> **New racism** the expression of prejudice in talk or text in a manner which attends to potential inferences of appearing to be prejudiced.

appeals to 'facts' or to 'obvious truths' about the targets of their prejudiced in setting out their claims. Another strategy 'new' racists may employ is the construction of a positive sense of their own group which is often accompanied by negative representations of 'the other'. Such constructions allow the racist to represent what is being said as not really racist, given what one 'knows' about the generosity or kindness or whatever of the nation to whom the speaker belongs, together with what one 'knows' about the venal attributes of those others about whom the speaker is expressing prejudice. They also point out that, somewhat ironically, prejudiced talk is often accomplished by drawing on liberal arguments. So the existence of inequality or prejudice might be addressed by talking about liberal values such as majority opinions not being outweighed by minority opinions, or by extolling the virtues of hard work as a means of bettering oneself.

Another interesting feature of new racism talk identified by Augoustinos and Every is that prejudice is often expressed in non-racial terms by referring to national identities rather than racial identities. Here, concerns with the nation state and its interests are deployed in order to draw conclusions about who should and who should not be treated as 'genuine' citizens. As far as national identities are concerned, prejudice often flows around the question of immigration: who counts as sharing our national identity, and who should be allowed to acquire it if they do not already have it? So in exploring discourses of national identity and prejudice, we will focus here on this one topic.

Asylum-seekers people seeking to effect international migration by claiming entry into a host country as a result of dangers they face in their home countries.

As a first example of this sort of concern, we can turn to a study of official speeches in the Australian parliament about **asylum-seekers**. In this study, Every and Augoustinos (2007) identify a range of ways in which people can accomplish racist talk while negotiating the potential danger of acquiring an identity as a racist. In analysing how such talk can be understood 'simultaneously as racist and not racist', they identify a range of potential instances, including the deployment of categorical generalizations such as 'Pakistanis', the unequal treatment of asylum seekers compared with other minority groups, talk of culture as talk of natural differences, and talk about national sovereignty. They point to one instance in which a speaker uses appeals to national sovereignty to defend himself against potential charges of deploying a racist agenda in arguing against the interests of asylum seekers. One of the other parliamentary speakers responds with the retort 'Heil Hitler', a move which the preceding speaker orients to as making precisely the charge of racism which he had sought to pre-empt.

So this alerts us right away to the fact that in contemporary politics, politicians are alive to the pitfalls associated with talk about immigration and refugees. Van Dijk (2005) draws our attention to this in an examination of the discourse of a political leader from the Catalan region of Spain, Jordi Pujol. In one of his speeches, Pujol suggests that people have been 'working for centuries' to establish a 'central culture of reference'. Van Dijk suggests that Pujol's claim here is that immigration must therefore be curtailed not because immigrants are bad in themselves, but because of the threat immigration poses to the nationalist programmes of developing a national identity. As a further example, we can turn to a study by Capdevila and Callaghan (2008) who examine a speech from the election campaign which took place in the UK in 2005. During this campaign, the Conservative party outlined a set of proposals dealing with the issue of UK immigration. Capdevila and Callaghan studied a speech made by the then leader of the Conservative party, Michael Howard, in which he talks about his party's plans to control immigration. In the following extract, Howard can be seen to describe what counts as a good immigrant:

Extract 2.9

4   Some people say that's racist. It's not. It's common sense.
5   I believe in controlled immigration for the most personal of reasons. I am the child of immigrants. As my parents always told me, Britain is the best country in the world. And one of the things, which make Britain so great, is our sense of fair play. We are a tolerant, generous, welcoming people with a profoundly compassionate nature.
6   We believe in immigration – in offering a home to people who want to work hard and make a positive contribution to our society. And we accept our moral responsibility to those fleeing persecution.

(Capdevila and Callaghan, 2008, p. 5)

Capdevila and Callaghan suggest that what Howard is establishing here is a sense of shared cultural identity. Britishness does not mean that a person has been born in the UK, rather it signifies an acceptance of a common way of life. In this respect, Howard presents himself as the epitome of the 'good' immigrant. So both by aligning himself with immigrants and by appealing to the positive aspect of the British identity, Howard is able to state his claim for immigration controls while, at the same time, avoiding any potential inferences about nationalist prejudice that might otherwise be associated with such claims. Naturally, such careful discourse is not the preserve of the UK politician. For example, we noted earlier (Wodak, 2007) that Turkey's entry into the European Union is a political 'hot potato'. Tekin (2008) draws attention to the way that French politicians construct Turkey's possible inclusion into the Union in a careful way, and often include **disclaimers** such as apparent denials of prejudice or the apparent making of **concessions** which are intended to defuse potential accusations of prejudice.

> **Concessions**   items of discourse in which someone apparently gives way on a particular point of argument.
> **Disclaimer**   a phrase that is designed to prevent hearers from drawing otherwise potentially available inferences.

Similar findings are reported by Every and Augoustinos (2008b), who draw attention to inclusive and exclusive features of nationality talk in their discussion of the construction of Australian national identity. They point out that Australians have become increasingly aware of the issue of immigration into Australia, particularly the rising incidence of asy-lum-seekers attempting to enter Australia. As might be expected, a range of previous studies (e.g. Lynn and Lea, 2003) had reported that talk of nation and national char-acteristics is routinely deployed in formulating this issue, with a focus on arguing for exclusion by drawing distinctions between the needs and concerns of the nation on the one hand and the illegal status of asylum-seekers on the other. However, given what was said earlier about the variety and flexibility of nationality talk, it should not be surprising to discover that this is only part of the story. And indeed, what Every and Augoustinos found was that characterizations of Australian national identity were drawn upon both by those who argued against further immigration and by their opponents. Thus, for example, the representation of the Australians as peo-ple who are generous and believe in a 'fair do' could be used to argue either that further immigration should be allowed, because it is fair to the immigrants, or that it should not be allowed, on the grounds that Australia, being a generous society, had already 'done its bit' in resolving the immigration issue. (Interestingly, Every and Augoustinos have noted elsewhere (2008a) that the same variability in characteri-zation also extends to descriptions of asylum seekers themselves, with liberal discourses of moral responsibility being set up in opposition to the negative char-acterizations of asylum seekers produced by opponents of immigration.)

No matter how careful the politicians' characterizations, many immigrants and refugees are themselves only too well aware of the potential hostilities that they face. Leudar and colleagues (2008a) found that when refugees constructed their own identities this happened in a particular way. The refugees displayed awareness of and concern with widespread media representations of them which involve hostile descriptions such as representing immigration in terms of natural disasters through terms such as 'floods of immigrants'. Moreover Leudar *et al.* note that such hostile representations have consequences for their targets. In particular, they suggest, since 'the self' is a social construct, these negative representations are a potential source of harm to the personal well-being of those people being char-acterized in such negative ways. So in presenting their own identities, the refugees who participated in this study would routinely make reference to these hostile characterizations precisely in order to demonstrate the ways in which such descrip-tions did not fit them. For example, refugees would draw on particular aspects of their own biographical histories in showing that such hostility was unwarranted in their cases. Thus, in a process of 'identity loss and reconstruction' Leudar *et al.* note that one of their refugee participants, M, draws on two distinct sets of life experiences based on living first in Iran then in the UK. In the first extract below, M describes his life in Iran and in the second his life in the UK.

Extract 2.10

36 M: I got to finish MS (.) at university. I have- I have to- I have
37 to pass the entrance exam. After that went to university and finish this course
38 MS- MS in textile engineering.hhh and after that (.) >err during this time I

39   worked- I worked< in three in three factories >in three textile factories< to get
40   some (.) experience about (.) mm: my job

(Leudar *et al.*, 2008a, p. 205)

Extract 2.11

107   M: I have to spend my time (.) hh just going to college (0.2) without
108   any work
109   JH: mm
110   M: .hh even <u>even</u> any voluntary work

(Leudar *et al.*, 2008a, p. 206)

Leudar *et al.* note M emphasizes the continuities in his self (as hard-working and conscientious) even as he describes the discontinuities in his life as a result of moving to the UK. In this way, M both displays an awareness of the sort of criticisms levelled against refugees which focus on describing them as lazy and waiting for government handouts but also demonstrates how such views cannot possibly apply in his case.

Of course, negotiations of who can appropriately be considered to be members of the national group, and resistance against the **attributions** associated with problematic national status, involve other identities as well. In a study of interviews of applicants for 'green card' status in the United States, Johnston (2008) shows how immigration applicants and those supporting them seek to draw on a variety of different social identities in pursuing their case. For example, applicants and their sponsors might draw upon identities of being parents or upon occupational identities in order to indicate to the immigration officer dealing with the case that they share a relevant social identity. Johnston suggests that by foregrounding co-membership of a particular social identity, the applicants seek to establish a sense of rapport with the immigration officer in order to facilitate the outcome that they will be perceived as appropriate candidates for national membership. In this way, the negotiation of the refugee identity is an arena in which other identities get brought into play. Van de Mieroop and van der Haar (2008) touch on a similar theme in their account of a female Afghan refugee's interactions with Dutch social services. In this study, they examine the way in which the female refugee negotiates several different identities, including that of 'the fearful woman' as a means of negotiating her refugee status in a foreign country.

> **Attributions** explaining actions and events by ascribing causes to them.

And if this is true of refugees, it is equally true of those who express forms of national prejudice against them. We can see this in a study by Condor which looked at how racist talk can be 'woven through and anchored in the delicate choreography of everyday sociability' (Condor, 2006a, p. 15). Condor points out that such talk may be used to display intimacy or solidarity, or to shock, or to mark the identity one is claiming for oneself during the current conversational interaction. So although, as Condor demonstrates elsewhere, people may sometimes 'dodge the identity of prejudice' by presenting racist views in a very careful, circumscribed manner, this is not always the case. Sometimes, people are concerned with other features of identity:

Extract 2.12

6   Gem I hate the Welsh
7   ((laughter))
8   Katie Yeah. Sheep-shaggers.
9   ((laughter))
10   Chloe They're not as as bad as the French though (1.5)
11   Susan What's wrong with the French?
12   Chloe [I dunno]
13   Katie [They eat] horses
14   Gem An' frogs. An' they are frogs so that makes them cannibals
15   ((laughter))
16   Chloe Yeah. And the Chinese, they eat dogs [and stuff]
17   Katie [Yeah]
18   ((laughter))
19   Chloe Sweet and sour Doberman
20   Gem Tastes like dog shit anyway
21   ((laughter))
22   Katie Yeah. They're terrible, the Chinkies
23   Gem Not as bad as the Pakis though. [I hate Pakis].

(Condor, 2006a, p. 12)

What Condor shows us in this extract is that her participants are quite willing to produce prejudiced talk about other nationalities of the most blatant sort. Now this might seem to contradict previous research which demonstrates that individuals are careful in how they produce prejudiced talk. But Condor's argument is that concern with 'dodging the identity of prejudice' is only one sort of identity project that can arise in talk. In this extract, we see quite different sorts of identity concerns. First, it is clear from the laughter that the participants are in some sense enjoying the collaborative achievement of working up this joint presentation of themselves as being prejudiced people. The re-presentation of different nationalities in terms of stereotyped descriptions of national activities is done in order to achieve comic effect. For instance, at line 14 Gem introduces a play on words, based on the popular English convention that French people can be referred to as 'frogs' because they eat frogs. And at lines 19 to 22, Chloe and Gem draw on popular English understandings of Chinese eating habits to produce an ironic **evaluation** of Chinese nationality. All of this is set, Condor suggests, in some sort of imagined hierarchy of disparagement in which 'the Welsh' give way to 'the French' who are in turn supplanted by 'the Chinese' and finally 'the Pakis'. Part of what is going on here,

> **Evaluation**   talk which situates the relevant topic in a comparative frame indicating features such as levels of goodness or worth.

according to Condor, is that the young female participants are using this sort of extreme prejudiced talk to mark out themselves as different from the interviewer in terms of age, education and social class.

Discussion

Our first foray into discursive research on identities has helped to illustrate their complex nature. National identities are not rigid self-categorizations that draw upon easily recognizable features of the external world. Instead, they turn out to be ways of viewing the self and others whose nature is essentially variable and interwoven with the specific context of their production. In part, it has to be this way. Identities have this fluid characteristic – but so do nations. Even the idea of an 'imagined community' does not fully capture the dynamic nature of the nation. Just as identities are constructed within local contexts, to meet specific interactional needs, and in response to other interactional goals, so too the nation itself appears as a discursive accomplishment, with its various features being managed, negotiated, accepted or rejected as individuals pursue the given identity project at hand. This is not to say that features of time and place are not relevant to national identity. But their relevance lies in how the speaker or author draws upon these notions, and what this drawing upon process enables the individual to say about self and other. Equally, other aspects of the 'imagined community' play a role. We saw, for example, how the formulation of Australian culture as one of fairness can be brought into play. But the essentially constructive nature of national identity was revealed in the way that this particular cultural feature can be seen to motivate different and competing perspectives on who is and who is not an Australian. At the same time, we also saw how important it is to understand that constructing a sense of one's own national identity is often bound up with constructing a sense of 'the other'. This can, of course, represent dangers to those whose national identity is in doubt. It allows the politician to present a version of national identity that excludes them. But, equally, it represents a resource for immigrants or refugees, because it allows them the discursive 'room' to present a version of themselves as people who do not have the sorts of problematic identity that their opponents might wish to foist upon them. As we moved towards the end of this journey into national identity, we discovered another important feature. The construction of oneself as a particular type of person in respect of others' national identities is only one of the 'identity projects' which an individual may have in a given interaction. As Condor shows, sometimes other identity concerns come to the fore, and in these cases sensitivities about prejudice in respect of nation give way to other interests. This idea, that we play an active role in managing (or not managing) perceptions of prejudice about ourselves is something that we return to in the next chapter. It is also clear that the media represent an important locus for identity construction but, for the moment, we must leave the newspaper and television tycoons for another occasion. It is now time to turn to the over-lapping concepts of ethnic and religious identity. We said at the start that nationality and other features of identity such as ethnicity are 'shifting sands' and that the one may often merge into the other. It is this notion that we will pursue in the next chapter where we will see that the shifting sands may also involve that aspect of the self which reflects our religious beliefs.

Chapter Summary

This chapter begins with a discussion of what we mean by 'national identity' and demonstrates the complexities involved in providing such a definition. 'Identity' is hard to define – but so is 'nation'. We end up with a sense of 'national identity' as something that people produce in discourse by drawing upon a variety of aspects such as communal understandings, common histories and shared geographies. A further key element of such discourse is producing a sense of oneself as distinct from 'the other'. We saw that these discursive constructions are often un-remarked upon and 'banal' parts of normal lived experiences. But where people do turn to give consideration to national identity, we discover that this is often bound up with other projects and goals that people might be seeking to achieve in interaction. The chapter moved on to consider two clear examples of this sort of process: national identity as it relates to time, and as it relates to place. We examined a range of examples where professional politicians and 'ordinary' people could be seen to talk about themselves and their nations in historical and spatial terms. Sometimes, people even draw upon both forms of talk, as we saw in the case of the 'English incomer'. In producing this kind of talk, people manage to create a sense of national identity. But, in addition, they can also often be seen to achieve other effects, such as excluding certain others from that identity. We pursued this theme further by examining instances of prejudice against other nationalities. We noticed that some people are careful about how they evince such prejudice. But we also saw that, on occasions and for the particular purpose at hand, sometimes people can reproduce nationalistic prejudice in more blatant forms. Finally, we noted that an important locus for many of these sorts of concerns is within media such as newspapers or television.

Connections

The most obvious links to this present chapter are based in the material on ethnic and religious identities which is presented in the following chapter. In many respects, national, ethnic and religious identities merge into one another. However, nationality can of course become a legal issue, so studies such as that of Kjaer and Palsbro are also relevant to material presented in Chapter 6.

Further Reading

Condor, S. (2006b). Temporality and collectivity: Diversity, history and the rhetorical construction of national entitativity. *British Journal of Social Psychology, 45,* 657–682.

This study looks at the way temporal discourse is brought into talk of national identity. ('Entitativity' in this case refers to the 'whole-ness' of the national group as opposed to viewing the nation as a group of discrete individuals.)

McKinlay, A. and McVittie, C. (2007). Locals, incomers and intra-national migration: Place-identities and a Scottish island. *British Journal of Social Psychology, 46,* 171–190.

This study explores the ways in which English people who move to a remote part of Scotland deal with the perhaps unexpected ways in which the Scottish locals view them.

Activity Box

It is unfortunately the case that instances of international tension and rivalry are frequently discussed in the media. One way to explore this is to get together a small group of friends and watch a television programme (or listen to a radio broadcast) which 'covers' one of these topics. Listen to the ways in which competing descriptions of national identity are produced. Can you identify other goals which the speaker might have had in mind as he or she produced just *these* characterizations? (At the time of writing, examples might include: discussions of Scottish independence; tensions in the Middle East between Palestinians and Israelis; and the ongoing debate between French and Dutch speakers in Belgium.)

3

Ethnic and Religious Identities

Topics Covered in this Chapter

Key Terms

Accountability

Acculturation

Affiliative stance

Code-switching

Discrimination

Framing

Hybrid identities

Hyphenated identities

Idiomatic expression

Integration

Marginalization

Primordialism

Reformulation

Reframing

Scepticism

Identities in Context: Individuals and Discourse in Action, First Edition. Andrew McKinlay
and Chris McVittie.
© 2011 Andrew McKinlay and Chris McVittie. Published 2011 by Blackwell Publishing Ltd.

THE head of a UK group that promotes tolerance and cohesion between ethnic and religious communities has robustly defended his open invitation to post Irish jokes on his blog. ... 'the idea that you can police jokes or humour which is not calling for anyone to be killed but is simply humour, is simply a nonsense. The law cannot legislate about humour. ... It is not the law's business and the faster people grew up and learn that the better.'

Mr Murray has been head of the Centre for Social Cohesion since 2007.

Belfast Telegraph, February 2010

In this chapter, we turn our attention to ethnic and religious identities. However, it is worthwhile recalling what we said at the very beginning of this book. Chapter headings like 'national identity' or 'ethnic identity' are here intended merely as conveniences for the reader. We will see, for example, that the distinction between 'national identity' and 'ethnic identity' is a very finely drawn one. However, we will also see that in some respects contemporary research has been particularly interested in the more 'cultural' aspects of ethnic identity. For this reason, we have chosen to set side-by-side contemporary findings from discursive research in the domains of ethnicity and religion. But the reader should remember that, like all discourse, these same issues could have been 'talked about' in a different way. That said, the aim of this chapter is first to explore what we mean by 'ethnic identities' and then to examine how and why ethnic identifications arise in everyday talk. We will then move on to a similar consideration of religious identities. Finally, we will spend a little time thinking about issues of prejudice as they arise in respect of either identity.

Ethnic Identities

Ethnic versus national identities

Before examining the findings that have been produced as discursive researchers explore ethnicity and ethnic identities, it is worthwhile pausing for a moment to consider the relationship between ethnic identities and the national identities we looked at in the previous chapter. In that chapter we presented a definition of 'national identity' centred on the discursive construction of a sense of oneself that draws upon commonalities with others, such as sharing a common history or heritage, or viewing oneself as sharing the same geographical space. However, concerns with commonality of history and heritage or shared co-location could equally be issues that are relevant to ethnic identity. On the other hand, we will see below that many researchers view ethnicity as commonality of symbolic features or a shared understanding of social norms and beliefs. But it is clear that such features could equally be said to be an aspect of national identity. So it turns out contemporary research on national and ethnic identities reveals that a very similar definition could be applied to both concepts. Both national identities and ethnic identities alike can be viewed as participants' own constructions of themselves and others. And given the range and flexibility of issues which people draw on in developing and maintaining such identities, it is perhaps not surprising that such constructive efforts could equally well be considered to be the identification of oneself in terms of either nationality or ethnicity. Indeed, it is for reasons of this sort that researchers such as Eriksen (2010), whom we discuss below, have even suggested that the idea of a national identity in many respects overlaps that of the ethnic identity, both being what he describes as 'kindred concepts'. Similarly, it is these features of identities that led us in the last chapter to note Lesser's (1999) comment about the 'shifting sands of nationality and ethnicity'.

   However, there are reasons for the analyst to cling onto some sort of distinction. Some ethnicities transcend national state boundaries. Some nations incorporate many ethnicities. In such cases, different ethnic identities within a single state can be socially arranged into power or status hierarchies. Perhaps more importantly, people seem to rely upon this distinction in making sense of themselves. For example, people who view themselves as strongly in favour of nationalism will represent themselves in terms of ideological views that emphasize the importance of the role of the state, and the state's relationship with other states, in civil society. In fact, as we examine the studies that are described in the first part of this chapter, we will find that drawing distinctions of this sort turns out to be a major preoccupation of people as they think about themselves and others. Of course, saying that a distinction between ethnic identity and national identity is important is not the same as saying that there is some sort of pre-analytic categorization to be put in place that readily parcels out some identities as national identities and others as ethnic identities. The approach we will examine here takes a quite different view. The distinction is important to analysts because, in their everyday interactions, people *treat* it as important. And what this means is that we will want, as analysts, to be able to understand how people themselves rely on this distinction when they are pursuing their own aims and agendas in discourse. Thus the question becomes not 'what is the analyst's distinction between national and ethnic identities', but rather what are the occasions in which individuals seek to establish the nationality/ethnicity distinction, and why is it important for them to do so? So the relevant point here is to understand that what counts as a national identity or an ethnic identity is not settled by analyst's fiat but is, instead, resolved by examining the ways in which people themselves orient to such identity concerns.

What are ethnic identities?

Eriksen (2010) provides a useful history of the terms 'ethnic' and 'ethnicity', with the former being traced back, at least in modern times, to mid-nineteenth century preoccupations with race. However, as early as 1922 the sociologist Max Weber

(1978) pointed out that the biologist's concerns with physiological inheritance as a determinant of natural types were of little use to the social scientist, since the practice of 'connubium' or inter-marriage meant that biological inheritance did not in itself mark out socially relevant groups. (Indeed, as Eriksen points out, similar considerations have led modern genetics to shy away from 'race' as a theoretical construct.) Of course, this does not mean that biologically inherited differences in physical appearance are irrelevant in social settings, but it demonstrates that it is how we as social actors respond to such differences that is important to the social scientist. For reasons of this sort, social scientists have come to consider ethnicity as in part a matter of commonality of culture rather than as an issue grounded in biological facts. However, this need not mean that 'biological facts' have merely been replaced by 'cultural facts' in such accounts of ethnicity. Contemporary researchers do claim that ethnic groups are people who share the same culture. And this may reflect shared symbolic aspects such as physical appearance or style of dress or food preferences or common languages or dialects. Or it may reflect common ways of thinking such as shared social norms or moral belief systems. But these features need not, themselves, be regarded as 'objective facts' of the sort that biologists or chemists take themselves to be concerned with.

In an influential paper on this topic, Barth (1969) points out that in most cases, the development of ethnic groups goes hand in hand with population movement and social mobility. This raises the question, he suggests, of what it is for an ethnic group to be distinct in some way from other ethnic groups: 'If a group maintains its identity when members interact with others, this entails criteria for determining membership and ways of signalling membership and exclusion' (Barth, 1969, p. 15). Barth points out that instances of 'ethnic identity change' do sometimes occur when individuals from one ethnic group assimilate into a different ethnic group. But what this alerts us to is the fact that ethnic identity is a form of self-identification: it is actors themselves who do the ethnic identifying. And what this means is that ethnic features are not 'objective facts' about us but instead are features of oneself and others which we draw upon as we create our own identities. Banks (1996) has described this view as revealing the socially constructive nature of ethnic identities. In establishing their own ethnic identities, actors will draw upon the sorts of cultural properties which can be associated with a specific ethnic group – for example, features of dress or common language, or broader cultural concerns such as moral values or social norms. But, says Banks, such features are selectively produced by actors within specific situations in order to construct a sense of their own ethnic identity, not merely to reflect a pre-existing natural order. Indeed, Banks points out further that such constructions are always relevant to a particular time and context (a feature that anthropologists have come to refer to as 'situated ethnicity').

Barth and Banks draw their conclusions from a consideration of social movement across ethnic groups and what that tells us about the nature of ethnic group boundaries. Fearon and Laitin (2000) draw similar conclusions from thinking about

Primordialism the reductive
view that ethnic categories are
grounded in more basic or
natural categories.

the way that violence can arise among such groups. They argue that such inter-ethnic violence cannot readily be explained by thinking about ethnicity in terms of **primordialism** – a view that ethnic categories are predetermined in nature (for example through bio-logical features). Instead, they argue that ethnic boundaries must be viewed as an outcome of social constructionism which could, for example, involve elite societal groups shaping ethnic identities to their own ends or the creation of ethnic identifi-cations in other ways, such as through the discourses of marginalized groups.

So what contemporary social research indicates is that ethnic identities are not a reflection of underlying biological facts but are, instead, social constructions cre-ated by individuals as they align themselves with particular ethnic groups. However, researchers such as Banks and Fearon and Laitin point out that this is a dynamic process. And Verkuyten amplifies this caveat when he points out that attempts to define ethnicity in terms of commonality of culture may 'underplay the impor-tance of creation and interactive use of cultural meanings' (Verkuyten, 2005b, p. 80). The key point here, then, is that the researcher must pay close attention to the detail of how such creativity is worked out in practice as ethnic identities are produced and taken up or challenged in social interaction. It is this task that the discursive researcher pursues.

Verkuyten himself provides an example that very neatly isolates the two issues that we have been discussing: ethnicity and nationality on the one hand and ethnic-ity and race on the other. In a study of third-generation South Moluccans living in the Netherlands, 40 young South Moluccan people were interviewed with the intention of learning how they themselves made sense of their own ethnic iden-tity. In analysing what these young people had to say, Verkuyten notes that his participants rejected notions of ethnicity as grounded in race. Instead, the concern they demonstrated in relation to their ethnic identity centred on cultural matters:

Extract 3.1

Too many Moluccan youngsters marry Dutch boys and girls, which will increase the number of half-castes. I'm afraid this will mean that we'll be left with totally Dutch children with a Moluccan surname. That's what you'll get. But I think these young-sters should be told where their name come from. This is what we should get into their heads. So that they, too, will understand that they should pass on their culture.

(Verkuyten, 2005b, p. 98)

What Verkuyten points out is that this speaker does not represent half-caste children as threatening some form of racial purity. Instead, the danger of such inter-marriage is that it threatens South Moluccan cultural identity. At other points in these interviews, Verkuyten's participants also discuss South Moluccan ethnic identity in terms of nationality, especially with reference to the possibility of an independent South Moluccan Republic (RMS).

Extract 3.2

The RMS is a lost cause. As far as I'm concerned, I don't think it's of any use. Of course you should show respect for what your parents fought for, but I don't think you should start fighting for it again. It's no longer realistic to do so

(Verkuyten, 2005b, p. 97)

So these young South Moluccans ascribed genuine desire for this sort of nation-hood to older generations, rather than to themselves. The point here, Verkuyten suggests, is that although the young people who were his participants were South Moluccans, they felt able to reject the view that there should be a South Moluccan nation state because this was a view that more properly belonged to an older generation than to themselves. And what this shows is that the relationship between ethnic identity and national identity is itself a social construction. In the present case, the claim that ethnic South Moluccans should have a separate national identity is made relevant, but is undermined by being ascribed to the 'older generation' who might, for example, be viewed as old-fashioned or too caught up with irrelevant historical events. It is also worth noting that this is a reminder that identities of ethnicity and nationality often surface alongside or even intertwined with other forms of identity, a notion we will see more of below.

In another study of ethnic identity that also draws on themes of nationality, Sala, Dandy and Rapley (2010) looked at the identity constructions of Italians who emigrated to Australia either as children or as adults. They found that the immigrants' discourse was concerned in part with the drawing of ethnic distinctions that helped to establish their authenticity as Italians.

Extract 3.3

108	CHIARA:	um (.) and um(.) and that, that there's that difference
109		um compared to the Anglo-Saxon <u>Australian</u> way of doing
110		things (laughs)
111	I:	mh hum
112	CHIARA:	yeah
113	GROUP:	(4.0)
114	PAOLO:	um (.) for me also um (.) being an Italian in Australia
115		for me also means I'm a migrant, so I believe (4.0) that
116		ah, I feel a migrant here, um (.) and (3.0) I don't know
117		I can see the way I live at home an the way I think and
118		(.) it's still the Italian way, um, the way I raise the
119		children, the way I <u>eat</u> (.) and it's still the Italian
120		way, I (4.0), we eat Italian at home.

(Sala, Dandy and Rapley, 2010, p. 116)

What Sala, Dandy and Rapley note is that Paolo establishes his Italian-ness by making references to a set of practices such as eating and child-rearing that make him Italian. So here we can see the sort of blurring of ethnic and national identifications that we have discussed. Paolo and his compatriots seek to establish a sense of themselves in terms of cultural practices that set them apart from Anglo-Australians. However, the very description of these practices such as thinking in 'the Italian way' draws upon national categorizations.

This point arises especially clearly in relation to language use. Verkuyten noted in his study that his South Moluccan interviewees viewed the use of the Malay language as very important in maintaining South Moluccan identity, and in discriminating 'real' Moluccans from others. Similarly, Sala, Dany and Rapley found that their participants treated the issue of whether and when to speak in Italian rather than in English as an important matter. Sala *et al.* noted, for example, that on occasions their participants would stress the importance of using their 'own' language and, interestingly, in doing so would often switch from English to Italian in order to make this point, which Sala and colleagues refer to as an 'ethnic category predicate *par excellence*'. Among linguistic researchers, this alternation between languages is referred to as **code-switching** (Gumperz, 1982; Su, 2009). These language researchers have noted that code-switching may be used for a variety of reasons, including establishment of a particular ethnic identity (Shin and Milroy, 2010). For example, Cashman (2005) points out that early views on code-switching saw social structures as primary and switches in code as merely reflecting such structures, with bilingual individuals selecting whichever language was appropriate to the current social setting. However, later researchers have come to view code-switching as a conversational resource in its own right. In particular, speakers may switch from one code to another in order to introduce a minority or majority cultural identity. For example, Cashman recorded spontaneous conversations that took place at a senior citizens' programme in Detroit, a city comprising varied ethnic groups including Latino, Anglo and African-American people. In one example, Cashman notes that even in the apparently trivial context of a game of bingo, her participants were able to use code-switching, and associated activities such as indicating relative success in the use of languages such as English or Spanish, to index ethnic identities such as the 'Anglo' or the 'Chicana'.

> **Code-switching** the use of more than one language in a single discursive episode usually associated with some attempt to mark this switch in language as significant.

> **Hybrid identities** identities that can be viewed as a mixture of more than one nationality or ethnicity.
> **Hyphenated identities** similar to hybrid identities, these mixed identities are so-called because of the nomenclature, e.g. Spanish-American.

Hybrid identities

This delicate negotiation of ethnic identity through language is associated with another phenomenon, sometimes referred to as the existence of **hyphenated identities** (Belanger and Verkuyten, 2010) such as African-American or Turkish-Cypriot identities. One

particular study of note here is Pichler's (2007) discussion of Asian arranged marriage practices in the UK. Pichler notes that the young British-Asian women who
were her research participants utilize a variety of discursive and cultural resources
to negotiate views and norms about marital relationships. She argues that cultural
understandings may be negotiated locally and in a number of cases remain implicit
in the young women's talk of marriage. In particular, Pichler notes that her participants are not 'passive victims' of cultural practices but instead play an active
role in reshaping cultural norms around marriage. So, although these young
women can be seen broadly to orient to available elements of gender in working
up their own identities, the precise detail of how these elements are taken up
within specific contexts is an important aspect of their identity formulations.
In consequence, Pichler argues, these young women are able to construct a fulfilling
identity which draws on positively evaluated aspects of the different cultural
resources which are referenced in their talk.

Extract 3.4

```
A    =YEAH: : [that's] true (.)
D              [yeah]      (.) yeah when they come to England
(21)
A                                        they just wanna get
H                    [(they just]xxx-)
D    yeah they just lea[ve you man]
(22)
A    married to girls from London [because like they are
V                                  [yeah because of the
(23)
A    Londoni] (.) yeah    [they are from London they are
V    passport] (.)         [they want their passport
D                   (ah[::)
(24)
A    British] they are British and they wanna come to this
V    inn]it
(25)
A    country as well
```

(Pichler, 2007, p. 208)

Pichler notes that in this extract her participants challenge the tradition of being
married to Pakistani men. The grounds they offer for this challenge are, in this
extract, rooted in their suspicions about potential grooms' motivations for
marriage. However, Pichler goes on to suggest that detailed argument of this sort
is set against a broader discourse in which it is not the Asian practice of arranged
marriages *per se* that the girls reject but, rather, particular versions of it. And what
is noteworthy here is that the girls rely upon characterizations of themselves as in
some sense British (e.g. as being British passport holders) in order to set out the

detail of their objections. In this way, Pichler's girls carefully construct a hybrid identity that reflects both their current nationality status and the traditions of their ethnic background.

However, it is important to note that the accomplishment of a hybrid identity is something that arises within a broader social context. For example, Burdsey (2007) analyses the way that the young British boxer, Amir Khan, was represented in newspaper coverage. Khan himself, Burdsey suggests, evidences a hybrid identity that is typical of young British Asians in that he frequently spoke of being British but was also 'openly proud of his Pakistani heritage and his Islamic faith'. One point of interest here, says Burdsey, is that although most of the newspaper articles to which he refers were positive towards Khan, they nevertheless discussed Khan and his achievements within a broader discourse of national and religious identity. Allied to this, says Burdsey, is the way in which Khan has been promoted by official agencies as a 'role model' for multiculturalism within the UK. So, Burdsey argues, Khan's perspective has been taken up in the media and reframed to epitomize the sorts of statements of loyalty to the UK that Muslims, but few others, are required to proclaim.

This latter issue, that hybrid identities are themselves open to renegotiation or even challenge, is also shown in a study by Norris (2007) of how ethnic and national identities can be simultaneously constructed. Norris examined discourses which arose at an official meeting of Hispanic/Latino Americans in Greater Washington which was attended by a number of businessmen and politicians. At this meeting, one speaker urged the multinational audience that it was in the best interests of the Hispanic/Latino community in America that they try to assimilate into the 'white majority group'. One point of interest that Norris makes clear is that the speaker foregrounds her ethnic identity as a Hispanic/Latino person while, to a lesser extent, representing her national identity as a Mexican, for example through the use of non-verbal gestures. However, Norris reveals that the speaker's assimilation proposal received a relatively negative reception from those in the audience who came from outside the United States. This, Norris suggests, indicates in part that the speaker was being treated as though she has only one singular identity, not a hybrid one that she shared with her listeners. Her claim for the importance of assimilation was directed toward the white majority group, who could be perceived as exercising power over job opportunities for new immigrants. However, this meant that the members of the audience who were Hispanic/Latino reacted in a negative fashion because the speaker had apparently selected the 'wrong' identity by affiliating herself with the aims and concerns of that white majority group.

We said earlier in discussing the South Moluccan study that ethnic identities can become interwoven with other sorts of identity in a way that transcends mere hyphenation. This is demonstrated in a study by Marra and Holmes (2008), who show how ethnic identities can be interwoven with other forms of identity in their New Zealand study of narratives within the workplace. They suggest that 'white' identity in New Zealand workplace settings can be taken as a cultural norm. In consequence, other ethnic identities may arise in workplace narratives in

New Zealand in a way that highlights their contrast with this norm. Marra and Holmes provide an example of this by analysing the ways in which a Māori identity is co-constructed by a group of co-workers in a media production company who are discussing a recent media awards ceremony. In particular, part of the workers' narrative turns to the issue of the way in which the awards ceremony presenter pronounces Māori words and phrases. According to Marra and Holmes this turns out to be a sensitive issue because people in New Zealand recognize that speakers will display a more or less **affiliative stance** towards the Māori in the way that they pronounce Māori linguistic terms. So those with a more affiliative stance take more care

> **Affiliative stance**   a position adopted in which one displays support for someone else.

to pronounce Māori words and phrases with a Māori accent, while those with a less affiliative stance adopt a more anglicized pronunciation. Marra and Holmes note that as one of the Māori workers in this media production company begins to discuss the presenter's introductions at the awards ceremony she provides ironic comment on the presenter's ability to pronounce Māori terms appropriately. This theme, although apparently subsidiary to the main topic of describing and evaluating the awards presented at the ceremony, is taken up by the other participants in the interaction who produce further ironic comment including mock repetitions of the presenter's use of Māori terms that emphasized their heavily anglicized pronunciation. So what is happening here seems to be that through their discussions, the workers are displaying an aspect of their occupational identities by displaying appropriate evaluative expertise and knowledge about matters related to media production. However, at the same time, they interweave into their narratives aspects of ethnic identity in which differences between Māori people and 'white' New Zealanders are commented upon in a manner which helps to establish the solidarity of their ethnic Māori identity.

Of course, this interweaving of ethnic identity with occupational identity can prove to be problematic, too. For example, Campbell and Roberts (2007) suggest that being interviewed for a job requires a special skill set. Candidates must be able to use a particular sort of discourse that combines talk of self with talk of the institution in order to produce an 'authentic' identity. This sort of identity successfully merges features of the self with features of the organization. Among successful candidates, features of the self are presented as fixed or essential and as measureable, in that the interview process allows interviewers to 'read' these features from the candidate's answers. Relevant features of the organization are the values and ideologies of the organization which the candidate is expected to recognize and endorse. However, in their study of a set of video-recordings of job-interviews in the UK, Campbell and Roberts draw attention to the ways in which foreign-born candidates may lack the relevant discursive skill to achieve this identity 'synthesis' of the personal and the organizational.

So what we have discovered is that discursive analyses of ethnic identities are strongly related to analyses of national identities. In part this is because the two notions overlap. But in part it is because people draw on ethnic and national identifications in a flexible way when they set out their own identities in talk. This is seen especially clearly in the cases of code-switching and hybrid identities. However, we have also seen that these identity constructions are not merely the product of a single individual. These formulations of self in terms of ethnicity are available to be taken up and challenged within broader social interactions. And this is an aspect of identity negotiation that is also a feature of religious identities, as we will now see.

Religious Identities

What are religious identities?

Christianity, Islam, Buddhism and Hinduism, to restrict oneself to the most 'popular' religions, jointly have adherents that number in the many billions. It is therefore in the nature of things that an adequate definition of 'religion' or 'religious belief' would probably encompass more than one volume all by itself. For this reason, we are going to have to restrict ourselves to a rough and ready working definition. One thing we can note is that in comparison with the national and ethnic identities we have already discussed, religious identity might seem to be something that is even more deeply personal and individual. This, at any rate, is the view of religious experience that Taylor (2002) ascribes to the philosopher William James. According to Taylor, the James view is that the social aspects of religion such as 'collective connections through sacraments or ways of life' are to be excluded from genuine consideration. This view has of course been challenged, perhaps most notably by those influenced by the work of Emile Durkheim. In his book *The Elementary Forms of Religious Life* (Durkheim, 1912), Durkheim reviews a number of possible definitional aspects of religion, especially the idea that it involves supernatural beliefs, or beliefs about a deity. He discounts these on the grounds that religions can be found whose adherents do not have these beliefs. He then draws attention to the fact that a religion is a system comprising many elements – myths, dogmas, rites and ceremonies – and concludes that it is better to understand each element in turn and then form a synthetic overview of what religion is once that prior task has been achieved. The essence of religion, he suggests, is that it comprises a set of beliefs which are representations of the religious aspect of the world (broadly the distinction of world features into 'the sacred' and 'the profane') together with a set of rites, which are the social practices such as particular forms of talk or action, performed by suitably qualified persons, that ensue from entertaining those beliefs. A consequence of such analysis, Durkheim asserts, is that religion is intrinsically a social phenomenon. On the one hand, religious beliefs or representations are shared representations. On the other, rites are activities that in principle are the sort of actions that are intended to engage broader social groups rather than just those who actually carry out the relevant actions.

Now one consequence of this latter view of religion as an essentially social process is its public nature. This aspect allows religion to become a locus for social action. For example, Chang and Mehan (2006) point to the way that US President George Bush deployed a mode of representation based on 'civil religion' to support and warrant the 'war on terror' and the invasion of Afghanistan. By 'civil religion', Chang and Mehan refer to a particular blend of discourse which combines American secular values such as freedom and liberty with an acknowledgement of a 'Supreme Being' loosely based on Christian teachings about God but not identical with them. The warrant provided through this discursive mixture was effective because it allowed Bush, and those others who took up this particular form of discourse, to present readily recognizable accounts of incidents such as the destruction of the Twin Towers that took place on 9/11. These accounts were developed around a simple dichotomy of good Americans versus evil terrorists. And by treating this dichotomy as having obvious evaluative overtones, Bush and others were able to treat their own claims for the need for a war on terror as self-evident and as standing in no need of further evidence.

So what we discover from this all-too-brief excursion into the history of the social science of religion is that we are apparently back at the place we started from at the beginning of Chapter 1. Accounts of religious identity will at times draw upon religious experience as an inward-focused aspect of the unique individual, and sometimes they draw upon the outward-focused notion of religion as a shared, social experience which represents a context in which social actions are performed. Hopefully, the reader will both be aware of the similarity of this to the discussions of identity and the self that we raised in Chapter 1 and will already be guessing the approach that we intend to follow as a consequence: for the discursive researcher, the key issue is to understand how participants themselves take up and negotiate these sorts of issues as they themselves develop a sense of religious identity as it applies to them and to others in interaction. It is to this approach that we now turn.

Religious leaders

One feature of religion as a social practice that we have noted is the idea that religions involve particular ritual practices which are to be conducted by appropriately qualified individuals. This, of course, raises the question of how people demonstrate themselves to be so qualified. In formal settings such individuals are often marked out by the roles which they occupy, and by the role's symbolic accoutrements such as robes, hats or belongings (such as special sticks or books) that those occupying the role ceremonially display. However, this is not the only means by which an individual may display such authority. Agne (2007) describes a stand-off that occurred in 1993, between law enforcement officials and members of the

Branch Davidian religious movement at a compound near the town of Waco, Texas. This event was to end in a disastrous fire in which 71 people were killed. In making sense of the events that led up to this tragedy, Agne points up the importance of **framing** and **reframing** in the interactions between the Davidians and the authorities. Reframing, he says, is a practice that allowed the Davidians to counter the ways in which FBI officials framed the ongoing negotiations. In the following extract, the leader of the Davidians, Koresh, challenges the spiritual foundation of the approach adopted by the authorities, here represented by the negotiator, Wren. Immediately prior to this extract, Wren has claimed that a particular individual who supports ending the stand-off has sought advice on the matter through prayer.

> **Framing**   a term deriving initially from Goffman to indicate participants' organization of their experiences into recognizable activities.
> **Reframing**   adopting a position in which a particular discursive framework of explanation is challenged.

Extract 3.5

399	Koresh:	[Well did God talk to him?
400	Wren:	He told me that he prayed to God and he came back with this with this
401		answer.
402	Koresh:	Okay. So God spoke to him then.
403	Wren:	That's that's correct.
404	Koresh:	Well why would God tell him one thing and me another.
405	Wren:	I have no idea but what uh what he's [telling you
406	Koresh:	[Maybe God's trying to get us to
407		fight or something.
408	Wren:	[No that's not it at all.
409	Koresh:	[You know you've got to watch this God

(Agne, 2007, p. 566)

Agne suggests that here Koresh adopts the identity of someone who is especially entitled to interpret God's wishes. Koresh introduces the notion of people not only praying to God, but receiving answers from him. Once Wren accepts that this is an appropriate way in which to frame the issue, Koresh then 'springs his trap'. Koresh reveals that God has also spoken to him, but told him something different, and implies that this is a problematic inconsistency. Koresh also indicates that he has a particular understanding of such issues, by warning Wren that God has to be watched, indicating that religious matters are not always easily grasped. In part, Agne suggests, what is going on here is that Koresh is establishing his own membership of the category of 'religious expert' by issuing a correction to Wren's interpretation of praying. And by doing this, Koresh is able at the same time to cast doubt on whether Wren is correct in claiming that the authorities' views on the stand-off have genuine religious foundations.

Of course, establishment of divine *bona fides* is sometimes a more subtle affair. Discursive researchers are in the business of making sense of people's identities from what people say and write. It is, then, somewhat ironic that on some occasions when someone is seeking to establish a divine origin for what they are saying, the speaker's utterances are designed to be unintelligible. In a study of a Cuban Santera ceremony, Wirtz (2007) shows how this apparent difficulty of unintelligibility is managed collectively by speaker and audience. Santera is an Afro-Cuban religion in which particular individuals, the santeros, are said to form a connection with deities who then 'speak' through them while the santero is in a trance-like state. The speech which is produced involves words and phrases interpolated into Spanish which are said to be drawn from the deities' own language, which only the santeros understand, although even they are taken not to understand it fully. In this respect, the discourse of the santeros resembles the 'speaking in tongues' which is sometimes observed in other religions such as Pentacostalism. Wirtz describes how the ritual unintelligibility of the deities' messages is produced as such in the way that both the santero and the audience orient to what is being said as standing in need of interpretation. This collusive activity extended into the 'translation' of the deities' messages, in that both santero and the audience would work together to 'disentangle' what it was that the deities meant. Now although this might seem a cumbersome way for the gods to talk to us, it does present the religious followers with several advantages. First, the very ambiguity of what is being said allows for a collective disambiguation in which all present can agree on the advice being offered, or the suggestions being made, or whatever. Second, the very need for a process of this sort allows the santero to establish himself or herself as someone who is being genuinely inspired by divinity. This is an especially delicate issue of identity for santeros, since not all trance-like states are accepted as genuine by their audiences. (It is amusing to note Wirtz's comment that it is other santeros who are often the most sceptical and nit-picking in raising doubts about the genuineness of a particular trance episode being evidenced by a rival santero.)

Followers of religion

Religions would not be religions without followers. So if it is important for religious leaders to construct a religious identity, it is equally important that their followers are able to do the same. Jaspal and Cinirella (2010) provide an interesting example of how ordinary people make sense of their religious identities in a study which examined how young Muslims who are gay make sense of their religious identities.

Extract 3.6

Interviewer:	And what's [which identity] most important to you?
Aziz:	Being a Muslim. That's my heart, my soul. I always try to be a good Muslim and sometimes it is hard but you got to try it.

| Interviewer: | Can you give me an example of this? |
| Aziz: | Even on 14th August [Pakistani independence day] I go out with my mates partying and sometimes I think 'This is wrong. Muslims are one.' Muslims aren't supposed to celebrate our national day because in Islam there's no nations. |

(Jaspal and Cinnirella, 2010, p. 11)

In this excerpt, Aziz is discussing the relationship of his religious identity to his national identity, and produces an account of religion in which the necessity of following religious principles is emphasized. This in turn leads to a negative evaluation of practices associated with his national identity. In this evaluation, he contrasts his religious beliefs about the non-existence of separate nation states with his practice in celebrating the date of Pakistan's independence. The depth of these religious inclinations, even given his apparent rejection of them in his actions, is indicated by his claim that his religion is 'my heart, my soul'. However, this religious identification poses particular difficulties for people who, like Aziz, are gay. As Aziz points out, his gender orientation can be viewed as incompatible with his religious affiliations:

Extract 3.7

Interviewer:	OK, so earlier you were saying that being Muslim is a beautiful thing, and er how do you feel about being gay? I mean, what does it mean to you?
Aziz:	It's wrong, really, isn't it?
Interviewer:	Wrong? Why's that?
Aziz:	In the mosque we're told that Shaitan [Satan] tries to tempt Muslims because he is evil and he makes us do evil things. I know that doing gay things is evil but I hope I'll change my ways and take the right path soon [..] It's all about temptation, really. Life is a big test.

(Jaspal and Cinnirella, 2010, p. 10)

So it turns out that Aziz's religious identity is not necessarily without its difficulties. It is in virtue of the deeply held nature of his convictions that other aspects of his life such as his sexual orientation become problematic. But it is noteworthy, Jaspal and Cinirella point out, that Aziz is able to formulate an explanation for his sexual activities which is, itself, grounded in this overarching religious identity. Aziz presents himself as someone who seeks to follow his religion's teachings but who is subjected to external forces in the form of 'temptation' that prevent him from avoiding evil. This religious view of the world is encapsulated in Aziz's gloss that 'Life is a big test', which makes available the inference that the world is to be considered in religious terms in which a deity or god is testing people in order to discover those who are appropriately faithful religious adherents.

However, spoken pronouncements of religious faith are not the only way in which followers can establish a religious identity. Chiluwa (2008), describing

Nigeria as one of the most religious countries in the world, explores the ways in which Nigerians use a particular means of establishing their religious group identities: vehicle stickers. Chiluwa argues that even the minimal discourse in these stickers constitutes a site for social action, notably one in which religious practices are constructed and, in so doing, allow an individual to present a version of himself or herself to the world. Thus, someone who sports a car sticker such as 'I am proud to be a Muslim' or 'I am proud to be an Anglican', is using discourse to establish a religious identity in a very direct way. More than this, however, is the way in which some of these stickers represent a particular version of what it is to formulate one's identity in this way. Thus some of the stickers observed by Chiluwa present a particular view of the world as perceived from the identity being established, such as hopefulness ('There is joy in the morning') or aspiration ('I am a winner').

What we have seen is that maintaining a religious identity is a matter which can arise both through talk and text. But it can be potentially problematic for the individual, even in cases where that identity is described as being 'core' to who that person is. Of course, it is a commonplace to observe that for society as a whole it is often taken to be the case that the biggest tensions in this area lie not within each individual but between individuals who espouse different forms of religion. As one example of this, Bowskill, Lyons and Coyle (2007) look at the way in which British print media have represented the debate within the UK about faith schooling. One point of interest here lies in the way in which faith schools provide information on how cultural variety within the UK is viewed, especially in terms of **acculturation**. 'Acculturation' describes a process in which different cultures undergo progressive degrees of contact, with subsequent changes to all of the parties involved. As such, those who advocate acculturation ought, in principle, to be willing to see their own culture altered as a result of interaction with other cultures. However, Bowskill and colleagues argue that discourses of acculturation can embed underlying discourses of **integration**, in which 'minority' cultures are expected to adapt themselves to the 'majority' culture. Thus those who apparently argue for acculturation may often be seen to be arguing for integration.

> **Acculturation**   a process in which the different cultural aspects of two groups are combined, usually indicating a more reciprocal arrangement than that found in integration.
> **Integration**   a process in which the different cultural aspects of two groups are combined, usually indicating that a minority culture has been subsumed within the majority culture.

Extract 3.8

The Daily Telegraph
… boys and their influential parents all seemed happy for the teaching to be in English, entirely by non-Muslims – sympathetic Christians to be more precise – working to a normal British curriculum. There was a room set aside for prayers but

I never saw anyone using it. … We even had a Christian Jordanian Arab boy in the school, totally integrated with the others and highly popular. … The modest princes mixed easily with everyone else and sang Amazing Grace in the music room as enthusiastically as the rest. But perhaps that was a step too far.

(Bowskill, Lyons and Coyle, 2007, p. 805)

Bowskill and colleagues note that the author of this letter (presented here in a condensed form) appears to offer support for the view that peoples from different cultures can live together in a fruitful way. However, this apparently progressive view towards minority cultures has a darker side. The author provides an example of this occurring in which boys of a variety of faiths were 'happy' to be taught by Christian teachers. Indeed, the potential difference marked out by difference in faith is minimized by the author in that although a prayer room had been set up he 'never saw anyone using it'. This situation is then further emphasized through reference to a particular case of a 'Jordanian Arab boy' who is described as having been totally integrated. The concern that Bowskill and colleagues note here is that a view which is apparently supportive of different cultures living in harmony within the UK in fact relies upon an integrationist discourse in which Muslims (or Arabs) are described as successfully living within the UK context when they are successfully integrated into a world of 'sympathetic Christians'.

Such tensions arise not only between religions but also between the religious and the non-religious. We noted above Chiluwa's analysis of religious car stickers. It is interesting to note here that atheists have struck back on the car badge front. In a number of countries, Christians have adopted the ichthys symbol, which is a stylized representation of a fish made up of two intersecting arcs. Atheists have responded by creating a variety of 'alternative' car badge versions, with perhaps the most common being an ichthys-like symbol which has 'grown' reptilian legs and contains the word 'Darwin' within its body. In part, this social development is interesting because Anspach, Coe and Thurlow (2007) have described atheists as experiencing **marginalization** in society. The prevalence of outward displays of religious identity can raise challenges for others such as atheists, who find themselves at odds with the religious perspective on the world. (It is interesting to note here that such marginalizing experiences are not limited to atheists. McVittie and Tiliopoulos (2007), for example, point to the ways in which the religious beliefs of those who interact with psychotherapists are routinely marginalized and viewed as 'getting in the way' of appropriate therapeutic delivery.) One means by which atheists deal with this marginalized status, according to Anspach and colleagues, is to invoke a 'more immediately recognized identity politics'. In particular, somewhat surprisingly, atheists sometimes present a version of their own social position that highlights similarities between their own position and that of homosexuals. They accomplish this by appropriating the metaphor,

> **Marginalization**   a process in which an individual or group faces social arrangements in which they lack the normal rights and entitlements of others.

common to homosexual accounts of identity, of 'coming out of the closet' as a means of describing their avowal of atheist principles. Thus, for example, Aspach and colleagues point to an entry on a web site, the Secular Web, in which a correspondent describes feelings of being surrounded by those who believe in God and having had to struggle to finally 'come out of the closet' and express his or her own atheist views.

Naturally, religious people will suspect that atheists feel challenged because they do not have an adequate account of the world which they can draw upon in justifying their atheism. Interestingly, there is some evidence to suggest that they may be right. We saw above that Durkheim was concerned to note parallels and differences between religions and magic. Both, for example, may draw upon notions of the supernatural or, to use more currently popular jargon, 'the paranormal'. This might indicate that people who adopt a **scepticism** 'take' on the paranormal should be in a position to explain why. However, Lamont, Coelho and McKinlay (2010) argue that

> **Scepticism**   the expression of disbelief in a claim or set of claims.

psychologists have traditionally approached belief in the paranormal as problematic in ways that disbelief is not. Implicit in this orientation is that believers are in some way at fault, and therefore carry a special burden of explanation when accounting for their beliefs, and that disbelievers are not similarly required to account for their disbelief. To make up for this, Lamont and colleagues designed a 'magic show' and invited along a number of paranormal sceptics. After the show, the audience members were asked how they would explain the apparently paranormal activities they had witnessed. What Lamont and colleagues found was not only that 'sceptics' themselves orient to their own accounts as though they do stand in need of justification, but found themselves in the somewhat embarrassing position of not being able to supply that justification. One way in which these participants addressed the problem of lacking details about how ostensibly paranormal events might be explained via normal means was by appealing to others' knowledge about such details and by attributing the events to the control of the performer. In the following extract, the participants are discussing an apparently mystical event involving dice and a cup.

Extract 3.9

124	A	So how how did you make sense of what was going on?
125	H	In relation to the dice? Or everything the ( )
126	A	Let's say in relation to the dice.
127	H	I mean I walked out of there and presume there's I mean I (.) I have to believe that the fix is in at some point.
128		
129	A	[Hehehe]
130	H	[Hehehe] <The next show it's going to be 6 and 1 and=
131	A	=Yeh

132 H you know and then maybe whatever but em. (2.0) >For the second one<I
        thought
132   well maybe is he is he jiggling the cup there ((sss)) you know is that.
        somehow
133   there's (.) Y'know I'm sure there's a (3.0) if you looked on those magic
        sites you
134   eh alluded to on the internet there must somehow there must be a way of
        doing
135   that. That's what I tell myself when I look at that. I'm eh the sceptic.
        Hehehehe It's
136   sort of ( )
137 M Hehehehe I agree I think that

(Lamont, Coelho and McKinlay, 2010, p. 550)

Reformulation   talk in which a partial or complete word or phrase is followed by a restatement in other words of what was just said.
Idiomatic expressions commonplace phrases or sayings that are found in everyday language and are difficult to challenge.

The initial response to the question asked indicates some form of dubiety. Following the **reformulation** of the question at line 126, the answer provided describes the speaker's standpoint as one which is sceptical in nature: 'the fix is in'. It is noteworthy here that although this sceptical position is initially presented as a presumption, it is then upgraded, at lines 127 to 128, to a belief that is held by necessity. However, the use of an **idiomatic expression** ('the fix is in'), rather than a literal avowal of scepticism, is treated as humorous by the interviewer and speaker, and avoids a potential criticism that a more literal avowal might provoke. In this way, the initial dubiety indicated in the speaker's first response provides a local context in which the relatively strong sceptical claim can be raised, albeit one that is not necessarily to be taken entirely seriously. So in this somewhat indirect way H is able to warrant his identity claim 'I'm eh the sceptic' without actually being able to explain away the events he has witnessed.

Our brief encounter with religious identities has shown that they are not necessarily associated with contexts of peace and harmony. The production and display of religious identities can be an unsettling matter for all concerned. However, to date we have not really plumbed the depths of this 'dark side' to identities grounded in religion. In order to do that, we will need to explore, once again, the realm of prejudice.

Ethnic and Religious Prejudice

Towards the end of the last chapter, we pointed out that episodes of directly prejudicial talk about other nations are regarded by contemporary social science as often having been supplanted by forms of new racism in which speakers accomplish prejudicial ends while managing their own self-presentation as non-prejudiced persons (Augoustinos and Every, 2007). As van Dijk (2006) has pointed out, discourse is not always 'ideologically transparent'. In the last chapter, we discussed this issue in relation to the question of national identification and immigration. However, new racism is just as likely to make its appearance when ethnic identities are made relevant. For example, Simmons and Lecouteur (2008) have discussed the ways in which Australian newspapers constructed different versions of two riots that occurred in New South Wales allegedly arising as a result of police **discrimination**. One of these riots involved indigenous Australians and the other did not, although both groups came from areas typified by low socio-economic factors. Simmons and

> **Discrimination** unfair behaviour directed at others as a result of prejudice.

Lecouteur note the way these riots were described in the media. The riot that involved indigenous Australians, unlike that involving non-indigenous Australians, was attributed to causes that were 'intractable' and unchangeable. Thus the problems involving indigenous Australians were presented in a manner which indicated that there was little point in trying to change the life-circumstances of the people involved. What is noteworthy here, of course, is that this claim, that the problematic aspects of life faced by non-indigenous Australians might be worthwhile trying to change but not those of indigenous Australians, is apparently racist. But it has been set out as a subtle argument in which directly racist talk is absent, and so accusations of racism are more difficult to establish.

As a term, 'new racism' seems to be explicitly directed towards forms of prejudice that involve either nationality or ethnicity. However, Ng (2007) has usefully extended this notion to other forms of 'subtle' discrimination such as discrimination in respect of religious faith. As an example of this broader sort of 'new' discrimination, we can turn to a study by Figgou and Condor which explores how subtle prejudice can be accomplished through the adroit production of membership categories. Figgou and Condor (2007) look at the ways in which category labels are negotiated in discussions about the Muslim religious minority who live in the part of northern Greece that borders Turkey. One feature of this particular situation is that a number of Greeks use the category label 'Turk' to refer to these individuals. This practice is, however, highly controversial. What Figgou and Condor note is that Orthodox Christian Greeks treat this as a highly sensitive matter, in which issues of 'Greekness' and indeed issues of categorization are brought into their talk in a careful manner.

Extract 3.10

Kiriakos: So much for the refugees (.) now about the others (1.5) the Turks (.)
               about the minority (1.5) the Muslim minority (4) but you know they
               themselves
               say that they are Turks (.) they never say that they are Greeks
Interviewer: hmm

Kiriakos: (3) they never say 'we are Greek Muslims' (.) they say 'we are Turks' (.)
                 Turks Turks (.) that's the way that they consider themselves (1)
                 although they have
                 the same rights that we have (Kiriakos, fireman, 42).

                                                        (Figgou and Condor, 2007, p. 449)

Figgou and Condor draw our attention to the way that Kiriakos corrects himself
by replacing the label 'the Turks' with the alternative characterization of 'the
Muslim minority'. This seems to indicate that Kiriakos is treating 'the Turks' as
a potentially problematic way of referring to this group of people. However, he
goes on to point out that these people do refuse to refer to themselves as 'Greeks'
and, instead, refer to themselves as 'Turks'. So Kiriakos is able to reintroduce the
notion that the people under discussion are not 'proper' Greeks because they
themselves do not use that label. The real issue here, Figgou and Condor suggest,
is that once this sort of talk is introduced, it allows speakers to move on to consider
whether the Muslim minority in Greece have the same civil rights as others. So, for
example, Kiriakos treats as mentionable the fact that they have these rights and,
elsewhere in their study, Figgou and Condor describe other participants as explicitly denying that Muslims in Greece should have these rights.

In another study, Lindgren (2009) explores the issue of how racism can be reproduced in news discourse by categorizing people in terms of a binary constructions
of 'us' versus 'them'. He examines a set of newspaper accounts of youth robberies
that occurred in Sweden. On the one hand, Lindgren notes that complaints about
'the youth of today' can have a political purpose – if the media emphasize youth
crime, then politicians will benefit from calling for tougher laws. (It is interesting
to note that the negative views on 'the youth of today' have been around at least
since Plato and Aristotle.) On the other hand, Lindgren points to the way in which
Swedish newspapers add a particular slant to this age-old story by focusing on the
over-representation of ethnic minorities in such crimes. Lindgren's suggestion is
that by drawing on ethnic identities of criminals in this way, Swedish newspapers
are able to construct an easily identifiable 'other' who is both different and bad, in
contrast to self-respecting Swedes.

Of course, just as 'extra' membership categorizations such as religious or ethnic
affiliations can be introduced into discriminatory discourse, so existing categorizations can be blurred. Wood and Finlay (2008) examined the discourse of Lee
Barnes, one of the leaders of the UK's British National Party (BNP), a far-right
political organization. They selected for study comments made by Barnes subsequent to events in 2005 in which bombings that took place in London were found
to have been carried out by Islamic extremists. One of the findings they report is
that the BNP sought to use reference to these bombings as a means of establishing
that all people who profess the Islamic faith, not just extremists, are terrorists and
therefore undeserving of British citizenship because they constitute a threat to the
'British' way of life.

Extract 3.11

The terrorists who attacked the tubes and bus in London on 7/7/05 were not long bearded, hook handed, one eyed ranting lunatics in white robes handing out videos with beheadings of Ken Bigley on them. They were your next door neighbour, the son of the chip shop owner down the street, Jaz down the road and the local supply teacher at the primary school. They drove Mercedes cars, dated your sister and integrated into mainstream British culture. And it was all a lie. (Barnes, Article 2)

(Wood and Finlay, 2008, p. 713)

Wood and Finlay note that Barnes introduces a particularly extreme vision of the terrorist as someone who is a 'long bearded, hook handed, one eyed ranting lunatic'. They point out that this is hearable as a reference to an extremist Muslim cleric, Abu Hamza (who is bearded and uses a prosthetic hand), who at the time was mentioned frequently in the British popular press. This figure is contrasted with the ordinariness of those responsible for the London bombings. The point of this contrast is to indicate to the audience that Muslims who set bombs are not distinguishable from everyone else in the way that people like Abu Hamza are. The implication made available here is, then, that the only distinguishable characteristic of these terrorists is that they are of the Muslim faith. Barnes' upshot of this argument is presented at the end of the extract, in which he indicates that attempts to integrate Muslims into British culture represent 'a lie'.

In part, the danger of discourses of this sort lies in the way that they become the single, authoritative discourse of such far right groups. For example, Atton (2006) examined the identities that are formulated on the BNP's web site. What Atton finds is that the discourse of the far-right, as represented by this web site, reproduces an ideological framework that curtails the appearance of different 'voices' within such discourse. By drawing on the everyday identities of those for whom it claims to speak, the BNP at the same time creates a space in which variation in identity is precluded. As an ironic note, Atton suggests that the means by which this is accomplished is by the representation of racist views through the medium of describing BNP supporters as, themselves, the victim of racism.

Buttny and Ellis (2007) have also explored the ways in which membership categories can be deployed in their study of how participants of a television discussion programme dealt with the issue of violence which arose during the conflict between the Palestinians and Israel in the years 2000–2005. What this examination revealed was that those participating in the programme developed differing versions of the violence which occurred during this conflict. In particular, Buttny and Ellis looked at the differing ways Israelis and Palestinians deployed membership categories in order to establish moral **accountability** for the violence they were describing. In the following extract, one of the television programme's Arab participants describes a particular episode of violence.

> **Accountability** responsibility, especially in relation to the speaker's responsibility in providing a particular account.

Extract 3.12

10   Israeli >residents bursted out< into the streets and eh ↑rioters actually
11   started attacking Arabs and Arab individuals everywhere (0.6) burning
12   Arab shops in mixed towns (1.1) and eh one (0.8) of the events was a mob
13   of three hundred four hundered Israeli racists (1.2) eh >de↑claring on the
14   radio that they're coming to burn my house< (0.6) and after midnight
15   organizing beating Arabs that they meet in the streets (.) and they come
16   with torches to my house after midnight to burn it (.)

(Buttny and Ellis, 2007, p. 145)

Buttny and Ellis point out that on a number of occasions, the television show's
participants can be seen to *position* themselves or others. What this means is
that the speaker adopts a particular stance, either to him/herself or towards
other people. In doing so, the speaker draws on particular features of an individual, such as elements of that person's identity, in order to 'notice' something
about that person such as his or her emotional state. In this extract, the speaker
positions Israelis as particular types of people: those who hate Arabs and are
violent towards them. In particular, Buttny and Ellis suggest, the speaker
accomplishes this by drawing on a number of membership categories such as
'rioters', 'mobs' and 'racists' and by providing action descriptions which are
associated with such category membership such as 'attacking Arabs' and 'burning Arab shops'.

The theoretical notion of positioning also appears in Verkuyten's (2005a) explo-
ration of talk of ethnic discrimination among majority ethnic Dutch people and
members of minority groups (Turks, Moroccan, Surinamese-Hindustanis
and Moluccans) in the Netherlands. He found that members of both majority and
minority groups used discursive strategies that denied the omnipresence of discrimination and that both groups also produced discourse which affirmed the
existence of racism and attributed it to the Dutch. In some ways, it is surprising
to discover that both groups relied upon similar discursive strategies (although
the reader may recall Atton's finding that British racists used anti-racism talk in
describing their own position). However, Verkuyten points out that the analyst
must be aware of exactly how these discourses are reproduced by being sensitive
to the way in which a speaker is positioning himself during the moment of
production. So, for example, at first blush there seems something odd about
minority group members agreeing with statements made by ethnic Dutch people
that minority group members are overly sensitive about discrimination, a claim
that apparently absolves the majority of Dutch from responsibility for discrimination. However, among minority group members this sort of talk arose in contexts
in which the speaker was establishing a sense of self as autonomous and self-
responsible and capable of upward social mobility. In positioning himself as that
sort of person, the speaker is less likely at the same time to successfully produce
a discourse in which he is also positioned as the hapless victim of discrimination.

(This has similarities with Condor's finding described in the previous chapter that people may sometimes be openly racist because, at that moment, they are seeking to display a rebellious or humorous sense of self.)

Fozdar (2008) reports a similar finding. She interviewed working-class New Zealanders and discovered that counter-racist forms of discourse are readily available to New Zealanders. She demonstrates that the same sorts of talk that are taken up by those who put forward racist views are also available to those who wish to challenge such views. As one example, Fozdar points to the way in which both racist and counter-racist arguments can be developed by appeal to temporal notions. We saw in the last chapter that temporality can be an important aspect of national identity negotiation. It is, then, hardly surprising that it also plays a role in ethnic prejudice. Fozdar describes how racist talk about the disadvantaged position of the Māori people in New Zealand sometimes draws upon talk of previous generations. The argument proposed is that while the present situation of Māoris may be unsatisfactory, it derives from actions performed by previous generations of white New Zealanders and that, in consequence, present generations cannot be held to account or expected to make reparations. What is interesting about this form of discourse, according to Fozdar, is that it is also taken up by those who oppose racism. For example, they too make references to not being able to change the past. However, unlike racists they use such references as a frame in which one can draw conclusions about whether past injustices ought to be continued into the present. So while all might agree that 'the clock can't be turned back' and that 'the past is another country', they use such talk in different ways, with racists deploying it to argue for the historical status quo while anti-racists use it to argue for a differentiation between what was wrong in the past and what should be made right in the future.

We began this section by reminding the reader about the review, that we discussed in the last chapter, of new racism studies produced by Augoustinos and Every. In that review, they point out that, since discursive research focuses on participants' own understandings and orientations, this can potentially leave the discursive researcher in a quandary. The problem here is something like the following. In new racism, people can be seen to use everyday talk to produce racist claims while managing impressions of themselves as being non-racist. This means that, if they are successful (or in cases where such talk is a joint accomplishment of more than one speaker), speakers may display no overt orientation to the talk being produced as racist. But discursive researchers are supposed to focus on participant's own orientations. So it seems that there will be occasions in which racist talk arises, but because it is not oriented to as such by the speakers themselves, analysts cannot produce analyses which identifies such talk *as* racist. In response to this problem, Augoustinos and Every suggest, some discursive analysts opt for 'door A': they accept that in such cases, it would be a mistake for analysts to describe such talk as racist. Other discursive analysts opt for 'door B': they refer to interactional features such as the surrounding

ideological frameworks in which such talk is produced, and claim that, as analysts, they can draw on those explanatory resources as identifying such-and-
such a pattern of talk as racist, even if the participants do not. For example, in
the study we discussed above of BNP discourses, Wood and Finlay note that
they have 'gone beyond the data' in their analysis by drawing on what they
know of far-right ideologies. In doing so, they align themselves with the 'critical
discursive approach' outlined by Wetherell (2003). Augoustinos and Every
themselves create a new door, 'door C' through which the analyst is described
as identifying 'a set of descriptions, arguments, and accounts that are recur-
rently used in people's race talk' together with 'discursive resources that perform social actions such as blaming, justifying, rationalising, and constructing
particular social identities for speakers and those who are positioned as other'
(Augoustinos and Every, 2007, p. 125). They suggest that by identifying such
accounts and resources, the analyst is able at least to demonstrate ways in which
people may 'dodge' the identity of being prejudiced, even if the analyst is reluctant to actually describe the talk under study as racist in itself. Among the language features that Augoustinos and Every identify are: producing explicit
denials of being a racist; grounding racist talk in 'rational' argumentation; the
joint production of positive presentations of oneself together with negative
presentations of 'the other'; the 'deracialisation' of discourse in which talk of
'race' is replaced by reference to other aspects of the world, such as economic
features, in order to produce negative formulations; and somewhat ironically,
the adoption of 'liberal' arguments in setting out illiberal claims of the sort
noted in Atton's study. The extent to which a project of this sort is successful
may, as yet, be unclear but it is already apparent that a number of the language
features to which Augoustinos and Every point are observable in the studies we
have examined in this section and in the previous chapter.

Discussion

What we have seen, then, is that ethnic and religious identities, like their
national identity counterpart, are best understood as constructive discursive
achievements. But we have also noted a darker side to this story. Just because
ethnic and religious identities can be constructed in discourse, this leaves open
the opportunity for people to construct ethnic and religious identities for others and, moreover, to do so in a way that accomplishes for them other social
actions such as criticizing, derogating, marginalizing, excluding or even insti-
gating violence.

There are some features of the discussion which we have followed up until now
that are worth noting. First, as van Dijk (2005) usefully points out, prejudice is not

just discourse. Marginalization, exclusion and violence are real social actions. And they involve aspects of institutional power and political realities. For example, Blackledge (2006) points to the way that forms of racist prejudice directed at ethnic groups in the UK such as people of black Caribbean heritage has in recent times been redirected toward Muslim people, often those whose heritage is in Pakistan or Bangladesh. He points to official reports that have revealed a rise in anti-Muslim discourses in fields as diverse as the media, education and the law. Thus the building of mosques or fasting during periods of religious observance have become representations in the media of the 'otherness' of Muslims within the UK. One consequence of these sorts of representation, he suggests, is that apparently coercive forms of legislation such as language-proficiency requirements can be presented as 'reasonable' responses to the otherness of Muslims and other religious and ethnic immigrant groups.

Second, it is also worthwhile remembering that not all expressions of prejudice are subtle expressions. But this does not mean that they necessarily lack any of the features of 'subtle' racist talk that Augoustinos and Every point to. For example, Finlay (2007) discusses the nature of extreme prejudice by exploring examples drawn from the writings of Nazis, white supremacists and extreme Zionists. What he seeks to do is to show how extremists 'normalize' their hostility by constructing particular versions of the groups that they seek to attack. Thus, for example, Jewish people were constructed by the Nazis as a threat to civil society and, as a result, were described in a manner which makes it 'obvious' that we should adopt a hostile stance towards them. At the same time, reformulations were provided of the attitudes and motivations of this group which were designed to undermine their legitimacy and so enable negative evaluations of those attitudes and motivations to be produced. And the question of why the ordinary person might be deceived into thinking otherwise was answered by appeal to the corrupting influence of the Jewish media. So even though by any stretch of the imagination anti-Semitic talk of the sort discussed by Finlay would 'count' as blatant prejudice, the authors of such talk still attended to the Augoustinos and Every dictum that racists are likely to at least attempt to propose their views as the outcome of 'reasoned' argument.

Third, it is important to consider whether prejudice is the sort of thing that can be challenged from the discursive perspective. Critical discursive theorists such as critical discourse analysts and critical discursive psychologists argue that the answer to this question is 'yes'. Broadly, the solution proposed is that prejudiced forms of discourse, whether overt or subtle, should be identified, challenged, and replaced with non-prejudiced discourse. However, other researchers such as Machin and Mayr (2007) express some reservations about the utility of shared discourses in tackling racism. In a study of anti-racist talk in an English regional newspaper, they point out that the newspaper aligns itself with those who oppose racism. But they also point out that the relevant texts that appear in the newspaper offer little by way of practical suggestions as to how racism can be tackled at the political level or at the level of social action within the community, beyond relatively bland encouragements to 'share' experiences. What they conclude is that in some respects, this form of anti-racist rhetoric represents little more than an ineffective 'talking cure' where it is merely assumed that talking about a problem is, in and of itself, a solution of sorts.

We have seen in this chapter that ethnic and religious identities sometimes merge into one another and that these, in turn, may blend into national identities. We also saw that expressions of one or other of these identities sometimes arise along with other identities, such as occupational identities. In concluding, we draw the reader's attention back to the story of Aziz and his struggles with his sexuality in the context of his religious faith. This provides us with an important indication that matters of nationality, ethnicity and religion may intersect with aspects of gender and sexuality. It is this theme which we explore in the next chapter.

Chapter Summary

The chapter begins with a discussion of the similarities and differences between national identities and ethnic identities. It is argued that in many respects these two forms of identity overlap. The notion of ethnic identity is traced back to mid-nineteenth-century preoccupations with race, but it is argued that contemporary social scientists view ethnic identities as cultural in nature, being best thought of as social constructions. A series of empirical studies are explored in which nationality is seen to overlap with ethnic identity concerns of the participants. Particular attention is given to hybrid identities in which people seek to establish a sense of self that draws on more than one ethnicity or nationality. The notion of 'code-switching' is also discussed. It is pointed out that ethnic identities are sometimes produced in contexts where other identities, such as occupational identities, are 'in play'. The chapter then moves on to discuss religious identities. A brief historical overview traces the view of religion as a social phenomenon to the work of Durkheim. The identity-work of religious leaders is examined, followed by a discussion of how religious followers formulate their religious selves. The tensions that can arise out of the display of religious identity are discussed, in respect of atheists and inter-faith rivalries. The chapter then moves on to review some recent discursive work on prejudice in respect of ethnic and religious identities. The notion of 'new' or 'subtle' prejudice is outlined, and a number of empirical studies are introduced which describe this phenomenon. In particular, processes of categorization and positioning are shown to be relevant in the formulation of prejudiced talk.

Connections

It will now be clear to the reader that the studies presented in this chapter are closely linked to the sort of work that was outlined in Chapter 2. We will also see that issues of ethnicity are often caught up with issues of gender, which we will explore in the next chapter. Of broader interest, it is useful to note that national and ethnic identities may arise in contexts where other identities are made relevant, and so some of what is discussed here in relation to the link between ethnic identities and occupational identities is relevant to material that is discussed in Chapter 7.

Further Reading

Agne, R.R. (2007). Reframing practices in moral conflict: interaction problems in the negotiation standoff at Waco. *Discourse and Society, 18,* 549–578.

In this study, some of the disastrous consequences of the stand-off between the Branch Davidians and the US forces of law and order are traced back to David Koresh's development of a religious leader identity.

Jaspal, R. and Cinnirella, M. (2010). Coping with potentially incompatible identities: Accounts of religious, ethnic, and sexual identities from British Pakistani men who identify as Muslim and gay. *British Journal of Social Psychology, 49,* 1–22.

A fascinating account of how people with deep religious convictions struggle to come to terms with a sexuality that their faith proscribes.

Sala, E., Dandy, J. and Rapley, M. (2010). 'Real Italians and Wogs': The discursive construction of Italian identity among first generation Italian immigrants in Western Australia. *Journal of Community and Applied Social Psychology, 20,* 110–124.

The authors explore with their participants the alternative ways in which different generations of immigrants preserve a sense of their ethnic identity.

Activity Box

We discussed the fact that religions involve public displays of ceremonial worship. On occasion, such events are so important that they become headline news around the world. For example, at the time of writing the Pope is making a well-publicized visit to the UK that involves several public sermons. Try to gather media coverage of one such event (perhaps via radio or television news broadcasts or via internet reports). What do these texts tell us about how religious identities are celebrated and confirmed in such events?

4

Gender Identities

Topics Covered in this Chapter

Key Terms

Agency

Couple identity

Cultural specificity

Disempowerment

Empowerment

Extreme case formulations

Feminism

Gender-blind

Gender-specific

Hegemony

Heterosexism

Macho identities

Performative

Sex

Sexism

Situated accomplishments

Swinging

Variationism

Women's liberation

Identities in Context: Individuals and Discourse in Action, First Edition. Andrew McKinlay
and Chris McVittie.
© 2011 Andrew McKinlay and Chris McVittie. Published 2011 by Blackwell Publishing Ltd.

Seven naked women on billboards across Poland are stirring passions in the coun-
try's already overheated election campaign.
  The poster is an attempt by the newly founded Women's Party to alert female vot-
ers to what it believes is the real political problem in Poland: male chauvinism.

The Times, September 2007

Just as was the case with national, ethnic and religious identities, gender as an aspect of the self has been a focus of interest for writers and researchers through-out the ages. In more recent times, the rise of socio-political movements such as **feminism** has brought gender to the forefront of social scientific research. Discursive researchers, too, have a long-standing concern with gender-related issues. In this chapter, we seek to introduce some of this discursive research by exploring the gender identi-ties of women and men. To accomplish this within the confines of a single chap-ter, we must present these research findings in a somewhat limited fashion. So in discussing women's gender identities, we will in the main restrict matters to the identities that women construct around interpersonal relationships. In discussing men's identities, we will mainly restrict ourselves to examining 'macho' male iden-tities. Of course it will be clear to the reader that there is nothing 'natural' about this particular organization of content. Women can adopt macho identities, and men can adopt relationship-centred identities. However, the arrangements that are set out here do reflect the findings of contemporary discursive researchers in that these are two regular ways in which women and men talk about themselves. As with previous chapters, we will then move on examine the issue of prejudice in respect of this particular identity.

> **Feminism**   the view that men and women should be treated equally.

What Are Gender Identities?

What marks out the discursive approach to this topic as distinctive is the discursive researcher's view that gendered identities should not be accepted as self-explanatory or as straightforwardly reflecting biological differences between individuals. For example, Eckert and McConnell-Ginet (2003) note that we are pervasively sur-rounded by gender as an apparently 'natural' distinction, but they argue that it is this very 'self-evident' aspect that ought to lead the analyst to look at gender more deeply. The task for the analyst, they suggest, is to uncover the processes of social construction that leads to this state of affairs. In beginning this task, they distinguish between biological **sex** and gendered performances, and note that it is a purely social convention that the one should be mapped onto the other. Indeed, they point out, sex itself is a biologically complex

> **Sex**   the biological distinction between men and women.

affair, with 1 in 100 individuals being born with bodies that differ from standard male and female bodies. And yet somehow these individuals usually end up being ascribed to one or other of the two sexes, male or female. This indicates that even sexual categorizations have a social origin, not a biological one. The importance of social construction is even more readily seen in relation to gender, which Eckert and McConnell-Ginet treat as a process of creating distinctions between men and women by socially establishing what is to count as 'normal' differences between them. The experience of social development that children undergo as they grow up in society means that they gradually learn about these differences and about the differential social practices in which they are to engage if they are to be counted as male or female. In this sense, gender is not part of one's essence but instead should be viewed as an achievement arising out of a set of social practices through which people construct and claim a gender identity for themselves. And a keystone in this development is the way in which gendered identities are constructed through discourse.

The subtle interplay between discourse, gender and other elements of interaction is well-described by Holmes and Meyerhoff (2003), who point out that the contemporary field of gender and language has moved beyond concerns with describing women's talk in terms of its syntactic or prosodic differences from men's talk. It has similarly moved beyond the treatment of gender as a proxy indicator for underlying power asymmetries within society. Instead, contemporary treatments of language and gender lay stress on the 'subtle and nuanced ways' that analysts have sought to explain language and gender interactions. Holmes and Meyerhoff suggest that one consequence of this is that the very notion of 'gender' is itself problematized in a variety of modern approaches to the issue. This means not only that essentialist views of gender as grounded in biology are rejected, but also that simplistic accounts of gender differences as an obvious cause of social effects are also treated with suspicion. Indeed, other researchers draw attention to further complexities. For example, as Stokoe (2005) points out in her review of the Holmes and Meyerhoff text, the precise status of 'gender' as a constructed entity is not always clear even in analyses which emphasize the **performative** nature of 'doing' gender.

Performative   a description of particular actions that emphasizes their role-like properties over suggestions that such actions arise from objective or natural causes.

In line with the basic assumptions of the discursive research approach, contemporary studies of gender have also emphasized the ways in which gender concerns are dealt with at the most local level of specific interactional contexts. It is these sites of identity formulation, maintenance and contestation that underpin the more generalized conclusions that gender researchers seek to draw about society at large. Holmes and Meyerhoff do take pains to point out the importance of these more generalized issues, where gender distinctions extend beyond their immediate context of production. But as was the case with the ethnic and nationality distinction we looked at in the preceding chapter, gender distinctions are of general concern to the analyst not because they reflect a general and pre-analytic notion of gender that is usefully drawn *a priori*, but because people in their everyday talk orient to what they and others say as though the issue of male-female gender identity is relevant. In a related vein, Eckert and McConnell-Ginet (2003) argue that local episodes of interaction are the contexts in which the seeds of 'larger societal discourse' of gender are planted. And this notion is, of course, consistent with the broader identity project within discursive research. It is in the particularities of situations that the accomplishment of identities is to be found. But the identities that arise, whether national, ethnic, religious or gendered, become ways of understanding self and others that permeate broader society.

So a key aspect of the contemporary approach to the study of gender is the view that gender identities have to be examined in a local context for their relevance to the participants themselves, rather than assumed to be self-evident objective features of a broader social landscape, even though such locally produced versions of gender identity may turn out to influence that landscape. Holmes and Meyerhoff highlight the socially constructive nature of this view of gender identity in saying that gender is an 'accomplishment and product of social interaction'. On a similar note Stokoe, in a discussion of the ethnomethodological background to the study of gender and feminism, draws attention to the ways in which gender-based identities are negotiated in talk: 'the gendered properties of social life, routinely taken-for-granted as natural and trans-situational, are best understood as situated accomplishments of local interaction' (Stokoe, 2006, p. 468). Of course, identities based on gender, understood in this sense as **'situated accomplishments'**, and the inferences that they make available are open to negotiation in a range of different ways. Speakers, for example, might take up and adopt forms of potentially gendered speech, or alternatively resist or rework versions on offer depending upon the demands of the local context in which they are located. It is to these discursive efforts that we now turn.

> **Situated accomplishments**
> a term used to describe social actions whose full meaning can only be understood by relating them to their context of production.

Women's Gender Identities

We have seen that the connection between immediate contexts of interaction and broader social notions of gender is a complex one. Nevertheless, there is evidence that women appear willing to draw upon these broader societal notions in developing their own gender identities. We can see this if we restrict ourselves to female gender identities as they are made out in terms of heterosexual relationships. Sandfield and Percy (2003) studied a number of women who had recent experience of being single. The women ranged in age from 20 to 48 years of age. What Sandfield

Heterosexism   a form of
thinking that views
heterosexuality as normative.

and Percy found was that their interviewees formed a version of their gender identities that drew upon **heterosexist** societal norms. In particular, the women appeared ready to provide self-descriptions which incorporated negative evaluations of women who are outside 'stable' relationships. The status of being single was presented as being an undesirable one and was for-mulated as a temporary life phase which should be treated as 'naturally' leading to an enduring relationship with someone. In producing these versions of themselves, the women in this study provided explanations for their single status in terms of the breakdown of a previous heterosexual relationship, a breakdown for which they blamed themselves.

Reynolds and Wetherell (2003) have also noted that single women display a defensiveness about their single status. In the following extract, one of their participants is responding to questions about how she views singleness:

Extract 4.1

Jay   I think my images when I was growing up were largely negative ones. . . . But certainly, or through literature I suppose … the sort of Victorian image of the spinster in the family who had to be supported somehow by the men in the fam-ily. And who was erm, not quite a whole person in some way. So I suppose I grew up with those images, erm, and with an expectation that it wasn't me, it wasn't going to be me, I was heterosexual I was erm at some stage going to get married and have children

(Reynolds and Wetherell, 2003, pp. 8–9)

Reynolds and Wetherell note the way in which singleness as a 'deficit' identity is positioned here, drawing on culturally available notions of the single woman as a negative character. Reynolds and Wetherell go on to describe how their female participants attempted to disown an identity of this sort by, for example, seeking to distance themselves from the 'typical' member of the category 'single women'. The reason for this, Reynolds and Wetherell suggest, is that the negative quality of the single woman identity is so socially pervasive that such women appear forced into evolving defensive strategies to cope with potentially unfavourable inferences about them grounded in their 'single' identity. Singleness thus is a discursively formulated social category that commonly is treated as a 'noxious' identity in rela-tion to which women without partners have to make sense of their own experi-ences and positions.

Another way in which women appear to draw on culturally available notions of female gender identity is in relation to parenthood. For example, Ulrich and Weatherall (2000) carried out a study of how women responded to issues of moth-erhood and infertility. What they noted was that the women who participated in their study appeared to readily equate womanhood with motherhood. Ulrich and Weatherall suggest that these sorts of constructions can be seen to reflect broadly held beliefs about the set of normative practices that surround being a woman, especially in respect of child-rearing and family care. Now, as with issues of single-ness, this might seem a somewhat surprising result. In some senses, it is shocking to discover that women develop a sense of their gender identities that is so close to other characterizations of female gender identity that could be taken to represent heterosexism or **sexism**. Developing a sense of women's gender identity by formulating that identity as more or less exclusively built around success in interpersonal relationships and in child-rearing sounds

> **Sexism** prejudice against others in respect of their gender.

uncomfortably close to the sort of comment that the average male sexist might share with his friends in the pub on a Friday night. For one thing, a focus on relationships and child-rearing seems to exclude from consideration other candidate aspects of identity that otherwise could be produced as relevant to a woman's sense of self, such as occupational status.

However, given what was said above about the nature of gender identity as a 'situated accomplishment' we should be cautious about assumptions that the women in these studies were 'social dopes' whose views of themselves were com-pletely conditioned by social pressures. For example, Reynolds and Wetherell point out that one can only understand what their participants are saying once one takes on board the idea that identity is a 'negotiated performance'. And if we look at the detail of such performances, they suggest, we find that their participants designed their self-descriptions in a way that inoculated them from the sorts of negative inferences that we have been discussing. Thus, their participants were able to for-mulate accounts of singleness in which positive evaluations could be inserted, such as emphases on the independent lifestyle and freedom of choice that such a status provided them with. In a similar vein, Coates (1996) has suggested that although 'heterosocial relations' are viewed by women as normative, they are nevertheless able to generate 'resistant' discourses, even though this may lead to forms of talk that are apparently contradictory. In this way, she argues, women are able to occupy a range of different 'possible selves'. Other researchers have demonstrated a simi-lar flexibility in the presentation of issues of relationship status. For example, in a study of individuals' constructions of marriage, Lawes (1999) notes that marriage, its foundations and consequences are open to somewhat differing versions depend-ing upon the argument that is being advanced. Marriage can of course be pre-sented in terms that rely upon notions of romance, commitment and permanence, in order to argue for it as a particular form of social arrangement. However, marriage – especially in relation to its failure – can also be presented as being grounded in more everyday concerns, such as difficulties with fidelity, or poverty, which make it appear to reflect concerns that are more 'realistic' than the com-monly assumed but idealized suggestions of romance and love.

Similarly, Croghan and Miell (1998) have examined the ways in which women faced with a particular challenging gender identity, that of being a 'bad mother', deal with this potential difficulty by challenging 'professional' discourses of

Hegemony a social arrangement in which particular views are treated as being normal or unremarkable, viewed as problematic where such views favour social elites in some way.

motherhood and attempting to construct a positive sense of self within 'good mothering' discourse. It is interesting to note that Sheriff and Weatherall (2009) also claim that motherhood is still **hegemonically** related to womanhood. However, in a critical discourse analysis of a number of articles drawn from the popular press, they note that a possible alternative

discourse is becoming more common, centred on women's experiences once their children have left home. This discourse is built around descriptions of women who are described as successfully negotiating the challenge of suffering traumatic loss when their children leave behind an 'empty nest'. For these women, a 'modern woman' discourse is available which emphasizes being 'fit' for a busy and engaged social life. However, it would appear that this particular identity is only regarded as legitimately available to women who have gone through this traumatic process of adjustment to loss – otherwise women who seek to take up this particular identity run the risk of being viewed as cold and heartless.

Kendall (2008) provides another example of these sorts of delicate identity formulation in her study of meal-time family interactions. She describes the way that the mother and father create gendered identities through their talk over the dinner-table. What is especially interesting, Kendal notes, is that these gendered identities are constructed in the process of enacting other social identities. For example, at times the mother adopts a position of 'moral guardian', in which she displays interest in the child's activities, but also exerts a regulatory force in determining whether the child has behaved appropriately. The father, on the other hand, at times seems to undercut the mother's disciplinary role by adopting the position of 'rebellious comedian' in which what he says can in part be interpreted as undermining the mother's authority.

Extract 4.2

1   Mark: You want another bowl? ((HOST))
2   Beth: Ew.
3   Mark: Hm?
4   Beth: No! They're disgusting.
5   Elaine: Excuse me. ((LANGUAGE MONITOR))
6   Beth: Sorry!
7   Elaine: Just say 'no thanks'.
8   Beth: No thanks!
9   ((6 seconds))
10 Mark: (chuckling, whispered) Disgusting.)
11 Beth: (scoffs)
12 Elaine: Go take your vitamin. ((CARETAKER))

(Kendall, 2008, p. 561)

Kendall notes that the mother, Elaine, adopts a monitoring position by correcting her daughter, Beth's language. At first, her correction seems to stand. But it is

Mark, the father, who then reintroduces the problematic term in a humorous way, thus apparently undermining Elaine's exercise of parental authority. Kendall's suggestion here is that in taking up these respective positions the parents are, at the same time, enacting gendered identities, with the mother adopting a feminine role as care-taker, engaged in activities such as feeding and bathing, while the father adopts a normatively recognizable masculine role of someone who engages in enjoyable activities with his children. Thus, gendered identities come to be made out through the establishment of other identities in this local interactional framework.

A further example of this sort of negotiation of gender identity is represented in a study by McKinlay and McVittie (2011). In this study, they interviewed a group of fishermen's wives living in a remote cliff-top village in the north of Scotland. One of the research interests here was to discover how the women produced a version of their gender identities that balanced the relatively demanding social norms of this remote community with other concerns such as displaying a sense of oneself as autonomous and independent.

Extract 4.3

AD: how would you see yourselves
    (2)
VB: Um (.) certainly not women's libbers
PM: (.) oh no
VB: No. We like to have a man to bring home the bacon
PM: Yes
VB: (.) em I don't think <u>either</u> of us would want a man coming in every night=
PM: =No
VB: That aspect would (.)
PM: (.) not after 24 years, no
VB: We think we've got the ideal situation where we (.) have a man part-time and
    the rest of the time we have complete liberty to come and go as we like
                                                        (McKinlay and McVittie, 2011)

In this extract, VB introduces a categorization that is not included in the question: **'women's libbers'**. This category makes relevant one particular socially prevalent view of women's experience which centres on ideas of freedom, independence and socio-economic

> **Women's liberation** a social and political movement begun in the 1960s that strove for equality for women.

status. Moreover, the category itself is produced in highly idiomatic terms, indicating the speaker's understanding that the sorts of views about women's experiences to be attributed to a 'women's libber' stand in no further need of explication. Now this version of women's identity stands in stark contrast to the 'traditional' views of gender roles that are prevalent within remote fishing communities of this sort. However, this categorization is introduced merely in order that VB may deny that she is herself a member of this category. And this seems to indicate that her

own gender identity is to be thought of in terms of these more 'traditional' characterizations. Following PM's agreement, VB develops her description further by
reference to what can be heard as a traditional stereotypical characterization of
the relationship between men and women in that it is men who 'bring home the
bacon'. This further description can be heard as confirming her rejection of
belonging to the category 'women's libbers' and is also agreed by PM.

VB's rejection of the 'women's libber' label therefore seems to set out one candidate identity for VB. However, the remainder of her response offers a somewhat
different version of how she understands the relationships that she and PM have
with their husbands. As she continues, VB states that she would not 'want a man
coming in every night'. This statement indicates a preference on VB's behalf, but
also goes beyond that, in that it casts doubt on what might be inferred to be one
feature of a 'traditional' husband and wife relationship. Following PM's agreement
with this statement, VB and PM collaboratively work up an explanation for VB's
claim. The terms of this explanation, 'that aspect' and 'not after 24 years' are not
fully spelt out but rather are treated by VB and PM as shared knowledge that does
not need to be made explicit to the interviewer. Although unspecified, this explanation paves the way for VB to provide an upshot to
the exchange. The upshot that comes, moreover,
stands in stark contrast to the earlier part of the
response. The **extreme case formulations**, 'the ideal
situation' and 'complete liberty' serve to emphasize
VB's positive evaluation of her life. We should note
that this evaluation remains set within a gendered category framework in that it is
bound up with a particular categorization of having 'a man part-time'. It is this
construction of men in a certain time-limited role, however, that allows VB to
argue that for most of her life, she has options available to her to live in ways
entirely of her own choosing.

Extreme case formulation
a discursive construction which
uses the strongest version of
comparative terms or phrases.

So it turns out that the idea of gender identity as a 'situated accomplishment' is
after all a useful one. Indeed, research reveals that the same sort of negotiation
of meaning can arise in the accounts that women offer of relationships themselves. For example, in their study of the practice of
'**swinging**', which involves partners in mutually
agreed sexual relationships outside of the partnership,
de Visser and McDonald (2007) examine one particular interactional difficulty which can arise in such situ-
ations. Even though 'swinging' may be mutually agreed, it is still possible that one
or both partners might experience jealousy at the thought of the other engaging
in sexual activities with someone else. However, this raises the question of whether
experiencing jealousy in this way is necessarily nega-
tive and harmful to a relationship. In particular, de
Visser and McDonald were interested to discover
whether couples manage such feelings so as to enhance
their own '**couple identity**'.

Swinging   a practice in which
couples exchange partners with
one another for sexual reasons.

Couple identity   a sense of self
that is grounded in a relationship
with someone else rather than in
oneself as an individual.

Extract 4.4

Amy   it's done for the sole purpose to enhance what we have together as a couple
        and that's the probably best way I can describe why we do it

(de Visser and McDonald, 2007, p. 466)

What de Visser and McDonald note here is that the notion of individual identity is 'played down' in order to privilege the notion of a 'couple identity'. In particular, they argue, what claims such as this demonstrate is that people can draw on the notion of shared experiences, which by definition involve more than a single individual. Thus the desires and motivations of the individual are supplanted by the desires and motivations of this larger 'couple identity'.

Interestingly, in their study of non-monogamous relationships, Finn and Malson (2008) point out that in many cases, research in this area privileges monogamy and sexual exclusivity as the best form of human relationship. Indeed, they point to previous research which indicates that in many cases even the people involved in non-monogamous relationships often rely on discourses of love and intimacy in a way that treats monogamous relationships as normative. And yet research in this area often demonstrates the ways in which non-monogamous relationships can be sites for the negotiation of self-invention. However, Finn and Malson argue that the discursive representation of issues such as love and intimacy are constrained by a 'regime of containment' in which socially prevalent understandings of interpersonal relationships condition the sorts of descriptions of non-monogamy that those involved in such relationships produce.

Men's Gender Identities

Of course, the scope for the negotiation of a gender identity as a 'situated accomplishment' within a context of broader social understandings is not restricted to women. Researchers such as Edley and Wetherell (1999) and Willott and Griffin (1999) have long argued that individual understandings of masculinity found within talk are influenced by hegemonic social constructions of what it is to be male. Here, we can gain an understanding of such claims by considering the ways in which men deal with one particularly prevalent social form of masculinity: the **'macho'** male. For example, in a study of young men's narratives of violence, Andersson (2008) draws upon the notion of the 'hero' identity introduced by Wetherell and Edley (1999) in their analyses of the talk of macho males.

> **Macho identities**   masculine identities in which 'traditional' views of men associated with power and control are highlighted.

Andersson examined the ways in which a young man's narratives of violence were constructed so as to establish a particular sort of self-presentation. Salim, 17 years old, was a resident in a youth detention centre in Sweden. In studying how Salim talked about himself, one of Andersson's aims was to understand how identity construction arises within such narratives. According to Wetherell and Edley, 'heroic positions' are imaginary positions that male speakers adopt in order to emphasize 'masculine' characteristics such as control, courage or physical tough-ness. However, for Salim, to talk in this way raises a potential dilemma. Since he is incarcerated in a detention centre, questions of the extent to which he has victim-ized others are clearly relevant. So how does Salim manage to portray a heroic, masculine identity while attending to possible negative inferences about him as a person? Well, according to Andersson, one possibility for Salim is to talk about fighting but to do so in a way which minimizes his own responsibility.

Extract 4.5

1	S	and it's never me who has started /
2	K	Na /
3	S	that's the thing /
4		OK with one /
5		but /
6		no it wasn't even me who started /
7		I took his knife an' /
8		he tried to threaten me once /

(Andersson, 2008, p. 148)

In this extract, we can see Salim introducing the notion that he himself has engaged in a violent confrontation involving a knife. But, Andersson points out, this aspect of his self-narrative is carefully negotiated to demonstrate that Salim's actions were not instigated by him. Instead, his involvement arose as a consequence of the actions of someone else. Thus, although Salim is able to draw in notions of vio-lence or toughness into his account of himself and his actions, he is able to under-mine potential problematic inferences about whether he is the perpetrator of violence upon innocent victims.

The 'macho' identity is, then, one whose production requires careful handling. The position is made more complex by the fact that men often appear to seek to juggle this identity with other forms of self. Gough (2006) looks at the way men's health is portrayed in a UK national newspaper. He notes that in a number of arti-cles, men are portrayed as obviously different from women in that men's health status is at risk as a consequence of their masculinity. Gough suggests that these sorts of popular representations of men promote a 'compromise identity' of men which incorporates potentially conflicting male identities of being 'macho' while at the same time being a 'new man'. In consequence, he suggests, representations of men and health take for granted everyday notions of masculinity which con-struct men as essentially disinterested in their own health. A particularly interest-ing version of this juggling act is seen in Seymour-Smith's (2008) study of the identities of men and women as they develop in the context of self-help groups.

She interviewed a group of men who took part in self-help groups organized by men with testicular cancer and women who were involved with a breast-cancer self-help group. In the following extract, the speakers had been discussing the difficulties of getting men to join self-help groups of this sort.

Extract 4.6

1	Paul	I think they expect to come along and find a load of ill people=
2	Cal	=yeah yeah (laughs)
3	Paul	[and you know (inaudible due to over talking)
4	Sarah	[yeah
5	Cal	[yeah it's er I think it's erm a bit of a I always use this one
6		but a bit of an alcoholics anonymous thing (2)
7	Sarah	yeah
8	Cal	stand up you know my name's Cal Jackson I've had testicular
9		cancer and then burst into tears and all that sort of thing and
10		blokes don't like that sort of [thing
11	Sarah	[they just think I'm not going to do that
12	Cal	I don't want anybody to cry in front of me or anything like
13		that=
14	Sarah	=no
15	Cal	so they don't want to come along

(Seymour-Smith, 2008, pp. 790–791)

Seymour-Smith draws attention to the way that Cal produces a stereotypical description of self-help groups by likening his support group to an Alcoholics Anonymous meeting. In presenting self-groups in such a stereotypical way, Seymour-Smith suggests, her participants achieve a number of goals. It allows them to introduce forms of activity, such as crying, without necessarily explicating what it is that might be troublesome about such activities. Further, it allows them to do so within a gendered context in which some activities are presented as being not relevant to men. In so doing, the speakers are able to present a version of themselves which is distanced from these potentially difficult identities in which, for example, women but not men might be taken to find crying an acceptable activity within such settings.

The difficulties of the 'macho' identity are also highlighted by Harding (2007), who notes the way in which cultural views on masculinity encourage two separate views of male nurses. On the one hand, nurses working within the general nursing sphere are perceived as being gay. On the other, nurses working in specific areas such as mental health nursing are viewed as 'macho'. So this places those men who wish to enter into the nursing profession with a difficult choice, if they happen to be heterosexual – they can either have their sexual identity undermined, or they can be presented as the type of people whose talents and tendencies mean that they are only really suitable for employment in very restricted areas of that profession where the potential difficulties of handling unruly patients can be met with a 'macho' approach. (We return to this issue in Chapter 7.)

A variant on the 'macho' identity has been revealed by Marley (2008) in her study of how metaphors are deployed in contact advertisements. She draws her data from dating ads that appeared in a national UK newspaper, the *Guardian*. Marley notes that, since such advertisements are necessarily brief, economy of expression is paramount. Her interest is in the way that the authors of advertisements of this sort incorporate 'ready made' identities which are already established through the means of familiar metaphors. The following extract is one of the advertisements that she studied.

Extract 4.7

Gallant knight, 25, seeks vivacious damsel to dirty his armour & find fun & adventure with.

Lndn.

(Marley, 2008, p. 564)

One resource that advertisers draw upon is fictional characterizations. These provide several advantages for the advertiser – they are presented as identity claims that are not intended to be taken as literally true; however, at the same time, they convey to the reader the sense that they are nevertheless appropriate characterizations. In this advert, the author has set out two candidate identities – gallant knight and damsel – that clearly draw upon narratives of chivalry and thereby indicate something about the form of the relationship that is being proposed. It is noteworthy that a particular **gender-specific** set of roles is outlined here, with the advertiser setting out a view of self as the active agent who is doing the seeking and the sought-after companion being cast in the role of passive recipient of the knight's attentions.

> **Gender-specific** understood as being relevant only for men or for women.

Gender and Other Identities

As will now hopefully be apparent, gender identities share discursive features with other forms of identities in that they are all occasioned constructions that are produced in discourse. And these are not just surface similarities. National, ethnic, religious and gender identities share discursive features in part because they are merely different ways in which self projects can be made out in discourse. One consequence of this is that gender identities can become interwoven with other forms of identity. This is a view presaged by Tannen (1999) who has argued that the relation between gender and language is one which is best conceived of as 'coming into view' when talk is directed towards other aspects of the world.

In previous chapters, we have looked at how talk of nationality 'blends' into talk of ethnicity. But in the example of the young Asian women we discussed in the last chapter (Pichler, 2007) we also saw that gender identities can be wrapped into ethnic identities. Some discursive researchers view this as an important aspect of gender identity. For example, Brenner (2009) notes that in the US Bush Administration of 2001–2004, talk of 'women's rights' began to enter political discourse. However, she argues that on many occasions such talk drew upon gender-stereotypical notions and that this prevented the establishment of genuinely 'feminist' policies. However, she does suggest that 'the ways that gender, identity and belief came to intersect with political realities' means that such talk represented more than mere strategic political manoeuvring. Because the politicians involved took themselves to be representing their own views about US national identity, there is at least some sense in which their talk of women's equality transcended mere political rhetoric. However, Shepherd (2006) makes a more critical point about Bush's war rhetoric, noting the ways in which women at home are portrayed as passive victims in the face of terrorist attacks and women abroad are portrayed as the passive victims of social norms that are oppressive of women. In a related vein, Das (2008) draws on critical discourse analytic methodology to examine how gender, nationalism and national insecurities are made out in discourse. In particular, Das points to the ways in which international tensions between Pakistan and India are represented in political talk by drawing on notions of gender.

Extract 4.8

In the history of all violence against our women either the Indian Muslims or their extended hand Pakistan has been the abductor community / country that has revealed a lustful behaviour of its males towards our women. If there is any reprehensible past which we cannot forget and forgive, it is the abduction and torture of Hindu women by Pakistan during partition.

(Ram Kumar, BJP member, interview, New Delhi, 2002)

(Das, 2008, p. 214)

In this quotation from a member of the Indian Parliament, the current tensions between India and Pakistan are made vivid by references to past and possibly present gender issues, in which Indian women are portrayed as the potential victims of the 'lustful behaviour' of Pakistani men.

Talk of ethnicities and nationalities ought to also alert us to another aspect of the discursive analysis of gender identities. Some researchers feel it is important to understand the **cultural specificities** of gender identity construction. For example, Zubair (2007) examines the ways in which Pakistani women use Pakistani metaphors to construct gender identities. She notes that when her older female participants

Cultural specificity the property that some aspects of social arrangements or normative ways of thinking possess such that these aspects and ways of thinking are unique to a particular culture.

described their lives, they relied in part on a metaphor of 'silent birds' to make sense of their experiences. This metaphor conveyed how these women felt: that, as a result of cultural pressures within Pakistan, female identity was one which was not only restricted in scope but was marked by silence and disengagement with wider society. Now this finding, that female participants may adopt culture-specific forms of discourse to make sense of their culturally related gender identities, may turn out to be an important issue, if there is evidence that the outsider's understandings of such identity constructions are similarly culture specific.

We can see how potential difficulties might arise if we look at Korteweg's discussion of the way in which debates within Canada on women's position under Sharia law represented a racialization of Muslim immigrant women that is 'clearly gendered' (Korteweg, 2008). In 2003, the Islamic Institute of Civil Justice announced that it would offer arbitration in a range of disputes, including family disputes. Korteweg notes that in response a number of interest groups expressed the fear that the introduction of Sharia law in such matters would set back the women's equality of rights movement. Subsequently the Premier of Ottawa announced that he would seek to ban such Sharia processes. In

> **Agency**   the property of being the source or cause of action or events

examining this case, Korteweg draws on the notion of 'embedded **agency**' as a process of actively shaping one's life, which can be distinguished from resistant agency whose sole purpose is to undermine hegemonic processes. Korteweg indicates that Western value systems often position Muslim women as objects and as people with limited agency. However, such appeals to liberal theories of freedom are, says Korteweg, overly limiting and ignore other ways in which Muslim women's agency can be expressed as women's active engagement in Islamic revival movements. In settings such as this, agency can be construed as related to structures of subordination rather than to 'freedom' *per se*, with agency in such cases being safeguarded by appeal to alternative power structures such as the Canadian government. In the following extract, a female Muslim journalist, Seema Khan, sets out this position.

Extract 4.9

… too many unqualified, ignorant imams [make] back-alley pronouncements on the lives of women, men and children. The practice will continue, without any regulation, oversight or accountability. […] [W]e have missed a golden opportunity to shine light on abuses masquerading as faith, and to ensure that rulings don't contradict the Charter of Rights and Freedoms.

(Korteweg, 2008, p. 445).

Korteweg here suggests that Khan has successfully set out a version of 'embedded agency' in which Muslim women are enabled to act 'informed by religiosity'. What Korteweg suggests is that Khan is proposing an alternative to 'Westernized' views of Muslim women as having only limited capacity to act within Sharia law. The account offered by Khan is that this view is only warrant-able because there are 'unqualified, ignorant imams'. However, if the Canadian state can ensure adequate safeguards, the Sharia-based tribunals need not be seen as contradicting Canadian values of gender equality in the way that Western-based feminists might suspect.

Prejudice

As we have already seen in earlier chapters, the production of an identity is, at the same time, the production of grounds for someone else to develop preju-diced views towards one. This is as true of gender identities as it is of national, ethnic or religious ones. For example, Lillian (2007) suggests that although 'male' and 'female' are terms that are treated by society as simple and self-evident cat-egories, sexism perpetuates and reproduces this simple dichotomy and so simple categorizations such as 'men' and 'women' are intrinsically problematic.

As a first example of this, we can turn to a study conducted by Smithson and Stokoe (2005). Their interest was in looking at workplace practices in respect of flexible working. What they discovered is that 'official' formulations of work-ing policies which are couched in **'gender-blind'** terms are often contradicted by the discourses of managers and employees. In making sense of this, Smithson and Stokoe suggest that gendered account-ing practices are particularly amenable to member-ship categorization analysis. Gender, as Sacks notes in his *Lectures on Conversation* (1992), provides a cat-egory set that is available for identifying any mem-ber of a given population. The category to which an individual is allocated

> **Gender-blind** a property of processes such as formal organizational equality policies in which individuals are to be considered while ignoring their gender.

within this routinely occurring set, as with any categorization, immediately makes available to a listener a range of inferences about the individual who is categorized. Thus categories such as 'professional worker', 'breadwinner', and 'woman' may have associated with them activities such as 'working all hours', 'caring', and 'looking after children'. Moreover, these inferences are treated ordinarily as being 'common knowledge', in that the attributes of a categoriza-tion are not made explicit but are taken to be immediately evident. In this way, such categorizations can be an important means by which gendered assump-tions are perpetuated. Sacks observes that ascription of category membership is a matter for negotiation by members and categorizations do not reflect cate-gories that have self-evident bases lying beyond the context within which they are located. However, Smithson and Stokoe point out that some forms of cate-gorization are so 'taken-for-granted' that they can be difficult to identify, much less challenge.

Extract 4.10

```
 6  I   Do you see any advantages from a business point of view,
 7          giving people flexible working schedules, giving people management
 8          of their own timetables, letting them working from home?
 9  D   Yes. The main advantage is the retention and attraction of,
10          sort of like, particularly female, female members of staff who
11          tend to be more the ones who'll be thinking of having kids,
12          things like that.
```
                                              (Smithson and Stokoe, 2005, p. 154)

In this extract, D, a male accountant, reformulates the interviewer's gender neutral use of 'people' as 'female members of staff' and goes on to state that workplace flexibility is a property that is particularly relevant to female workers. This is accomplished by means of an explanatory account in which it is explained that it is women who 'have' children. What Smithson and Stokoe suggest is that in this talk we can 'track' D's 'common-sense' perspective that women are mothers and therefore it is women who are flexible workers. So despite the diversity of working practices rhetoric represented by formal policy statements, in practice issues such as work-life balances are often characterized by their participants as essentially women's matters. Thus accommodations to the demands of home and family life come to be represented as concerns for women, rather than men, an apparently sexist consequence that undermines 'official' gender-neutral policy statements.

In her discussion of feminist practice, Lazar (2005) points out that although prevailing gender ideology is hegemonic, this does not mean that it is not contestable. And in part such contests may draw upon alternative identities than those which are on offer within a gender-ideological framework. We have already noted that expressions of identities and of prejudice associated with identities arise within specific local contexts of production. We saw in Chapter 2 that Condor's young women were happy to display apparently racist views because they wished to establish a particular view of themselves as rebellious and unshockable. A similar feature of talk can arise in respect of sexism. For example, Richardson (2007) examines the way that young African-American women use language to construct or resist the identities that are available to them. In her study, she focuses on the ways in which a group of young women respond to hip-hop videos. In her study, she asked the women to watch a number of videos, including one in which gangsta-rap style lyrics predominated. This particular discourse is often described as incorporating sexist and patriarchal language, and Richardson's interest here is in discovering how the participants are nevertheless able to negotiate a sense of black women that challenges notions of subordination. In the following extract, the young women are discussing a particular scene from the video.

Extract 4.11

BE: Look how she act like she havin sex with her.

ED: Like she hittin it from the back.

ET: Yeah.

BE: Them the girls that be getting more tips. Guys like that kinda stuff. Look at her. She ri: din. (Using tonal inflection and vowel elongation to underscore and emphasize the intensity of the sexual motion being portrayed, represented by the word 'ridin'. The colon marks elongation)

ED: She look like she fo*real*. (stress on real, indicated by italics)

BE: That's why I think she got paid though. She ri: din. (Tonal emphasis) Yeah, the whole video, she was workin like fo*real*. (stress on real)

(Richardson, 2007, p. 800)

Richardson suggests that hegemonic views of femininity encode rules for the way that women ought to behave, which includes the idea that women will not have sex with other women. So when BE and ED draw attention to the activities of two of the women from the video in this way, they are potentially making salient a socially transgressive act. However, this is not how Richardson's participants represent what is going on in the video. Instead, they characterize the women's activities in terms of their work, and evaluate the performance in terms of how well that work is being carried out. Moreover, the emphasis on 'ri: din' demonstrates that the participants are treating as being unproblematic the notion that women might have active sexual natures and that this might include homosexual as well as heterosexual activities. "Traditional" discourses of patriarchy might analyse the contents of the video in terms of women being objectified and degraded. But, says Richardson, the girls who are her participants subvert the supposed 'power' of males by emphasizing the way that women are free to act as they wish, and 'have the right to express their sexuality in both homo- and heteroerotic ways', and, in doing so, can achieve financial success.

However, what counts as a successful challenge to hegemonic patterns of sexism is in itself a debatable issue. Whitehead and Kurz (2009) explore this issue by examining different discourses associated with the phenomenon of recreational pole dancing. They note that this activity is constructed in terms of discourses of fun and fitness and that recreational pole dancing is contrasted with professional pole dancing. This latter is constructed around themes of lack of **empowerment** and objectification of women who are **disempowered** by being required to 'sell themselves' in order to gain an income, in contrast with recreational pole-dancers who are empowered through their ability to expend money on their preferred activity. Whitehead and Kurz, however, raise questions as to whether such 'empowerment' discourses adequately address concerns that feminists might raise that

Empowerment giving people power to make appropriate decisions about their own lives and experiences.

Disempowerment the removal of the ability to be a competent social actor with agentic status.

pornographic or pseudo-pornographic activities inevitably reproduce patriarchal power struggles, even if women are acting as the consumers. They summarize this concern by suggesting that acts that may be individually liberating may reinforce societal notions of masculine and feminine sexuality and thus covertly secure societal oppression.

Indeed, this potential ambiguity is not merely a participant's concern, but arises with equal force at the level of analysis. Earlier, we discussed the way that on occasions women's views of gender identities veer closer to the views of the Friday-night pub sexist than we might find comfortable. This is an interesting finding if only because, as we have already noted in respect of 'new racism', research indicates that forms of gender-based prejudice are often produced in a somewhat careful manner that relies upon routinized ways of talking about gender differences (Weatherall, 1998). We should therefore remind ourselves of the discussion presented in the last chapter – the vexed notion of when and how analysts are 'allowed' to talk about theoretical notions of nationality, ethnicity, religion or gender or about the prejudice that can be associated with such identities. In the preceding chapter, we discussed the point raised by Augoustinos and Every (2007) that ironically the discursive approach to racism sometimes appears to mean that researchers cannot refer to racism in their analyses because participants do not orient to what they are saying as racist in the talk that is being analysed. Holmes and Meyerhoff (2003) make a similar point in relation to gender. If participants themselves do not bring up or make relevant gender-related issues in their talk, then some analysts will claim that, for example, imputations of sexism cannot be produced as an outcome of the analysis of such talk. An example of the sort of meta-theoretical debate which this issue can generate is seen in a paper by Wowk (2007) in which she criticizes feminist conversation analytic approaches to understanding sexism (Kitzinger, 2000). The combination of feminism and conversation analysis is intended as a contribution to research on sexism through its examination of the ways in which everyday conversation encodes or represents as commonplace features of gender such as heterosexuality or other gender-based assumptions that are treated in talk as unremarkable. However, Wowk argues that Kitzinger wrongly attributes a social constructionist motivation to the conversation analyst's work. One consequence of this is that Wowk rejects any suggestion that gender is merely social performance, and argues that to some extent there are social facts that underlie such performances. Another is that Wowk is suspicious of Kitzinger's claims that a conversation analytic approach can coherently be combined with feminism. Feminism relies on describing society in terms of 'macro' structures of power and oppression which stand as pre-analytic categories, and this is just inimical to the conversation analyst's concern with participants' categorizations. So on the one hand, some discursive researchers seek to avoid treating 'macro' perspectives on gender as relevant while, for others, this is a necessary feature of gender identity analysis. It is this latter thought that leads analysts such as Swann (2002), for example, to suggest that prior assumptions about gender in such research are probably unavoidable.

Discussion

We have seen that the study of gender identities has come a long way in the last 15 to 20 years. A concern with gender as 'situated accomplishment' has replaced more reductive approaches to the topic. Of course, treating gender identities in this way is not incompatible with making more basic discoveries about how people use gender language. In some studies of language and discourse, researchers are interested in **variationism**, that is, examining 'variations' in the discourse produced by men and women. For example Macaulay (2005),

> **Variationism** the view that different categories of people such as men and women produce language that varies categorically.

from a sociolinguistic perspective, identifies clear gender-based differences in talk. But other discursive gender researchers are social constructionists of the sort we discussed in Chapters 2 and 3. This seems to indicate a methodological tension. However, this tension between gender as a pre-analytic variable and gender as a social construction may be less worrisome than it seems. As Macaulay points out, the analyst is well advised to adopt caution in attributing meaning to observable gender-differences in discourse because in many cases a discourse feature does not 'create' meaning but, rather, takes its meaning from the context of its utterance. If the social constructionist's further claim that contexts, themselves, may be reflexively determined by the discourses that comprise them is taken into consideration too, then it may well seem that this theoretical tension is more apparent than real.

In passing, as we have discussed gender identities, we have noted some similarities among the ways that national, ethnic, religious and gender identities are understood from the discursive research perspective: gender identities like those other identities are socially constructed and can be associated with problems of prejudice. It is also useful to note at least one other similarity. We saw in previous chapters that national, ethnic and religious identities intersect with other identities. The reader may, for example, remember from Chapter 2 that in Condor's study (Condor, 2006) Gem, Katie, Chloe and Susan formulated racist versions of themselves in part to look rebellious or unconventional. Eckert and McConnell-Ginet (2003) note the same thing about gender identities. For example, it is a social convention that women, more than men, should avoid the use of profanities when they speak. Eckert and McConnell-Ginet suggest that women may sometimes reject this social norm. But this does not necessarily mean they are seeking to adopt a male identity. It is just as likely that, in the momentary context of a specific local interaction, they are seeking to be 'cool, modern' or 'in your face'.

In concluding, we might usefully return to a theme that we introduced towards the end of the previous chapter. There we briefly raised the question of whether discursive approaches to identity are capable of offering up potential solutions when prejudice in respect of one identity or another occurs. One approach to this, as common in sexism research as in racism studies, is to indicate that the analyst's main job is merely to expose prejudice and to delineate its discursive features to make it recognizable. Now this might seem a modest enough goal but, as we saw towards the end of the last section, even this may be a tall order for the discursive researcher. On the one hand, issues can arise, such as recreational pole dancing, where there is no easy answer to the question of whether such activities challenge or are complicit with sexist and patriarchal societal structures. On the other hand, there is deep theoretical debate within the discursive community over how issues such as racism or sexism are to be approached at a methodological level with, for example, some people advocating conversation analysis mixed in with other approaches and others suggesting that this is an incoherent strategy. Moreover, proponents of more 'critical' forms of discursive research would insist on going much further than mere identification of sexist or racist talk. The point, they would argue, is not to understand the world but to change it. Now in this project, they either implicitly or explicitly assume the support of 'everyday people'. There are just not enough critical discursive researchers to go around. But this notion, that everyday speakers might become reflexively aware of what they say and how they say it, needs careful handling. If talk arises among a group of like-minded souls, then their collective abilities to recognize what they are saying as prejudiced is limited – that, in a sense, is what we mean by hegemony. But if, on the other hand, we have an awkward interlocutor who is capable of reflexive reflection, one has to wonder whether this is much of an improvement. Of course, such a person could continually nag at interactional partners whenever issues of prejudiced talk arise. But the practical question, the question that those who are all for practical outcomes presumably want answered, is whether someone who is a constant source of correction and admonition would be interactionally successful in the long run. There are, of course, more practicable suggestions. For example, critical researchers such as van Dijk (2005) have pointed out that in many instances prejudiced discourse derives from elites. So if the researcher can persuade them to change their ways (e.g. through active engagement in the process of media management and production) then this may have some sort of long-term societal benefit.

Chapter Summary

This chapter begins with a discussion of the nature of gender identity as it is viewed from the discursive research perspective. It is noted that earlier conceptions of gender have, in more recent times, given way to a more 'nuanced' view in which gender is viewed as a 'situated accomplishment' brought about through discourse. The chapter then moves on to discuss women's gender identities. A range of studies have shown that women draw upon notions of interpersonal relationships in constructing a sense of themselves. It is pointed out that this can seem puzzling, since talk of women in terms of marriage and children seems to negate other identity projects such as viewing oneself in terms of occupational success or socio-economic standing. However, these constructions, being situated accomplishments, involve more complex detail than would be found in similar sorts of talk produced from a purely sexist perspective. Women are able to produce identities of this sort which nevertheless allow them to display positively evaluated features of the self such as autonomy and independence. The chapter then moves on to discuss men's gender identities from one particular viewpoint: the 'macho' male. A variety of research is presented to show how men both adopt such a sense of self and yet, at the same time, orient to such an identity as potentially problematic. The next section of the chapter discusses the ways in which gender identities overlap with other forms of identity. We then go on to raise the issue of sexism as a form of prejudice. A preliminary example of sexist discourse is offered, and then the focus switches to whether and how women's discursive practices represent a challenge to such sexism. As the discussion unfolds, we return to an issue hinted at in the previous chapter – that discursive researchers face internal disputes in how best to characterize prejudice.

Connections

We have been keen to stress the ways in which national, ethnic and religious identities can be seen to be associated with gender identities. For that reason, depending on the particular 'slant' on gender identity that is being followed, this chapter can be seen as being related to Chapters 2 and 3. The reader may also be interested to pursue the ways in which gender identities are made out within the legal domain (e.g. in discussions of the crime of rape) in Chapter 6 and within the organizational domain (Chapter 7).

Further Reading

de Visser, R. and McDonald, D. (2007). Swings and roundabouts: Management of jealousy in heterosexual 'swinging' couples. *British Journal of Social Psychology, 46,* 459–476.

A surprising account of how some people develop a sense of 'couple identity' that in some respects overshadows their gender identities.

Kendall, S. (2008). The balancing act: Framing gendered parental identities at dinnertime. *Language in Society, 37,* 539–568.

This is an entertaining account of how men and women construct gender identities within the everyday setting of home life.

Reynolds, J. and Wetherell, M. (2003). The discursive climate of singleness: The consequences for women's negotiation of a single identity. *Feminism and Psychology, 13*, 489–510.

A study that shows how women reflect social views on singleness but are also able to react against such positioning in constructing their own positive identities.

Activity Box

We said at the start of this chapter that gender distinctions between men and women seem to be socially pervasive. But we have also seen how men and women react against societal expectations of gender. And we have also seen the hope expressed by some critical discursive researchers that the more negative aspects of sexist views on gender identity can be tackled through 'passing the message' on to those who work in elite areas of discourse such as the media. So, think of a popular movie or television show that you have enjoyed watching. Are there elements of characterization or storyline involving male and female characters that show whether 'the message' is getting through? Select examples of dialogue from your chosen movie or television programme and show how the gender identities on display are, or are not, seen to challenge 'traditional' views on gender.

5

Health Identities

Topics Covered in this Chapter

Key Terms

Authority to speak

Expertise

Individual pathology

Moral imperative

Natural language generation

Nature

Nurture

Objective evidence

Patient information leaflets

Patient journey

Rapport

Small talk

Subjective accounts

Troubles telling

Identities in Context: Individuals and Discourse in Action, First Edition. Andrew McKinlay and Chris McVittie.
© 2011 Andrew McKinlay and Chris McVittie. Published 2011 by Blackwell Publishing Ltd.

Patient died after being given wrong drugs six times

A WIDOW is considering legal action following the death of her husband who was given six separate doses of medicine prescribed for another patient.

   Joseph Gill, 58, collapsed after taking the tablets, but doctors at Aberdeen Royal Infirmary later decided he'd recovered and was well enough to undergo a scheduled lung cancer operation …

   Mrs Gill said yesterday: 'It was all meant to be routine. This is like a bad dream. Joe said the nurses had been calling him "George" and had given him the wrong pills.'

   (*Daily Express*, www.express.co.uk/posts/view/133743)

Contexts of health and ill-health, as much as any others, foreground issues of identities and the social actions associated with identities. How individuals are identified (or not identified) brings consequences for the interventions that are deemed to be appropriate in terms of treatment or lack of treatment. The tragic case of Joseph Gill outlined in the extract above serves all too well to illustrate the issues that can arise when a particular identification brings with it consequences that differ from those that would be considered appropriate. Of course, the identities ascribed to individuals in such contexts are relevant not just for those who will receive or not receive certain forms of intervention. In play also are the identities of healthcare professionals who are responsible for determining the interventions appropriate in specific cases and who are expected to do so in ways that exemplify expert knowledge and practice. Further, as this extract also demonstrates, the identities that come to be ascribed to individual patients and to professionals carry implications also for the broader management of health and ill-health and for its place within broader patterns of social relations including those of the media and perhaps in some cases those of the legal system. It is such identities, those located in immediate contexts of health and ill-health and their relationships to broader social concerns, that we shall consider in this chapter.

Identities and Health

To be healthy or to be ill is not simply a matter of introspecting upon and reporting one's state of being, whether physiological or psychological, at any given time. Rather it can be understood as a process of negotiating who we are in ways that will be understandable to ourselves and to others and which we anticipate will be taken up in particular ways. Moreover, health identities are not readily amenable to negotiation in any manner of our choosing; they carry with them a range of inferences about the person being identified. The inferences drawn from people's descriptions of being well or being ill in turn shape the listener's response, and have consequences for whether a proposed health identity is accepted, challenged or otherwise dealt with in the interaction that follows.

Being ill

Commonly, issues of health and illness take place against a background that advantages certain forms of identity over others. Being healthy is viewed as a preferred and socially desirable identity, one that usually requires little or no justification. Individuals are taken to be healthy unless and until established as otherwise. Narratives that suggest that people can deal with difficulties are routinely treated as demonstrating abilities to overcome adversity and as reflecting socially meaningful and coherent forms of identity (Carless, 2008; Ryan, 2006). By contrast, talk of illness is often treated as a highly sensitive matter. Accordingly, even speakers with recognizable health problems will aim to present themselves as being healthy. For example, speakers with communicative difficulties such as aphasia attempt so far as possible to appear linguistically competent rather than incompetent, and listeners encourage such attempts (Wilkinson, 2007). Being healthy therefore is treated as preferable to being ill. This, however, is no simple preference for one identity rather than the other, in that such identities are inextricably bound up with moral considerations. In short, there is a **moral imperative** for people to be healthy. We expect people to be well

> **Moral imperative**   an obligation to act in certain accepted ways.

and someone claiming to be ill will be required to produce evidence for such a claim to be accepted. Moreover, not all evidence produced will necessarily be accepted as conclusively pointing to illness. Routine medical evidence, such as readings obtained from measuring instruments, outcomes of investigative procedures and diagnoses given by professionals are readily treated as independent of the individual's own account of experience and as comprising **objective evidence** of health or ill-health. By contrast, individuals' own reports of their states of health are open to being treated as potentially motivated by the interests of the person making the claim and as providing **subjective accounts.** Evidence of this sort, although derived from first-hand experience, will not be accepted in all cases as convincing proof of ill-health.

> **Objective evidence**   evidence, such as measurements or readings, that is not treated as dependent upon any individual view.
>
> **Subjective accounts** descriptions provided on the basis of an individual's own view or perspective.

Differences in the status accorded to different forms of evidence have effects for how descriptions of illness are treated. Particular considerations come into play where people claim to be suffering from conditions for which no objective evidence is available and, in many cases, their claims are as likely to be contested as they are to be accepted. Take, for example, the condition of myalgic encephalomyelitis (ME, otherwise known as chronic fatigue syndrome) for which no medical tests have been identified. Notwithstanding that ME sufferers report that they experience debilitating illness, the absence of any objective evidence often leads to their accounts being met with some resistance from sceptical health professionals and others. In addition, even where ME is accepted as being a recognizable disease, this is not the end of the difficulties. Lack of evidence of any physical cause can easily result in reports of ME being treated as reflecting problems that are psychological rather than physiological in origin. This type of construction can easily result in the sufferer being identified as mentally weak instead of being unwell and unfortunate. People claiming to suffer from ME therefore face two identity challenges: (1) to establish that ME represents a genuine illness; and (2) to convince others that they are unfortunate rather than weak in having this condition. One way of dealing with these challenges is to argue that ME is a serious and enigmatic illness that to date has confounded health professionals (Guise, Widdicombe and McKinlay, 2007), and that individuals who suffer from it are not weak but active in seeking solutions to their illness and recovery to full health (Guise, McVittie and McKinlay, 2010). An alternative way of negotiating these identity challenges, paradoxically, is to accept that the scepticism surrounding ME is in many cases justified; that is, that people do make claims that are unfounded or are weak in having psychological and not physical problems. Such descriptions work to build up an identity of people who simply 'jump on the bandwagon' by aligning themselves inappropriately with the identity of ME sufferer. This identity of non-genuine claimant provides an opportunity for sufferers to distinguish their own experiences from the experiences of those who 'jump on the bandwagon' and so to argue that they by contrast are genuine ME sufferers (Horton-Salway, 2007).

Accountability for illness

Other issues of moral responsibility equally arise in relation to health. The moral imperative to be well means not just that people are expected to be healthy but also that they are expected to take appropriate steps to remain healthy. Thus, those who become ill through their own actions might well receive medical treatment, but at the same time can be treated as to some extent personally culpable for their problems. Cancer, for example, is commonly presented as having potentially severe health consequences but not as arising through any individual fault. Binge-drinking, by contrast, might also lead to negative health outcomes but often is presented as a negative lifestyle choice rather than an unavoidable illness. Each illness therefore brings its own identity considerations for those who suffer from it.

In order to explore further some of these issues, let us consider eating disorders. As is suggested by the name, such experiences are commonly recognized as comprising 'disorders' in that they are exemplified by physiological and psychological changes within the person. Eating disorders, however, are frequently categorized as instances of **individual pathology**, in that the person affected is constructed as being individually responsible for his or her eating patterns and thereby as potentially accountable for the resulting disorder.

Individual pathology   disorder or problem that is treated as located within the individual person.

Brooks (2009), in a study of calls made by individuals with eating disorders to phone-in shows on major UK radio stations, notes that callers commonly orient to issues of accountability for their eating patterns and for the outcomes. In describing their experiences, callers do so by referring to anxiety, phobia or addiction, all factors that are immediately recognizable in medical terms. They also commonly externalize the disorders, presenting these as not being part of themselves, and as exerting power over which they have no control. These accounts allow the callers to argue that eating disorders do not arise through individual choices and that it is the disorders and not the callers themselves that are accountable for the resulting problems.

Often when we talk of eating disorders we refer to disorders that result in people becoming markedly underweight, with potentially severe consequences. More recently, however, considerable attention has come to focus on different weight-related conditions in the form of being overweight. Within the National Health Service in the UK, increasing numbers of patients are coming to be diagnosed as obese, a condition that is commonly associated with individual overeating. The health consequences of obesity therefore are often taken to be self-inflicted and to arise through behaviours for which the individual is accountable. It is unsurprising that accountability is as much a live issue for those diagnosed with obesity as it is for people diagnosed with other forms of eating disorders. Sally Wiggins (2009), in a study of NHS Weight Management Discussion groups, notes that members attending these groups describe their disorders in ways similar to those found by Brooks (2009) in her study of calls to phone-in shows. Thus, a first means by which group members seek to avoid blame is by denying that they have been involved in any culpable eating activities. Below, we see an extract from a group discussion in which Melanie, the group leader, has asked group members about their diets. This exchange comes immediately after Melanie has described to group members the dietary recommendations contained in a 'balance of good health' chart.

Extract 5.1

1.	Melanie:	can you see: (.) >wh- ↑what's th' difference about<
2.		(0.6) what you eat at the ↓moment compared to that
3.		kind'v bal↓anc:e
4.		(2.4)
5.	Paul:	act'lly not a ↑thing cos that's:: (.) what we eat
6.		(0.6) >ah m'n< (0.8) we don't eat >a lot.of
7.		fat(ty) < foods:,
8.	Melanie:	righ',
9.		(0.4)
10.	Paul:	an::d,
11.		(0.8)
12.	Paul:	I don't take su:gar in ma- (0.4) coffee >anythin'

13.   like tha',<
14.   (1.0)
15.   Paul: it's s:kimmed ↑milk we use (.) °but°=
16.   Melanie: =righ',
17.   Paul: we still cannae lose <u>weight</u>

(Wiggins, 2009, p. 378)

Melanie's question at lines 1 to 3 suggests that the diets followed by members of the group are different from the dietary recommendations for healthy eating that she has just outlined. Paul, one of the group members, responds by denying that there is any difference between what he eats and these recommendations. He also provides examples, at lines 6 to 7 and at lines 12 and 15, of the foods that he eats and those that he does not eat. Paul uses these examples to argue that he is familiar with principles of healthy eating and that he eats healthily in his daily life. By describing his diet in these ways, Paul denies that it is his unhealthy eating patterns that have led him to be in the Weight Management Group. The cause of his health problem is thereby presented as a puzzle instead of a matter of personal accountability.

Describing behaviour in ways that make it reasonable and not blameworthy offers one way of denying personal accountability. An alternative way of avoiding blame is to attribute responsibility for a disorder to factors that are not under personal control and for which the individual cannot therefore be held accountable. In the following extract, we see two group members Elaine and Jennifer (with a minimal contribution from Melanie as group leader) discussing the factors that might be involved in being overweight.

Extract 5.2

1.   Elaine: =but <u>ah</u>'ve always been like this: >fae the day ah
2.   was born< my nickname, (0.6) my uncle gave me (0.8)
3.   was 'baby ele↑phant'
4.   (1.2)
5.   Jennifer: well my dad used to call me ↑(unclear)
6.   (0.5)
7.   Jennifer   (y'know) af[ter the cartoon character
8.   Elaine: [the reason, (0.4) an' ah was in ma
9.   mum's ↑arm[s when ah got that nick↑name
10.   Jennifer: [uh huh (0.4) mm hm
11.   Elaine: good God woman she's like a baby ele:phant, (0.4)
12.   >cos ah was< <u>mass</u>↑ive,
13.   (0.8)
14.   Melanie: mm
15.   Elaine: and ah've always ↑been like tha' (0.6) ↑see up until
16.   ah- (0.2) ah actually went to the hospital when ah
17. ·   was eighteen, for- (0.2) to help me lose <u>weight</u>

(Wiggins, 2009, pp. 381–382)

Here, Elaine describes her weight as unrelated at all to her eating patterns, arguing that she has had difficulties in being overweight since birth. This argument takes weight out of the realm of individual choices and thereby beyond personal account-ability. More than this, Elaine describes her previous attempts to address her weight problem and argues that she has been deterred in pursuing these attempts by the inappropriate responses of health professionals. As a result, her current attempts to deal with being overweight appear appropriate and indeed commendable in that she has not been deterred by previous difficulties. Elaine therefore becomes someone who has tried against the odds to address a problem that has arisen through circumstances beyond her individual control, instead of being accounta-ble for causing her health problem and for failing to address it.

We can see people dealing with similar issues of identity in relation to a range of health behaviours and conditions. For example, dependence upon drugs can easily be treated as arising through personal choice rather than uncontrollable factors, and makes available a highly negative identity of illegal drug user. Even dependence upon a prescription medication, such as amphetamines, can lead to unfavourable inferences being drawn about the person who is dependent. People who are potentially ascribed such identities might therefore seek to present the dependence as being associated with a different form of identity that does not carry the same negative evaluation. Accordingly, individuals who use amphetamines can seek to explain this behaviour in terms of an identity of being a patient with a recognizable condition, that of attention deficit hyperac-tivity disorder (ADHD). Negotiating an identity of ADHD patient instead of illegal drug user works to present amphetamine use not as an illegal and mor-ally reprehensible activity but instead as part of the treatment of a recognized medical condition and thus as morally justifiable and acceptable behaviour (Schubert *et al.*, 2009).

Doing professionalism

Of course, in the realm of health it is not only identities of patients that are in play. Health professionals too have to negotiate, across a diversity of contexts, who they are in relation to the everyday practice of health. Much of this negotiation consists of doing **expertise**, in displaying to patients and to fellow professionals attributes that are associated with being a professional. In part, this involves the sorts of activities that we routinely associate with the practice of health. Psychiatrists, for example, are expected to ascribe to patients states of sanity or insanity. The ascription of sanity or insanity, of course, might well reflect common-sense or mundane forms of reasoning rather than the application of highly special-ist knowledge (Roca-Cuberes, 2008). Nonetheless, we associate professional

> **Expertise** specialized understanding of, and practise within, a particular field of activity.

psychiatric practice with the production of diagnoses of sanity and insanity, and routinely treat professionals' diagnoses as exemplifying the actions that are consistent with such an identity.

As is the case in relation to identities of patients, identities of health professionals are bound up with negotiating the meaning of evidence relating to such identities. For professionals, this issue becomes all the more salient against a prevailing background of evidence-based practice, or evidence-based medicine. A major principle expressed in relation to evidence-based practice is that practice should be based upon evidence of the effectiveness of different healthcare interventions and of success rates in individual cases. Again, this raises the question of what is to count as evidence in arriving at particular decisions. We noted above in relation to patient identities that much discussion focused on the status accorded to evidence that was produced in relation to their claims. It is perhaps unsurprising, but nonetheless interesting, to note that similar discussions are found in professional talk about evidence. Thus professional contexts, such as that of a drug committee, become less a matter of evaluating uncontested results of clinical trials than of interpretation and reformulation of the evidence that is produced in any particular case (Jenkings and Barber, 2006).

Authority to speak   acceptance that a speaker is suitably qualified to make definitive comments on a topic.

In contexts such as these, other matters also come to the fore. Just as evidence and available conclusions are open to professional reworking so too is the **authority to speak** on such issues. By authority to speak we mean the relative and relevant expertise to be accorded to the speaker on the matter in hand.

Much of the time, professional working relationships and the identities of those involved in them are taken to be established and rarely provide scope for contention. We expect cardiac surgeons to perform heart operations when required to do so, anaesthetists to administer anaesthetics, nurses to provide nursing care, and in these ways much of the practice of medicine in health gets done on an everyday basis. Working patterns of this sort, however, can all too easily become disrupted when previously established patterns become changed. One such example comes from a study by Schryer and colleagues (2007) of how two groups of Canadian eye-care practitioners, optometrists and ophthalmologists, negotiate their particular realms of professional practice. Optometrists are generally involved in the examination, diagnosis and treatment of disease and disorders of the visual system, whereas ophthalmologists are physicians who perform surgery and prescribe medications for eye conditions. Often patients reporting visual problems will come into contact with both professions, necessitating co-management of patients and inter-professional communication. In recent years, however, optometrists have sought to expand their professional practice into areas previously associated with ophthalmology, a move that has been resisted by ophthalmologists and that has led to tension between these groups of practitioners. As Schryer and colleagues note, the resulting tension is played out in changes in the referral letters and consultant reports being exchanged between these professionals. Increasingly, ophthalmologists fail to respond to communications from optometrists or only respond using standard forms. The tensions between these two professions, in the form of who has authority to speak on matters of eye-care, are thus reflected in poorer communication between individuals who are negotiating the scope of their professional identities in their everyday working lives.

Contexts of Health and Identity

Social contexts of health

We have already seen in this chapter some ways in which individual identities are inextricably interwoven with broader understandings of individual health and illness. The moral imperative to be healthy comes to be reflected in everyday contexts and in how other people respond to individuals' claims to particular forms of identity. At the same time, descriptions of individual experiences are oriented towards prevailing understandings of particular conditions. For example, the ways in which ME sufferers seek to make sense of their condition orient not just to the immediate contexts in which they find themselves but also to widely available constructions of ME as 'yuppie flu' or similar. By contrast, cancer is frequently described in terms of metaphors such as 'cancer is war' that frame it in somewhat different terms (Williams Camus, 2009) and that make for illness identities that are unlikely to be challenged. The ways in which health and illness are constructed of course have implications also for healthcare professionals and how they make sense of their practice. For example, constructions of mental illness as dangerous activity or as medical disorder call for markedly varying responses from psychiatrists, while suggestions that mental illness can reflect socio-political upheaval place psychiatric practice in an altogether different relationship with individuals and with social conditions (Bilic and Georgaca, 2007).

Changing social understandings of issues such as these of course will have their own effects for how individual patients and practitioners are constructed at different times. One recent change in the delivery of healthcare has been an emphasis on empowerment of recipients of healthcare. In terms of empowerment, patients are regarded not simply as passive recipients of healthcare that is provided to them but instead as people who should be appropriately informed to make meaningful decisions in relation to that care. One example of this changing identity of patient is evident in the context of **patient information leaflets**. Prior to 1992, within the European Union, pharmaceutical manufacturers could opt whether or not to include with their medications leaflets that offered patients more detailed

> **Patient information leaflets**   leaflets issued with medications to provide patients with details of the products and how to use them.

information about these products. Since 1992, however, in terms of EU law, manufacturers have been required to provide patients with relevant information to accompany any medication that is supplied. This change in legal requirements has been accompanied by a change in the form of information that is given. Whereas the leaflets that were available in the early twentieth century were designed to emphasize the medical expertise of those who compiled them and the effectiveness of the medications, leaflets in recent times have focused on patients as consumers and on the steps that they should take as individual consumers of these products. Thus, in patient information leaflets, the previous relationship of expert professional and passive patient has given way to one that recognizes the patient as someone who has power to make choices relating to his or her treatment (McManus, 2009).

At the same time, health and illness are not isolated elements of human experience. Rather they are inextricably linked to other understandings of who we are, in our dealings with health professionals, and with others such as family members, friends, work colleagues and others. Health identities inevitably intersect with a diverse range of other identities. Part of understanding identities of health and illness therefore requires us to examine how these become interwoven with social understandings of other forms of identity. For example, much debate within psychology has involved discussion of issues of **nature** – that is, the extent to which human attributes are innate to an individual – and **nurture**, the extent to which attributes are acquired in the course of living

Nature   the influence of innate factors in human behaviour.
Nurture   the influence of social and environmental factors on human behaviour.

one's own life. We saw above, in the context of the weight management group, Elaine arguing that she had been overweight since birth and thereby claiming that she was overweight due to nature and not due to nurture in the form of her own life choices (Wiggins, 2009). Such discussions of nature and nurture also surface in debates as to whether or not people are genetically predisposed to particular medical conditions (Lehtinen, 2007). Reference to the relative contributions of nature and nurture is found also where health-related behaviours are in issue, such as discussions in antenatal classes regarding the breastfeeding of infants. In such instances, health professionals such as counsellors can draw upon nature, nurture or indeed both in attempting to persuade parents-to-be of the benefits of breast-feeding infants and to argue for individuals attending these classes to take up and enact particular mothering identities (Locke, 2009).

In a similar way, understandings of health and illness often become caught up with social understandings of gender and their implications for individual men and women. Much work has pointed to ways in which prevailing forms of masculine and feminine identities come to be reflected in how individuals interact with others. Gender becomes relevant in health contexts in a number of ways. For example, certain medical conditions are routinely associated with particular groups of people. Thus, although illnesses such as influenza or the common cold are taken to be potentially relevant to everyone regardless of gender, other conditions are presented as gender-specific in being relevant only for men or for women. One such example is that of anorexia nervosa. Commonly anorexia nervosa is described as predominantly affecting women, especially young women and adolescents. Such descriptions draw on a long history of the origins of anorexia nervosa and how it has come to be understood (see Hepworth, 1999, for a discussion) but are played out in everyday discussions of the condition. Faced with the possibility that anorexia nervosa might be relevant for men, male interviewees reject any such suggestion and attribute to male sufferers identities that distance them from dominant masculine identities. Instead, men will construct sufferers as being feminine or mentally weak, or argue that they suffer from a different (non gender-specific) condition that does not comprise anorexia nervosa (McVittie, Cavers and Hepworth, 2005). These forms of everyday talk function to maintain established social understandings of gender and of illness identities. Gender can also be seen to be reflected in health identities in other ways. Dominant forms of masculine identities are usually associated with attributes such as power, invulnerability and stoicism in the face of adversity. These attributes, in contexts of health, are often taken up in identities that deter men from accepting vulnerability to illness and from seeking appropriate help from health professionals, even in contexts where help is clearly required. Men seeking help in such circumstances might require to move from an identity that is consistent with prevailing notions of masculinity to one that more readily allows for help-seeking actions (McVittie and Willock, 2006).

Identities of health and illness then are interwoven with broader understandings of these matters, understandings that change over time in ever-changing social contexts. Health and illness have to be understood also in relation to other available elements of identity, such as nature and nurture and gender. However, we cannot assume that these elements of identity will always be relevant in similar ways. Descriptions of nature and nurture can be very different in discussions of genetic predispositions or of breast-feeding. Understandings of gender might be relevant across a range of contexts of health and illness but this is not to say that masculinity or femininity will be salient in every case for every individual man or woman. To understand identities, therefore, we need to consider if and how individual people orient to these broader considerations in their everyday lives in making sense of themselves and of others (McVittie, 2006; McVittie and Goodall, 2009).

Professional/patient interaction

Interactions between individuals and health professionals provide some of the most common contexts for the identities considered above. It is in such settings that descriptions of health and illness, the evaluation and application of available evidence, and the expectations surrounding patients and professionals become especially relevant. These are linked also to other interactional features. For example, the topics discussed within such encounters are likely to be rather more circumscribed than those found elsewhere, reflecting a focus on accomplishing health in practice. Of course, the topics and interactional forms found in particular instances will inevitably vary with the form of professional expertise being practised. Issues of importance to a counsellor will differ from those considered relevant within an emergency department, as we will soon discover should we attempt to have them considered there! Below, we consider some specific features of psychotherapeutic settings, caring relationships and emergency departments. First, we turn to aspects of what is perhaps taken to be the most prototypical form of health-related encounter, the consultation between doctor and patient.

Doctor/patient consultations

Typically, doctor/patient consultations involve not just particular interpersonal contexts but also physical ones. Surgeries or consulting rooms both provide the settings within which healthcare is delivered and also comprise one element of that delivery. Stethoscopes, thermometers, blood pressure monitors and similar instruments all enact for us the practice of medicine. The measurements obtained through the use of these tools exemplify the focus of healthcare on obtaining, wherever possible, objective evidence of illness that might point to a particular cause and thus indicate the intervention appropriate in individual circumstances. One part of such practice is the familiar file of case notes comprising a record of previous consultations and their outcomes. In doing so it both provides a history of past health and illness and offers a resource for the current encounter in that its contents can be made relevant in the present at any point of the ongoing consultation (Frers, 2009).

   Alongside these aspects of practice, we of course find discussion of the issues of potential relevance. The usual expectation is that those who consult doctors make explicit the reasons for doing so. As we noted above, patients are expected to demonstrate illness and might be treated as morally responsible if that illness appears to result from their own actions. On such matters, professionals reach conclusions as to the well-being or otherwise of the patient and of the course of action to be followed. Individuals who consult doctors usually are well aware of these considerations and tailor their communications accordingly. For example, people making requests in out-of-hours telephone calls to doctors often tend to introduce these requests using terms such as 'I wonder if' (Curl and Drew, 2008). Presenting requests in this way marks them out as different from more everyday requests and demonstrates that patients understand that acceptance of their requests is contingent upon doctors treating them as reasonable and attending to what is being sought. The substance of patient requests, and indeed the negotiation of health and illness in these encounters, is likely to take the form of what we understand as **troubles telling.** In

Troubles telling   talk that is designed to be heard as a report of recent or current difficulties.

troubles telling, the patient will describe the issues and experiences that have led him or her to consult the doctor. Here, of course, the preferred response from the doctor is one of acceptance of the patient's problems and the display not just of professional expertise but also of compassion. Thus, being a doctor is associated with a particular interactional stance towards the patient in that patients look to doctors to be sympathetic towards their problems and to be motivated to help in the resolution of these problems. For their part, doctors commonly orient to these expectations, demonstrating that they understand the problems that patients describe to them and affiliating with the patients in negotiating what should be done to address these problems (Ruusuvuori, 2007).

Troubles telling then comprises what we might consider to be the main business of consultations between doctors and patients. The relevance of the experience that the patient describes and the ways in which this is presented in large part shape the interaction that ensues. These features, however, are not the only communications found in such interactions. Indeed, often these consultations involve some communication that is not focused at all on topics of experience, evidence, diagnosis, or associated matters. When turning to matters that are not of immediate relevance to the health or ill-health of the patient, these interactions can then take on a form that more resembles aspects of everyday conversation than the routinized format of medicine in practice. Talk of this kind we think of as **small talk** that is not directly related to the topic of health but instead to the process of maintaining interaction in itself. Small talk in these contexts offers benefits

> **Small talk** talk that relates to commonplace topics and which is not directly relevant to the main topic at hand.

both for doctors and for patients in negotiating the encounter to an agreed conclusion. For doctors, small talk can be particularly useful in allowing them to direct attention away from matters, such as the introduction of intrusive procedures, which are not to be pursued as topics of discussion. Equally, it can direct attention away from other topics, such as patient complaints or concerns, that will not be taken up and pursued further. Small talk brings advantages also for patients where they do not seek to continue difficult topics. Where doctors make recommendations that are unwelcome or provide advice that is troublesome, patients too can seek to move the interaction onto less challenging ground. Thus small talk provides for both parties the possibility of avoiding antagonistic exchanges and conversational difficulties that might otherwise arise (Maynard and Hudak, 2008).

Small talk or no small talk, there are occasions on which conversational difficulties do arise, however. A common feature of doctor / patient interactions is that doctors ask questions to elicit information about patients' experiences and actions and it is expected that, in answering such questions, patients will provide the information that is sought. Often, the process of question and answer presents few difficulties as doctors and patients collaborate to arrive at an understanding of health or ill-health and the steps to be taken (if any). In other cases, however, questions produced by doctors are more likely to lead to interactional difficulties. Consider, for example, questions seeking information about patients' alcohol consumption or use of tobacco products. For some patients, answering such questions openly might reveal information that is potentially relevant to their state of health but which could be deemed culpable and thus be met with rebuke. One interactional strategy available to patients for dealing with such questions is to provide an answer that does not offer the potentially damaging information, in other words to lie. For their part, doctors have available to them various means of discouraging patients from lying, such as asking general questions, using strategies that circumvent these issues or by using explicit frankness in framing their questions. Notwithstanding these attempts, however, patients are likely to treat questions on a range of topics as problematic (Vincent, Laforest and Bergeron, 2007) and to provide answers that are somewhat 'economical with the truth'!

Psychotherapy and mental health

Questions, then, in the context of doctor / patient interaction, are commonly designed to elicit information from patients that can be used to inform decisions as to health or illness, and possible intervention where appropriate. The questions found in other health settings, however, can function quite differently. In psychotherapy settings, the questions that practitioners ask are not wholly oriented to discovering information but function also to establish and to maintain the interaction itself. Here, questions are designed to allow therapists to display sensitivity to the issues that are presented, and moreover to do so in ways that accept the clients' subjective accounts of their experiences as in themselves sufficient evidence of clients'

Rapport   sensitivity to and empathy with a conversational partner.

troubles. This sensitivity to clients' descriptions of their own understandings is commonly termed **rapport**. Sequences of therapists' questions and clients' troubles telling often are followed by therapists providing some summary or interpretation of the subjective account

that is on offer. In these, the experiences of clients as narrated come to form the focus of the interaction, emphasizing the 'here and now' in making sense of individual experience in a therapeutic setting (Leudar *et al.*, 2008b).

Interactions such as these, as well of course as being the immediate focus for those involved, come to be recognizable as what we usually expect of psychotherapy as practised. These sorts of encounters, thus, can be seen as working both on an interpersonal level and on an institutional one. It is precisely by engaging in these ways that psychotherapists do psychotherapy and demonstrate their professional expertise. These two simultaneous orientations are played out throughout the course of the psychotherapy session. Questions, although part of maintaining rapport, provide at the same time a means for therapists to define the clients' experiences in therapeutic terms and so make their troubles amenable to psychotherapeutic interventions (Bartesaghi, 2009). Similarly psychotherapists' summaries and interpretations of clients' stories work to frame these in ways that are appropriate to the psychotherapeutic domain (Bercelli, Rossano and Viaro, 2008). For example, professional interpretations that rely on commonplace or idiomatic expressions (e.g. 'at the end of the day') display understandings of clients' troubles in ways that are difficult to challenge while also bringing these troubles within the remit of the therapeutic encounter (Antaki, 2007).

Psychotherapy then, privileges subjective accounts of clients' experiences while bringing them within the recognizable practice of psychotherapy. Other forms of mental health practice work similarly in treating the experiences of clients or patients as the main topic of discussion. Indeed on occasions that clients seek to formulate their accounts in terms of other forms of social practices, such as religion, professionals attempt to rework these so as to make them more recognizable in therapeutic terms (McVittie and Tiliopoulos, 2007). Thus the individual client and his or her experiences become foregrounded within interactions in the mental health domain. This particular focus is especially evident in two further ways. First, if clients produce accounts that do not refer to themselves or to personal experiences, psychotherapists design their questions and interpretations so as to encourage descriptions that take on this form (Kurri and Wahlstrom, 2007). Second, little attention is given to the contributions of practitioners that lead up to these descriptions, and the resulting accounts come to be treated as reflecting solely the experiences of the individuals rather than as interactional achievements (McKinlay, McVittie and Della Sala, 2010). In these ways, mental health in practice works to locate its focus within the individual client or patient instead of examining broader social patterns of meaning.

Care and identity

We noted above the current emphasis in healthcare on empowerment, that is, the changing identities of individuals from being passive recipients to people who should be able to make meaningful decisions in relation to all aspects of their own lives. One context within which empowerment has become a particular focus is that of care. Many people who are ascribed an identity of being intellectually impaired, such as one of having learning disabilities, receive care either on a residential or on an attendant basis. Here, the current stated policy of the UK Government is that people with learning disabilities should be empowered to participate meaningfully in all decisions and practices that affect them and so have control over their lives.

However, the extent to which the principle of empowerment is reflected in the everyday identities of people with learning disabilities is somewhat less clear. Where new forms of care relationships have been devised to promote empowerment, evidence suggests that these have to at least some extent been successful in facilitating such identities. For example, one consequence of current policy is that the costs required for obtaining care at home are now paid to the individuals who receive that care in order that they can employ care assistants. The effect of this change in arrangements is to make potentially relevant identities of employer and employee that operate alongside alternative identities of care-giver and care-receiver. These identities now available can address the asymmetry often found previously in personal care relationships, leading to a blurring of the boundaries between personal and professional identities seen in more traditional care arrangements (Williams *et al.*, 2009).

Elsewhere, however, findings suggest that the identities on offer for people who have learning disabilities fall short of carrying the full rights and entitlements that would ordinarily accompany having full and meaningful control over their lives. In residential care settings, members of staff continue to ascribe to residents identities that are associated with lesser abilities than would be attributed to other people. For example, when members of staff and residents are discussing topics that are potentially important to residents, staff members often seek to guide residents' talk and these discussions are marked out as different from other forms of conversation. In effect, staff members' efforts can be seen as coaching residents in what is deemed to be relevant and so proceed on the basis that residents have limited abilities to engage in such discussions on their own behalf (Antaki, Finlay and Walton, 2007). On a similar note, staff members who are looking to organize residents' time by suggesting that they attend external events propose these events in very particular ways. As Charles Antaki and colleagues (Antaki, Walton and Finlay, 2007) note, members of staff routinely propose external activities by referring to social or emotional features of what is suggested rather than describing the activities themselves. Thus, a member of staff suggesting that a resident attend a concert might ask 'do you want to go to a concert with Bill' instead of referring to the music that is to be played there. The effect of this, according to Antaki and colleagues, is that staff members encourage residents to participate in social networks and events but undermine their intellectual abilities to make choices on a range of other grounds. Moreover, in describing their everyday practices, members of support staff continue to attribute to people who have learning disabilities problematic features of identity that they would not attribute to other individuals. Everyday practices of care thus in many respects fail to treat residents as empowered service users and make relevant rather more limited and problematic identities (Jingree and Finlay, 2008).

In view of the negative attributes that are commonly associated with an identity of having learning disabilities, and the difficulties of securing full and meaningful social participation, it is unsurprising that many people who face being identified in these ways seek to engage in more wide-ranging negotiations of identity. One way is to resist ascription of the identity itself and instead to identify oneself in other ways. Part of this resistance inevitably involves non-alignment with the category label and refusal to accept such identification. This, however, in itself is potentially not sufficient, for the reasons we have seen, in that the identity might be inferred from descriptions of lesser abilities or from the orientations that others take up in discussions or conversations. Those looking to resist being ascribed this problematic identity therefore attend not just to the identity itself but also to any ascription of impaired abilities, relying upon favourable comparisons with others to present themselves as fully capable individuals (McVittie, Goodall and McKinlay, 2008).

Health and the hospital

We are all familiar, to a greater or lesser extent, with hospitals as sites where certain medical procedures are carried out. Commonly we might think of hospitals in a physical sense, as buildings designed to allow for these procedures to take place in an efficient manner. Hospitals, however, are at the same time complex expert systems within which medical expertise is negotiated in ways that orient to the institutional demands of making sense of medicine. If we think back to the example with which we began this chapter, it is clear that the practice of medicine within hospitals is associated with a range of expectations as to how treatment is to be delivered and as to the identities that are bound up with such practices. Medicine as practised in hospitals then can be understood as a set of collaborative processes that are oriented to meeting these varying expectations as much as they are to specific tasks to the solving of problems that occur along the way (Maseide, 2007).

One example of how the differing expectations of medical practice unfold in everyday life comes from a study by Slade and colleagues (2008) of communication within the emergency department of a large public teaching hospital in Sydney, Australia. In this context, healthcare professionals are required to deliver high-quality care to numerous patients in the course of a busy working day. Patients attending the emergency department, however, look for professionals to provide attention that will allow them to make sense of their conditions and experiences. The attendant features of each identity are likely to make for a mismatch of expectations in the interactions found within the emergency department. At the same time, the negotiation of identities in this context is highly important as any breakdown in communication can lead to unforeseen incidents that are to be avoided. Diana Slade and colleagues offer some examples taken from the **patient journey** through the procedures in the emergency department. The extract below comprises an exchange between a doctor and a young female patient.

> **Patient journey** the course of an individual's various experiences of dealing with health professionals in, for example, a hospital.

Extract 5.3

Doctor: Might even ( ) Um, I think given that you're having a scan, a CAT scan, um, at some stage today.
Patient: You're alright.
Doctor: But I'll keep you informed.
Patient: ( )
Doctor: Alright?
Patient: Did you get all that? (To the researcher).
(Recorded in a consultation room)

(Slade *et al.*, 2008, p. 277)

What this exchange illustrates clearly is the patient's unfamiliarity with hospital practices, both in the form of the procedures used and of the language that is used to describe them. At the end of this exchange, we see the patient display to the researcher (rather than to the doctor) her lack of understanding of what is going to happen to her at this stage of her journey through the hospital. Such interactional difficulties are by no means restricted to exchanges that describe specialist procedures. Below we see an example taken from an exchange between a doctor and a patient and also involving the patient's family.

Extract 5.4

Doctor:	Have you been eating and drinking sort of reasonably normally?
Patient:	I drink but I haven't been eating.==
Family:	==She hasn't been eating well because she's just had a recent death in the family.==
Doctor:	OK==
Family:	== A couple of days ago.==
Doctor:	OK.==
Family:	==Which is her grandmamma.==
Doctor:	OK.
Family:	So she's been spending a lot of time at her mother's house and no she hasn't been eating well obviously distressed because of that.
Doctor:	OK. Sure but you've been keeping up your fluids and drinking and==?

(Slade *et al.*, 2008, p. 279)

Although the exchange above begins with a question from the doctor relating to the patient's eating and drinking patterns, this quickly becomes caught up with descriptions of her personal and social circumstances as introduced by family members. It is noteworthy that the doctor does not pick up on these concerns prior to returning to the initial topic. Instances such as this one reflected a general interactional pattern in which clinicians paid little attention to information that was deemed not to be of direct relevance to the clinical encounter and that they rarely sought information from patients as to their own views on their health problems. Instead, within such interactions, doctors focused almost exclusively on pursuing their own goals of obtaining information deemed to be of direct relevance in a narrow bio-medical sense. Given these recurrent difficulties, it was often left to other professionals in the emergency department setting to pick up on such aspects of patients' concerns, as seen below.

Extract 5.5

Nurse:	They think you've got gout (to elderly, hard of hearing male patient)
Patient:	They're going to kick me out?
Nurse:	No, we think you've got gout.

When the doctor arrived later she asks the patient:

Doctor: Have you ever had gout?

(Slade et al., 2008, p. 282)

This exchange occurred at a point when the patient had experienced a long wait prior to being seen by a doctor. At such times, nurses would often seek to reassure patients by advising them of diagnoses that were likely to come and thus prepare them for a consultation that was likely to be experienced as unsatisfactory and as paying insufficient attention to their concerns. In these ways nurses, perhaps regardless of their designated professional responsibilities, would adopt identities as apologists of the hospital medical system and in so doing would enact the institutional face of caring for the patients in the emergency department. Such interactions, in which nurses took up identities associated with caring in broad terms, allowed patients to make better sense of their journeys through the system and all of those within the emergency department to overcome the interactional difficulties found elsewhere in the system.

Identity Challenges

Throughout this chapter, we have seen how contexts of health and illness routinely present challenges for individual identities. In presenting their accounts to practitioners, individuals orient to the moral and evidential dimensions of health and illness and resist unwelcome attributions to themselves and their actions. Healthcare practitioners too have to negotiate their ways through dealings with patients, with fellow practitioners, and in patterns of healthcare services in displaying the attributes that are associated with particular forms of expertise. For much of the time, management of these identities proceeds if not smoothly then at least without undue difficulties, and indeed people have available a range of discursive strategies for ensuring that health issues are dealt with in practice. We now turn, however, to consider two areas in which identity work of this sort can all too easily become challenged; first, where individuals' attempts to be healthy are undermined, and second, where professionals' expertise and authority to speak are contested.

Undermining health

In many ways, the patient and professional identities that we have considered relating to health and illness might be taken to be mutually complementary. For example, a patient's claims to be ill are consistent with a practitioner displaying expertise in attending to illness. Other issues might be contested but the attributes of each identity are ordinarily compatible in an interactional context. Other contexts of identity, however, make contention more likely; for example, in situations where the attributes of one identity are in large part dependent upon certain attributes being ascribed to another identity. In discussing care-based relationships above, we saw that in some respects the ways in which carers constructed their professional roles and activities were inconsistent with the changing identities of those who receive such care. There, emerging identities of care provider and decision-maker appeared to give rise to conflicts that had been less evident when residential care settings involved the previous identities of care giver and care recipient. Such conflicts in identities are likely to be all the more evident in personal caring relationships where, for an identity of carer *as* carer to make sense, it is dependent upon another person requiring such care. Jennifer Guise and colleagues (Guise, McKinlay and Widdicombe, 2010), in a study of the experiences of people who had suffered early strokes, noted that in group discussions many sufferers claimed to be recovering from strokes and to be regaining their health. These identity claims might appear consistent with the moral imperative to be healthy and to reflect an orientation towards health rather than illness. Various group discussions, however, also involved the carers of the individuals who had suffered strokes, making it problematic for sufferers to pursue their claims to health. For, in emphasizing recovery and relative well-being, the sufferers at the same time were potentially minimizing the need for, and meaning of, the role of their carers. We see below an extract from a group discussion involving Jennifer, the researcher, Eric and Euan who are both recovering after a stroke, and Alison, Eric's carer.

Extract 5.6

584	Eric:	but I would have taken the view. hh before the stroke that
585		I could have run this hospital you know. h I could have
586		been the. h the (1.0) manager of the place you know but
587		eh. hh now I just [blows out 'pwrr'] couldn't care less
588	Jennifer:	mhmm
589	*Alison*:	[that's not true that's not true to say you couldn't care
590		less
591	Euan:	[I could still I could still do I could still but I keep falling
592		asleep [[laughs
593	Eric:	[[laughs
594	*Alison*:	because you could care less and that's what's bugs you=
595	Eric:	that's the frustration yeah

(Guise, McKinlay and Widdicombe, 2010, pp. 82–83)

Extract 5.6 begins with Eric describing how he has changed as a result of having had a stroke. In doing so, he refers to a certain task, that of being able to run the hospital (where the group discussion was held), that he could have performed prior to his stroke. He explains that he would not want to carry out such work now, not because of any lack of ability but instead due to lack of interest in that he 'couldn't care less'. This claim suggests that any difference in Eric's aptitude for this task is attributable to a change in motivation rather than a change in his abilities, and suggests that he is quite able to perform this work should he choose to do so. However, Eric's claim that the difference is attributable to motivation is soon challenged by his carer, Alison. Following her challenge, Eric accepts Alison's argument that his motivation is not changed. The changes that he has experienced thus become attributable not to different motivation but instead to reduced abilities to perform certain tasks. Identity challenges of this sort provided a recurring focus for many discussions, undermining suggestions of recovery. Below we see an extract from a group discussion again involving Jennifer, the researcher, and Yvonne, Norman and Ian, all of whom are recovering after strokes.

Extract 5.7

853	Jennifer:	can anybody say in what in (1.0) what wa:ys would you
854		say that having had a stroke has affected you as a
855		person?
856		(3.0)
857	Yvonne:	impatient (1.0) e:h
858	Jennifer:	what make it has made you impatient
859	Yvonne:	mhmm
860	Jennifer:	yeah?
861	Yvonne:	[very quietly] aye
862		(3.0)
863	Norman:	yeah it's [unclear]
864	Ian:	it's maybe
865	Norman:	one of the things that trauma and shock bring on
866	Ian:	yeah maybe you should ask the carers rather than the. h
867		the sufferers of that [laughs]
868	Yvonne:	that's right

(Guise, McKinlay and Widdicombe, 2010, pp. 85–86)

In Extract 5.7, it very quickly becomes clear that the participants treat the question put to them as a sensitive matter. Although they are invited to discuss their experiences after suffering strokes, the discussion is punctuated by pauses and hesitancies and none of the sufferers seeks to discuss in any detail the changes that a stroke has made for him or her. Interestingly, towards the end of the exchange, Ian and Yvonne collaboratively propose that the question should be asked of the carers not of those who have suffered the strokes. Thus, the sufferers orient to the discussion as being too problematic for them to make any definite claims to identities or to health-related attributes. In a context within which any identity claims that they make are potentially likely to be met with challenge, the individuals involved offer only minimal subjective accounts. They become disqualified, in effect, from speaking about their own experiences of health when the identities of others present as carers are dependent upon them accepting identities associated with ill-health.

Competing expertise

As we have seen in this chapter, identities of health professionals are inevitably associated with practice that enacts expertise, in dealings with patients or clients and in interacting with other professionals, all within ever-changing contexts of health and ill-health. Particular forms of professional practice incorporate different forms of communication, such as the diagnosis of medical conditions, establishing rapport, offering interpretations, or providing care. Thus, in doing practice, health professionals display that they have authority to speak on the matter in hand, whether an individual suffers from anorexia nervosa or should identify more personally with an account of troubles telling. For much of the time, interactions that take these forms are treated as unexceptional and as consistent with broader social understandings of what it means to be an optometrist, a doctor, or a nurse. It is indeed for such reasons that the case of Joseph Gill, with which we began this chapter, stands out as exceptional in that the treatment he received differed markedly from what would be expected in these circumstances.

For some health professionals, however, matters are not as straightforward as this. Earlier we noted some of the difficulties that can arise when different professions make competing claims for expertise in delivering aspects of eye-care. Similar difficulties can arise across the spectrum of health and ill-health. Doctors are routinely accepted as having authority to speak on issues of medicine; other professionals are treated as somewhat less qualified to do so. Complementary and alternative medicine (CAM), for example, is often regarded as not being founded on principles of objective evidence and therefore is not always taken to be a form of expertise that can make legitimate claims in relation to medical issues. This potentially negative evaluation of their practice makes life difficult for CAM practitioners in working out their identities in relation to other professions and to patients who consult them. Homeopaths, for example, in their dealings with patients not only have to display understanding of troubles telling but also have to convince potentially sceptical patients and others of the efficacy of their approach to dealing with these troubles (Chatwin, 2008). Practitioners of acupuncture attempt to display expertise by referring to core principles of a particular version of healthcare and treatment (Ho, 2006). Negotiating professional identities on such bases of course is highly contingent upon practitioners' claims being accepted by those with whom they come into contact in their practice. Should the claims prove unconvincing, especially in comparison to other less disputed versions of practice, patients might well opt to stay with more familiar and recognized forms of medicine.

Widely recognized professional identities can of course bring their own challenges in relation to the extent of the expertise that is to be accorded to the professional. Increasingly, in the light of information available on the internet and other sources, individuals can gain much knowledge about health issues and are not solely reliant on professionals for the delivery and acquisition of details relating to their health concerns. What this makes for therefore are changing contexts in which patients potentially may lay claim not just to subjective knowledge of health matters but additionally knowledge derived from external sources. In short, professionals' claims to expertise in such matters become open to challenge by patients who are equipped to claim entitlements to knowledge. An example of one such challenging context is provided by Lehtinen (2007) in the form of genetic counselling discussions at a clinical genetics centre in Finland. Often genetic counselling is less concerned with producing diagnosis or offering treatment than with enabling individuals to understand genetic illnesses to make informed decisions about potential risks in living their lives. In these cases, clients potentially have access to knowledge that will not be available to doctors. Matters of family history, for instance, will be relevant but available to clients alone. Thus, where clients introduce such knowledge in the course of counselling sessions, doctors have to orient to the entitlement to such knowledge and to manage it where it appears at odds with their own expertise. In negotiating their identities as experts, therefore, doctors have to reconcile these very different forms of expertise to produce an outcome that will be accepted by the clients and not subjected to further challenge.

Discussion

In this chapter, we have examined many of the factors that accompany identities within the realm of health, looking particularly at those of individuals as well or unwell, and health professionals, across a range of contexts. The meanings of experience and understandings of practice are formed within and in turn shape the interactions that commonly recur in which these concerns are played out for individuals and which are accompanied by a wide range of actions. For the most part, these interactions appear to proceed smoothly; it is not by accident that we come to understand health in the ways that we do and recognize a diversity of forms of expertise. Testament perhaps to the ways in which health is routinely accomplished in social interaction is the extent of the problems encountered should one attempt to replicate it in other ways. Recently there have been attempts to devise artificial systems that can in some ways reproduce the sorts of communication otherwise found in particular health settings. Consider, for example, the setting of a busy neonatal intensive care ward in which end-of-shift summaries are used to communicate valuable patient information to nurses who are about to take over the care of the neonates. In this setting, could an intelligent **natural language generation** system produce textual summaries that sufficiently resemble those produced by expert nurses (McKinlay *et al.*, 2010b)?

Natural language generation the production by an intelligent system of linguistic output that is designed to resemble human language.

Well, the answer is no, not really. It is of course unreasonable to expect that a system of this sort would produce small talk or idiom to ensure the smooth course of communication. However, summaries that make little reference to the babies as individuals and that do not make available causal inferences stand in sharp contrast to the talk that we usually find in contexts of health and illness. In addition, communications taking the form 'The temperature sensor was re-sited' are in many instances of little help in identifying patients and the treatment that they should receive. Fortunately, the consequences in these cases were less extreme than the example with which we began: human professionals remained constantly on hand to display the expertise that we routinely attribute to them in providing care to patients who required just that attention.

Chapter Summary

Health and illness are not simply descriptions of physical or psychological states. An identity associated with being healthy or being ill is negotiated in ways that are recognizable to others and which orients to broader understandings of these issues. Such identities are bound up also with actions, whether receiving medical treatment, other interventions, or displaying professional expertise.

There is a moral imperative for people to be well. People who claim to be ill are expected to warrant these claims by providing evidence. Usually objective evidence, by way of measurements or outcomes of tests is preferred to individuals' subjective accounts. Subjective accounts, however, are the main focus of some forms of practice, such as psychotherapy.

People are treated as responsible for maintaining health wherever possible. They might be treated as accountable, and thereby morally culpable, if their own actions are deemed to have led to ill-health.

Professionals have to negotiate their expertise with patients and with other professionals. Displaying this expertise allows them authority to speak on the health topic in question.

Patients have increasingly been constructed as people who can make meaningful decisions in relation to their own heath and care. This principle of empowerment has become increasingly visible in contexts that include patient information leaflets and the provision of care.

Identities of health and illness are negotiated against a background of social understandings of other identity issues, such as nature/nurture and gender. The identities that individuals claim, resist or manage, however, have to be examined in everyday contexts.

Interactions between clients or patients and professionals involve elements such as small talk and rapport as well as troubles telling and discussion of the main health topics. The participants usually work to make these interactions proceed smoothly, although difficulties can arise when, for instance, patients are asked questions about actions that are likely to be treated as problematic.

Other people, such as carers, can undermine individuals' attempts to negotiate identities associated with recovery. In such circumstances, people are more reluctant to make definitive claims to certain identities.

Expert artificial systems cannot, at least as yet, produce any reasonable attempt at replicating human communications in relation to health. This failure and the material covered in the chapter, all demonstrate the intricate and complex ways in which we all negotiate identities of being well or being ill in everyday terms.

Connections

Arguments as to the relative contributions of nature and nurture to the development of identities are discussed in Chapter 1. Issues of gender and identities are more fully discussed in Chapter 4.

The internet provides opportunities for people to negotiate many different identities, including those related to health or illness. Support groups and discussion forums, in particular, make available contexts in which individuals can take up or challenge the understandings of health and illness found elsewhere. These issues are discussed in Chapter 8.

Further Reading

Jingree, T. and Finlay, W. M. L. (2008). 'You can't do it... it's theory rather than practice': staff use of the practice/principle rhetorical device in talk on empowering people with learning disabilities. *Discourse and Society, 19,* 705–726.

This study provides a useful example of how professionals attempt to deal with issues of empowerment in care settings. As the title suggests, much of this is taken up with justifications as to why empowerment as a principle cannot be put into practice fully.

Lehtinen, E. (2007). Merging doctor and client knowledge: On doctors' ways of dealing with clients' potentially discrepant information in genetic counseling. *Journal of Pragmatics, 39,* 389–427.

A good example of how genetic counsellors, as experts, and patients contest the weight to be given to very different forms of claimed expertise.

Slade, D., Scheeres, H., Manidis, M. *et al.* (2008). Emergency communication: the discursive challenges facing emergency clinicians and patients in hospital emergency departments. *Discourse and Communication, 2,* 271–298.

An illuminating study for anyone who has spent any time in a busy hospital department! This demonstrates the ways in which different health professionals contribute to the discursive management of patients and the hospital department (just about) manages to run smoothly.

Activity Box

Imagine that you were attempting to design an expert system to assist the communication of someone who had difficulty in describing their own daily experiences to healthcare professionals, family or others. This system would be required to describe the experiences of the individual in ways that made sense while conveying the appropriate subjective account of their experiences on a daily basis. What elements of the negotiation of such experience are most important to include in such a system? In considering the output of this system, how should it most usefully combine its descriptions of the person's activities into a summary that would be useful for people wanting to know what had gone on for that person?

6

Identities and the Law

Topics Covered in this Chapter

Key Terms

Analogy

Category incumbent activities

Cross-examination

Direct examination

Display talk

Dispreferred responses

Expert witness

Facework

Hybrid discourse

Institutional norms

Irony

Lay constructions

Mediation

Minimal response

Mitigation

Narrative expansions

Oral argument

Subjectivities

Identities in Context: Individuals and Discourse in Action, First Edition. Andrew McKinlay and Chris McVittie.
© 2011 Andrew McKinlay and Chris McVittie. Published 2011 by Blackwell Publishing Ltd.

Q: What was the first thing your husband said to you when he woke up that
     morning?
A: He said, 'Where am I Cathy?'
Q: And why did that upset you?
A: My name is Susan.

(Lederer, 1996)

Questions of identity are clearly important in legal processes. We all understand that the police should apprehend the right person, and we all expect that
the person who is convicted in court is the person who did the deed. But legal
issues of identity transcend such matters. As we have already seen in relation to
other settings, what happens in the courtroom depends crucially on how people are characterized by others, on how they characterize themselves, and on
the features of themselves as individuals that are made relevant during the
course of an interaction. In the above example, both questioner and respondent
understand that by allowing Susan to specify her name, they are making a range
of inferences available to the over-hearing courtroom audience. These inferences are associated with the normative expectations that a reasonable person

Institutional norms sets of
expectations or beliefs that are
taken to be rules of interaction
associated with particular contexts,
such as those observable in law
courts or other organizational
settings, and which differ from
expectations associated with
everyday conversation.

might have about marital relationships, such as the
expectation that husbands will not address their
wives by using another woman's name, especially
upon waking up in bed. However, as we have already
seen in the previous chapters and as we will see in
this chapter, developing, maintaining and challenging identities in some circumstances, such as in legal
settings, arguably incorporates a special feature
which is absent in other, more everyday settings:
institutional norms.

The role of the law as an institution is to preserve or
restore social order within society by defining and then regulating a wide range of
the relationships and interactions which underpin everyday life. Discourse analysis is
well-suited to the study of legal institutional practice, because most legal processes
involve either written or spoken language. Those who have never been involved in
legal affairs might assume that in this context language can be taken at 'face value',
and that what is written or said can be understood to be statements of fact. However,
legal contexts are often cases of adversarial dispute, in which police officers contest
versions of actions and events with suspects, and defence lawyers strive against the
versions that are produced by prosecution lawyers while both seek to control and
manage the contributions made by witnesses. And, of course, overlaid on these discourses are the contributions made by the judge. Another factor to be considered is
that speakers often design what they say for more than one audience. Thus a lawyer
may ask a witness a question which is specifically framed to allow the over-hearing

jury to draw a particular inference. Or a witness may frame an answer in a way that not only addresses a lawyer's question, but also presents a particular view of events to an over-hearing judge. (Indeed Luchjenbroers and Aldridge, 2007, have argued that frames are 'powerful tools' in the encoding of assumptions within the legal context so that audience perceptions of actions and events can be manipulated.) So legal discourse turns out to be a field in which the various parties involved attend to a wide variety of interests and direct what they say to a range of audiences as they engage in interactions in discourse. And this means that what they say, and how they say it, and the identities that appear and disappear in such talk, are likely to reflect those interests. It is this feature of legal discourse which makes the study of identities within the law an especially fascinating exercise.

In this chapter, we will explore how those involved in processes of law and order strive to maintain and challenge identities as they carry out their legal duties. It is worth remembering at the start that legal discourse arises in a wide variety of settings ranging from the courtroom itself through legal documents and legal textbooks to the informal chatter about the law common in the media which even appears in our everyday talk (Martinez, 2006; Trosborg, 1995). To begin with, we will turn to the discourse of lawyers. Theirs is the most obviously adversarial discourse, and so it is not surprising that contests of identity can be seen especially sharply in what they say and write. But, perhaps frustratingly for lawyers, legal matters are regulated by judges and so we will next turn to consider how their discourse displays what their identity concerns might be. Of course the law exists to regulate the activities of the person in the street, and so lay-people also make an appearance in legal processes, and so we will also examine how in their discourse they seek to present themselves and others as particular sorts of people in order to further their legal interests. Finally, the appearance of the lay person in a courtroom usually occurs only after they have been brought there by some due process, which in criminal cases involves the police. So we will conclude by briefly examining the way that issues of identity can arise during interactions between police officers and their suspects.

Lawyers' Discourse

Within the courtroom, lawyers and judges have entitlements to speak which do not exist for others such as witnesses, defendants and members of the jury. Lawyers and judges have the institutional power to demand answers to their questions. Witnesses and defendants are therefore not only required to answer, but they are required to give answers that can be taken to be relevant to the question. And, as anyone who has enjoyed television or film representations of courtroom drama knows, it is up to the lawyer, not the witness or defendant, to control the topic of what is said. Most of us can recall the look of chagrin on the face of a witness when the prosecutor leaps to his feet to call out 'Move to strike as irrelevant!' So in the contest of identities, it might seem as though lawyers have the upper hand. This is especially important since evidence suggests that lawyers already have, before they enter the courtroom, an established set of discourses which they reproduce later in court.

Constructing identities in talk

This is shown in a study by Pond (2008). They conducted a series of interviews with New Zealand lawyers in order to understand the **subjectivities** which arose as these lawyers talked about the people who are involved in domestic violence cases. So what they were interested in was to understand the sorts of discourses that inform lawyers' practices and interactions once they engage in legal discourse in more formal settings. They note that a variety of competing descriptions can arise. While in some cases men are portrayed as the aggressors and women the victims, they note that in other cases men can be described as victims through reference to the possibility that women might lie about domestic violence in order to gain advantage in the process of managing divorce or separation. Moreover, even in cases where it is accepted that men may have been violent towards their partners, such violence is often portrayed as limited in scope:

> **Subjectivities** forms of discourse in which actions and events are described in a way which highlights the partial or interested nature of what is said about them.

Extract 6.1

Alison: I just feel sorry for some guys sometimes, you know. They've screwed up their relationships. But they're not all bad … It's amazing how many guys hit their partners and never touch the kids. It's incredible.

(Pond and Morgan, 2008, p. 466)

One effect of cases of domestic violence is that fathers may struggle to obtain access to see their children. In consequence, some of the lawyers' discourse examined by Pond and Morgan focuses on the issue of whether men who have been violent towards their partners might nevertheless be safe around the children. In this extract, what is occurring here, according to Pond and Morgan, is the deployment of a 'violent partner; good father' discourse in which the nature of the partner as a violent person is being negotiated. Specifically, what such talk implies is that a man could be shown to be violent in one circumstance, when dealing with his partner, but not in other circumstances, such as in dealing with his children.

So it seems as though lawyers, those who have a large measure of control over the production of discourse within the courtroom, enter the courtroom with a variety of ready-to-hand descriptions of the identities of the people they are going to represent. And as Matoesian (2001) has pointed out, such discursive practices are the means by which lawyers make relevant the different legal and social identities that arise during the courtroom process itself. For example, in the course of the rape trial which he examines, Matoesian notes that the defence lawyer seeks to transform the identity of the person who was allegedly attacked from a victim identity to a non-victim identity. One of the means the defence lawyer draws upon is, perhaps surprisingly, a characterization of the people that the victim called after the attack. The victim called a friend rather than, say, a family member. In describing this event, the lawyer then describes this friend as an 'acquaintance'. So by carefully establishing that the friend who was called was not as close to the victim as a parent, for example, the lawyer is able to indicate that the events under discussion, the alleged rape, could not have been as 'serious' as the sort of thing that would have necessitated a call to close family members. In this way, by deploying a particular characterization of the relationship between the victim and the person she subsequently called, the lawyer is able to suggest that the victim identity of the person making the complaint is under question.

Perhaps one of the most compelling aspects of the spoken courtroom process is that, as a trial comes to its close, it is up to the competing lawyers to present a closing argument on behalf of their client. Pascual (2006) notes that the language-in-interaction which arises in the courtroom often takes the form of **display talk** in that the talk is produced for an over-hearing third party in contrast to everyday talk in which what is said is directed towards the person one is speaking to. In this respect, when lawyers interrogate witnesses, often what they say is in fact directed towards the jury. Sometimes, in pre-

> **Display talk**   talk that is designed not only to further an ongoing interaction but to present a particular perspective on what is said to an over-hearing audience.

senting their closing arguments, lawyers do directly address the jury. Interestingly, however, even in these closing monologues, lawyers frame some of what they say in the form of questions, even though, of course, under the rules of the court the jury are not entitled to speak in answer. The point here is that the skilled lawyer can introduce potential difficulties for his or her case through the means of such questions, and this provides a context in which he or she can provide answers to such difficulties. Indeed, Rosulek (2008) suggests that the closing arguments in criminal trials can be viewed as persuasive discourse in which two quite different and competing discursive representations of the people and events under discussion are produced. In discussing the closing arguments which occurred in a sexual abuse trial, Rosulek notes that the defence and the prosecution deployed different strategies in their representation of those involved with the case. The prosecutor's closing argument focused on what had happened to the victim and personalized her through references to her age, the use of her nickname and by describing her thoughts and what she said. However, in this argument the defendant was depersonalized, in that he was referred to not by name but as 'the defendant', and the focal point of descriptions was on his actions rather than on his thoughts and feelings. By contrast, the defence lawyer's closing argument presented a quite different persona for the victim, emphasizing her 'mature sexual understanding', while personalizing the defendant through the use of his name and by introducing descriptions of his thoughts and feelings.

Constructing identities in text

The discursive contest of identities is not merely a feature of spoken discourse within the courtroom. The law is an institution that is grounded in written texts. And so these texts represent important resources in understanding how the interplay of identities takes place within legal contexts. Scheffer (2006), for example, has pointed to the way that preparatory drafts and final written and spoken arguments all form a context in which actions and events are shaped within legal discourse. And in a discussion of legal texts that deal with divorce, Wharton (2006) argues that such texts represent not only a codification of institutional power, but are potentially constructive of the identities of those who find themselves involved in divorce proceedings. Indeed, not only do such texts potentially become involved in identity construction, they also establish power asymmetries between the identities thus constructed. These power asymmetries therefore are embedded in the adversarial subjectivities which such texts produce in legal divorce proceedings.

An especially clear view of how legal texts construct identities is well demonstrated in a study of a decision produced by the United States Supreme Court in the case of detainees held at the United States facility in Guantanamo Bay (Hobbs, 2007a). Here, Hobbs examined the written arguments put forward by both parties and the ways in which the written judgement reflected these arguments. It might seem as though, outside the hurly burly of courtroom context, calm and dispassionate written judgement would not reflect any of the efforts at identity construction through discourse which lawyers produce in their courtroom talk. However, Hobbs shows that this is not so. The issue which Hobbs studied was a case involving detainees who had been captured during the war against Taliban forces in Afghanistan in 2001. Having been captured, detainees then applied for legal processes to take place in which they could appeal against their incarceration. During this process, lawyers for the detainees and their opponents, lawyers for the US Government, sought to pursue their cases in part by presenting competing 'versions' of the identities of the detainees. In their written petition to the court, the lawyers for the detainees sought to distinguish them from other cases where such incarceration might be expected. In part, this relied on category contrasts such as contrasting 'convicted war criminals' with people 'imprisoned completely without legal process' and contrasting 'enemy aliens' with 'citizens of our closest allies'.

So by picturing the detainees as wrongly imprisoned citizens of closely allied countries, the detainees' lawyers sought to create a version of the detainees as the innocent victims of a tyrannical government. The government's lawyers, however, produced a quite different version. In the government's argument, the detainees were characterized as 'aliens captured and detained abroad'. This, says Hobbs, establishes a particular context of 'us versus them' in which the arguments put forward by the detainees constituted an attack on the military authority of the United States President. On this version of the detainees' identity, the consequences that follow upon offering them due legal process would be highly detrimental to the US, and highly supportive to US enemies. So what this study shows is that both defence and prosecution lawyers are able to deploy versions of identities of the people under judgement, and that even in the case of written submissions part of the legal process is the contest of these identities as that process unfolds.

When matters such as these are considered, the full impact and seriousness of the law comes to the fore. However, there are occasions on which lawyers and advocates, those skilled proponents in the use of language, draw upon other resources open to them in creating, maintaining or challenging the identities. For example, in a study of **mediation** in a civil court case, Hobbs (2007c) notes that lawyers may deploy humour to persuasive effect. In one case, the plaintiff, Carpenter, claimed to have slipped on a banana peel in the parking area of a shop called 'Arbor Drugs'. The formal written summary of the mediation process included a relatively lengthy poem produced by the defence lawyer, part of which is represented in the following extract:

> **Mediation**   service that aims to resolve disputes where other attempts have failed and intervention by an external agency is necessary.

Extract 6.2

There once was a man named Mark Carpenter
Who slipped in the parking lot at Arbor.
He said three banana peels caused his fall
And claimed he couldn't see them at all

(Hobbs, 2007c, p. 133)

It might be unusual to see poetic flights of fancy in dry legal documents. But, Hobbs points out, in the present case this rhyming rhetoric has a point. It helps the defence lawyer to establish not only that the case itself was frivolous, but that the plaintiff, Carpenter, was behaving inappropriately in making his claim. The use of comedic verse frames Carpenter's complaints in a particular way. Rather than treating Carpenter as the innocent victim of a negligently run business, the poetic treatment frames Carpenter as someone who is a suitable target for humorous commentary.

So what we see here is that, in what they say and in what they write, lawyers are able to deploy different forms of rhetorical identification depending on their persuasive goals. In describing their own clients, they construct identities that emphasize features such as probity and reasonableness and may strive to present their clients as personalized individuals. In describing their opponents' clients, they strive to do the opposite, by creating identities for them in which aspects such as lack of victim status are emphasized and in which the person is treated in a depersonalized fashion. However, what we also see is that the particularities of how this gets done depend on the nature of the legal issue under consideration. Thus it is in cases of domestic violence that good fathers are contrasted with bad husbands and it is in cases of international issues like Guantanamo that alien combatants are contrasted with victims of government tyranny and it is in cases of sexual abuse that sexually naive children are contrasted with the sexually mature. This is a feature of identity talk that we discussed in the first chapter. Identities are not constructed in a vacuum. They are produced and maintained or challenged as part of the 'business' of the interaction in which such productions take place. And so, in constructing identities, speakers draw upon the locally available resources in talk which those interactions make available. For the lawyer, the resources to hand are the details of the legal case in process, and so it is the particularities of that case that provide the 'raw materials' for their identity construction efforts.

Judges' Discourse

Judges construct others' identities

Now as the poetic example in Extract 6.2 demonstrates, one complexity here is that it is not always the case that lawyers in the courtroom are going to reproduce identity discourses directly. That is, a lawyer might not ask his client something like 'Although you are a bad husband, you are a good father, aren't you?' For example, in relation to gender identity Ehrlich (2002) notes that as the trial of a rape defendant unfolded, his lawyer attempted to deal with possible inferences about the defendant as someone accused of sexual assault by producing talk which diminished the agency of the defendant. The lawyer did not draw on discourses of gender identity to make this case. However, according to Ehrlich, the judge did. In his formally stated decision, the judge drew on discourses of male sexual drive to explain that the defendant was innocent of one of the charges levelled against him, because the female complainant should have realized that at certain points, men's capacity to control themselves is limited by hormonal urges. So just like lawyers, judges involved in legal processes display a cultural understanding of different identity discourses such as discourses of gender identity, and draw upon them in guiding their practices within the courtroom. And an important feature here is that judges, like the rest of the courtroom participants, are at times willing to 'push the boundaries' of what is to count as an appropriate interactional contribution. (For an interesting case of a judge even omitting his 'formal' opening statement, see Licoppe and Dumoulin, 2010.)

MacMartin (2002) demonstrates the importance of this in a study of the ways in which judges can reproduce versions of the actors involved in cases of child sex abuse. MacMartin notes that in such cases, the identity of abuser and victim are constructed in part by the projection of particular **category incumbent activities**. These are features of behaviour which can be inferred to belong to a person as a result of being categorized in a particular way. In the case of the trials that she studied, MacMartin notes that a judge's determination of whether a crime took place sometimes rested on what he said about the nature of the complainant's behaviour after the alleged attack. In some judgements, judges presented a version of children who had suffered abuse as traumatically affected by the experience. As a result of them being categorized in this way, the behaviour of such children was made inferentially available. In particular, one inference that followed on from such a categorization is that children in such a category would avoid their attacker in the future. The consequence of this, MacMartin suggests, is that in some cases judges ruled in favour of the defendant over the alleged victim, where evidence was produced that the alleged victim did not, in fact, avoid her attacker in the future.

> **Category incumbent activities**
> a set of activities that are presented as being normatively related to membership of a specific category.

Judges construct their own identities

It might seem odd that judges or those who hold relevantly similar positions such as quasi-judicial mediators display any concern with their own identities. However, as Garcia (2000) points out, people in these roles are walking a tightrope. On the one hand, they have their own interests and concerns and yet on the other hand, their role requires that they display impartiality. So the extent to which they can allow their own interests and concerns to appear in what they say is constrained by the need to appear to be 'above the fray'. This is quite unlike the position of lawyers, who are normatively expected to be adopting a clearly biased position in which the interests of their own clients take precedence. It is for this reason that those in judicial positions can be seen to present their own identities as bound up with impartiality. And where some sort of alignment is discernible, this is accomplished in a very careful manner.

We can see this in a study conducted by Heisterkamp (2006), who looked at the way people who act in a quasi-judicial role as mediators in court-based mediation sessions managed the requirement of steering the parties involved to a conclusion while at the same time 'displaying' themselves as holding a 'neutral' position.

Extract 6.3

24	M20:	My role is to be neutral and impartial.
25		(1.2)
26		Uhm- I don't make decisions for you.
27		I simply facilitate (.) uh an- and uh try to help you k- with with-
28		promote your ideas on how we can
29		come up to uh resolution to the dispute

(Heisterkamp, 2006, p. 2056)

Cases such as this typically arise during the mediator's opening statement, especially on those occasions in which the disputing parties may be unfamiliar with mediation processes. Thus, Heisterkamp suggests, by explicitly providing labels such as 'neutral' and 'impartial' for her own role, the mediator presents herself as being someone who occupies a particular sort of position in this interaction. This is given emphasis by the contrast she goes on to draw between the adjudicative role of making decisions and the practices she will engage in of not taking sides but merely encouraging the parties to come up with their own resolution. So what we see here is a relatively simple and direct claim about self and role which is produced during the business of mediation. However, as Heisterkamp points out, while claims of this sort may provide information to the uninitiated, the very simplicity and directness of this claim may limit the extent to which it is rhetorically persuasive for the parties involved.

Moreover, such tactics do not allow the mediator or judge to display their own viewpoints. Tracy (2009) has pointed out that a variety of different identities are made visible in the courtroom talk of judges. Her particular interest is in the way that talk 'sets in motion' inferences about features of the person such as social roles or interactional stances. In her study, Tracy examines the way that judges use questions to construct themselves as particular kinds of people by discursively representing features of the self such as attitudes, knowledge, moral standpoint, or political orientation. The context which Tracy selects is a set of **oral arguments** which took place in the New York Court of Appeals in 2006 after a number of same-sex couples had been denied marriage licences. (The Appeal Court judges' eventual majority decision was that New York State was not required to recognize same-sex marriages.) Oral argument is that phase of court procedure in which lawyers for the prosecution and defence present their arguments to the judges

> **Oral argument** within legal contexts, that form of discourse that arises in court in which lawyers present accounts of actions and events through speech rather than by the presentation of written argument.

who will adjudicate on the appeal. During the unfolding of this appeal process, Tracy notes, the judges who were to adjudicate the cases asked a range of questions. Now it might seem as though a judge in a courtroom asks questions in a purely 'forensic' manner solely in order to establish matters of fact or points of law. But what Tracy discovered was that the judge's questions in fact accomplished much more. The key to understanding what was going on, says Tracy, is that identities are constructed through talk. But in saying this, one must understand that such construction depends in part on the particularities of the institutional context in which such talk takes place. The institutional role of judges is one which provides a range of opportunities for judges to interrupt the talk of defence and prosecution lawyers by asking questions. And so, for judges in the courtroom, it is this practice of asking questions which provides an opportunity for them to construct their own identities through talk.

To make sense of what the judges were doing, Tracy draws on Goffman's (1967) notion of **facework** and its theoretical extension into 'identity-work' by Brown and Levinson (1987). Tracy notes that sometimes judges' questions are hostile, sometimes they are neutral,

> **Facework** Goffman's term for the negotiation of matters of face in everyday interactions.

and sometimes they are supportive of the case being advanced. In the latter case, Tracy argues, such questions allow the judge to display alignment with the case being presented.

Extract 6.4

A-K: … If you walk into a room and tell someone you're married to someone, that for all the reasons Ms. Sommer explains, connotes something in our society and our culture that civil union does not.

J-C: Even if you were to direct the legislature to um enact civil union legislation there are many benefits that could not be enacted by the state legislature, which would which um now inure to a married couple, federal benefits for example umm so wouldn't- it wouldn't really be a total [ah

A-K: [That is true. If- if we win this case and walk out of this courtroom tomorrow it would not be a total victory. I don't deny that.

(Tracy, 2009, p. 212)

In this extract, A-K is an attorney arguing the case for gay marriage and J-C is one of the judges. Tracy suggests that what is going on here is that Judge C's contribution indicates that even were gay marriage to be acceptable, the people involved would continue to suffer relative disadvantage. The implication here, presumably, is that gay people are so disadvantaged in society that they at least ought to be afforded the entitlements of marriage. So by asking this question, Judge C is able to present herself as someone who is aligned with the attorney's argument.

We saw earlier that humour can be a useful component of the lawyer's discourse. And of course, if lawyers can deploy humour, so can judges. So humour represents another 'indirect' means through which the judge can display his or her identity. In another of her studies, Hobbs (2007b) discusses a case in which one party's lawyers submitted court documentation four minutes past a relevant deadline. The opposing lawyers then submitted a legal motion to disallow the filing of these documents. Hobbs describes the way in which the judge's response, in rejecting this motion, humorously criticized the motion to dismiss, by using satirical language to imply that the motion was a waste of the court's time. She suggests that in cases such as this, judge's humour allows the judge to present a personality that is 'screened from view' by his official role.

Lay People's Discourse

Lay identities outside the courtroom

Preceding sections have indicated that lawyers and judges draw upon cultural frameworks of identity, such as gender identity or the identities of the abused, in order to establish points of view. But this is not a special feature of legal professionals. The ordinary person in the street is just as capable of generating versions of perpetrators and their victims which establish them as being particular sorts of people. This is well evidenced in a study by O'Byrne, Hansen and Rapley (2008). In this study, a group of heterosexual male students from Australia can be seen to draw upon an interpretative repertoire of 'mis-communication' to diminish the responsibility of men who rape.

Extract 6.5

413	Kyle:	Just something I thought and wondering how this ties into it yeah
414	M:	Yeah
415	Kyle:	It all does 'cause um
416	M:	Yeah
417	Kyle:	'Cause some people do play hard to get but that is no excuse for rape
418		(.)
		don't get me wrong'
419	M:	Yeah
420	Kyle:	But again (.) with regards to communication how (.) how does the
421		receiver in (heh)terpret a(heh)ll th(heh)at (.)um

(O'Byrne, Hansen and Rapley, 2008, p. 180)

In a section of their discussion which precedes this extract, the men discuss whether 'the perpetrator' might be confused by the signals that his victim gives off. O'Byrne notes that initially, in this extract, what Kyle says can be heard as establishing the position of someone who does not excuse rape. However, at line 420, Kyle's 'but again' indicates that to some extent he is about to undermine the claim that he has just made. What follows is a description that *reformulates* the identity of someone responsible for rape. Whereas the men had previously been referring to a rapist as 'the perpetrator', O'Byrne suggests that Kyle reformulates the identity of such a person through 'the receiver'. In what follows, the questionable and comical nature of the sorts of communication that such a receiver might receive (i.e. from the woman victim) indicates that the rapist should be thought of, not as a perpetrator, but as someone dealing with a woman who is unable to communicate properly.

Lay accounts of identity do not stop at the perpetrator. Such accounts can also be produced for victims. Tuffin and Frewin (2008) examined letters written to the editor of a New Zealand newspaper about the issue of indigenous land rights. This issue is a matter of ongoing concern in New Zealand, where the respective rights of Māori and non-Māori (Pakeha) New Zealanders continue to be debated, especially in respect of entitlement to live on, and use the resources from, particular geographical areas. Tuffin and Frewin were interested in examining the **lay constructions** of law which arose in these letters, and in understanding the ways in which different interpretations of legal and other issues in such letters could be seen to produce different effects. In Extract 6.6, a section from the letter of one of these correspondents, Schmidt, discusses the possibility of a separate legal system for Māori people.

> **Lay constructions** descriptions or accounts of practices and procedures that do not require expertise, often described as such in a context where professional discourse on the same topic is also available.

Extract 6.6

The likes of MJ argue for a completely separate criminal justice system for Maori because he sees the Maori and European systems as fundamentally incompatible. However, realistically, this could probably never work because of problems of jurisdiction. That is, how does one define who is to be classified as Maori and therefore dealt with under the separate system? (Schmidt)

(Tuffin and Frewin, 2008, p. 78)

In the paragraphs of his letter preceding this extract, Schmidt has been careful to argue that the New Zealand legal system should be pluralistic, in that it should attend appropriately to the varying cultural beliefs which separate Māori people from Pakeha people. However, as this extract shows, Schmidt is careful to distinguish claims about legal pluralism from claims about establishing separate legal systems. The rationale presented for this argument lies in the difficulty for those operating such systems in defining who is to count as Māori and who is not. In other words, the identity of 'Māori' becomes centrally problematic, and it is this problematic status that leads to the conclusion that there should not be separate land entitlement rights for the Māoris under the law. Of course, as Tuffin and Frewin point out, what is left unstated is the issue of why such difficulties would not equally apply to a 'pluralist' legal system in which Māori people were offered 'special treatment'.

Lay people as witnesses

Once the lay person sets foot in the courtroom, however, his or her lay accounts of identity come under close scrutiny. One area in which this occurs is during the evidential phase of a trial, in which lay people are called as witnesses in order to give testimony. This is a process in which someone provides an account of the individuals, events and circumstances which form the basis of the court case. How such accounts are taken up depends in part on the relationship between the witness and the lawyer. If the witness is providing evidence which supports the lawyer's argument, the form of questioning which arises is usually referred to as **direct examination** or the 'evidence-in-chief' portion of the trial. If the witness is providing evidence which the lawyer wishes to challenge, then the process is referred to as **cross-examination**. Here, the lawyer's concerns is to challenge or undermine the account on offer, either by challenging matters of fact or by establishing that the witness is a particular kind of person: one

Direct examination   the questioning of witnesses by the lawyer representing the party who has called the witness.
Cross-examination   the questioning of witnesses by the lawyer not representing the party who has called the witness.

whose statements ought not to be accepted by the judge or jury (e.g. because the witness is untruthful or unreliable). The lawyer's goal here is to emphasize those aspect of the issue that support his or her client's case while dealing with those other aspects that might potentially damage it.

Given what we discussed earlier about the institutional nature of courtroom interactions, it might seem as though all of the bases are loaded in favour of the lawyer as the process of questioning the witness unfolds. However, as Hansen (2008) has pointed out, it is clear that lay people share with professionally trained denizens of the courtroom the skills to distinguish between what is 'literally' meant by an utterance and what that utterance might actually mean within a legal context. Similarly, Gnisci and Pontecorvo (2004) suggest that things are not quite so simple. They suggest that both lawyers and witnesses have discursive strategies open to them. So while it is lawyers who get to ask the questions and control the topic of the interaction, witnesses have the opportunity, in their answers, to provide elaborations on what they are saying which carry particular rhetorical effects, such as the minimization of blame. And, say Gnisci and Pontecorvo, this need not even involve the witness in outright dispute with a lawyer asking a hostile question. Witnesses can use subtle means such as picking up on peripheral aspects of the lawyer's question and then treating those peripheral aspects as the salient part of their answers. In this way, they can provide answers which serve their own pragmatic ends while, at the same time, providing responses which have the appearance of being topically relevant to what the lawyer just said.

Galatolo and Drew (2006) explore one of the means by which witnesses achieve this effect in their study of **narrative expansions** in witnesses' answers. In these narrative expansions, witnesses' answers to yes/no questions can be seen to elaborate on the direct answer which the lawyers' questions are seeking to elicit. Given the institutional setting, witnesses understand that lawyers have a range of sanctions available to them if they do not answer 'properly'. And so, just as Gnisci and Pontecorvo suggest, any attempt to produce a rhetorical effect in their answers has to be carefully managed so that what

> **Narrative expansions** the provision of extended items of talk (or text) in which an initial response is followed by other discourse which is either presented as being relevant to that initial response or is concatenated to it by some discursive device (e.g. the use of terms such as 'on the other hand ...').

they say will still count as an 'appropriate' answer. This can be tricky, if the question posed seems to call for either 'Yes' or 'No' in response. This answer format would appear to limit the extent to which witnesses can develop their own representations of actions and events and of those involved in them. But, according to Galatolo and Drew, witnesses deal with this by providing yes/no responses which are immediately followed up with a narrative expansion in which witnesses can structure or restructure events. The trial which Galatolo and Drew examined involved the murder of an Italian university student, and they focused on testimony provided by three prosecution witnesses. In looking at their testimony, Galatolo and Drew noticed that the witnesses relied on different means of narrative expansion. One technique was to repeat a fragment of the question set as a 'springboard' for further talk, while another was the use of a conjunction (e.g. 'because' or 'but') which coupled the narrative expansion to the **minimal response** 'Yes' or 'No'. In this way, witnesses could provide information that was not asked for, or seek to contextualize events, in order to seek to avoid blame which might otherwise be conveyed by the question set. This allowed witnesses to offer up accounts in which they provided explanations

> **Minimal response**
> a conversational turn, produced in response to a prior turn, which is noticeably brief.

directed towards actions which otherwise might have been viewed as morally questionable. These accounts were designed to establish that the account-giver had good reason for committing (or not carrying out) the relevant actions. So narrative expansions represent an ideal means through which witnesses can attend to aspects of their own identity that might otherwise appear troublesome.

Extract 6.7

```
1  P:   with Urilli and Ba↑°sciu°
2       did you speak↑ (.)
3       [somehow
4  W:   [yes, (0.5)
5       yes I spoke with them
6       pt .hhh I d- (1)*I had this=eh
```

7	this thing inside
8	(.) to- to have
9	the possibility made manifest
10	with somebody at l<u>e</u>ast
11	with somebody who was near me=and
12	who belonged to the surrounding

(Galatolo and Drew, 2006, p. 688)

In this extract, the witness admits to having spoken about the murder with someone. However, in answer to a previous question she said that she had not spoken with anyone about the murder. So in saying 'yes I spoke with them' her present answer now seems to contradict something she said earlier. And the difficulty for the witness here, of course, is that she now begins to appear to be a particular sort of person: someone who is either lying or is confused. In order to deal with this potential difficulty, the witness provides an expansion to her initial 'yes' response in which she seeks to demonstrate that this particular episode of her speaking to someone about the murder should be treated as a sort of 'special case' which is not really inconsistent with her general behaviour in not speaking to others. Here, the witness provides an account of why she spoke about the murder which is grounded in something within her, a 'thing', that seemed to require that she 'made manifest' to someone else what it is that she wanted to say. Moreover, the special nature of this one occasion is underlined by the description provided in the account of the person or people to whom she talked: the 'thing' inside her seemed to involve talking to someone who was both near to her and 'belonged to the surrounding'. So the witness is able to deploy narrative expansion in order to present a particular version of herself: she was not lying about never having spoken to anyone because this particular instance of speaking to someone was a 'special case'.

Galatolo and Drew suggest that another means by which witnesses manage to add narrative expansions to their answers is to provide a minimal yes/no answer but to produce this answer via a rising intonation or 'rushing through' so that the minimal answer is swiftly followed by the expansion section. Interestingly, Innes (2007) provides evidence that the particular sort of strategy adopted by witnesses may in some senses be culturally specific. In a study of intonations in courtroom discourse in New Zealand, Innes notes that the adoption of a rising intonation at the end of declarative sentences is a feature of New Zealand speech. This form of intonation has been associated both with the asking of questions and with speech which is rated as relatively powerless. However, Innes suggests, rising intonation may prove useful to witnesses in the courtroom context for other reasons. One example he selects is the case of witnesses offering up **dispreferred responses**, in which witnesses appear to use this particular intonation to mark out that the response they are providing is dispreferred and, perhaps, to indicate some sort of **mitigation** of this dispreferred status.

Dispreferred responses conversational turns, designed as responses to a prior turn, in which what is said is taken to be potentially problematic for the recipient, e.g. turning down a request.

Mitigation the description of extenuating circumstances designed to reduce possible responsibility for otherwise blameworthy actions.

There is one witness identity which the lay person can assume in court which seems to offer even more discursive resources: the **expert witness**. As an expert witness, the lay person's status is peculiar. Expert witnesses may be 'lay' in that they possess no legal qualifications, but precisely because of the role they are asked to play they can lay claim to other qualifications. This means that what they say has a special status in that even the hostile lawyer is restricted in the extent to which he or she can question what it is that the expert witness says. This has been described by Stygall (2001) as a coming together of two separate 'discourses of elites' in which the language of, say, science, can clash with the language of the courtroom. What this means is that expert witnesses can draw on forms of talk which are not available to 'ordinary' witnesses, and because of this have more scope for producing explanations or conclusions which lawyers find difficult to challenge. Matoesian (1999) has shown the importance of this in a study of a physician who was accused of sexual battery. Matoesian's analysis shows that the physician was able to draw on his own medical expertise in framing himself as a person who was qualified to comment on whether the alleged victim's injuries did or did not provide evidence as to his own guilt.

> **Expert witness** a witness whose testimony is produced on the basis of his or her skills or knowledge.

However, it is important to note that when someone identifies himself or herself as an expert witness, this identification need not go unchallenged. Winiecki (2008) examined the way an expert witness was treated in trial involving a dispute between proponents of 'intelligent design' and those who opposed such a view from the perspective of evolution theory. Winiecki's interest here was to note the different ways in which membership categorizations were drawn on during these courtroom debates. Of particular interest here is the way that the lawyer speaking on behalf of evolution theorists constructed two different versions of the expert witness who spoke on behalf of the intelligent design perspective. On the one hand, the fact that the witness was a tenured member of staff at a university and had published scientific articles is treated as establishing him as a bona fide scientist. The lawyer takes some trouble to establish that such publications are a part of 'normal' science and so are an activity that marks out the 'normal scientist'. However, the lawyer's questions then go on to reproduce a quite different version of the witness. In this version, the fact that the witness has never published his views on intelligent design in peer-reviewed academic journals is made relevant. In this respect, the witness now becomes categorizable as someone who is a problematic member of the category of normal scientists. So according to Winiecki, what has happened here is that the lawyer has drawn out the set of normative expectations that are associated with the category of 'scientist' and then used these to establish the boundary between who 'counts' as a scientist and who does not. And this, of course, has implications for who ought to be allowed to appear in court as an expert witness based on their identity as a 'scientist'.

Lay people as defendants

Of course, as we saw in the Stygall study above, witnesses sometimes appear in court because they are defendants. And what this means is that defendants often rely on the same discursive moves as other witnesses in trying to represent a particular version of themselves. For example, Martinowski (2006) discusses a range of ways in which defendants seek to offer mitigation – excusing their actions without necessarily accepting responsibility. One of these is the provision of justifications:

Extract 6.8

1 D: 'yes: I had been drinking but not for any length of time in any case because I
2   had been taking Antabus during this whole spring then / until the eighteenth
3   eh the eighteenth of April I had been taking Antabus / and it [Valborg]
4   happened not so many days after that and and it actually takes eh / one and a
5   half weeks before the Antabus leaves THE BODY if one / has been taking
6   Antabus for so long I have not been able / ANY TIME a couple of days before
7   I could have started drinking'

(Martinovski, 2006, p. 2073)

This defendant's response occurs immediately following a question from the prosecutor about whether D had been drinking. What is noteworthy here is the similarity between D's tactic and those identified by Galatolo and Drew. D begins by offering a 'Yes' answer, but this is followed by a lengthy expansion prefaced with 'but'. So in this case, D's initial admission is then followed by a justification in which he provides a quasi-medical explanation for why his drinking should be regarded as limited in scope.

So in the courtroom, defendants can draw on the same sorts of discursive resources as other witnesses. However, the particular identity concerns of those actually accused of crimes do not begin in the courtroom. Before the defendant takes his place on the stand, it is likely that he or she will have already taken part in interactions with that other arm of the legal apparatus: the police. In such interactions, as in other legal contexts, there are institutional disparities among those involved. Police officers have formal authority both to detain individuals and to require that they provide answers to questions which they pose. In this process, the goal of the police is to gather evidence in respect of the crimes which they think have been committed. Thornborrow (2002) points out that in this process, police officers draw upon everyday conversational features of talk as well as upon those advantages which they derive from their official status. This 'interplay' between discursive role and institutional identity has also been recognized by Johnson (2005), who points out that police interviews can arise in an institutional setting in which 'policespeak' can be viewed as a **hybrid discourse** that incorporates both everyday conversational language and legislative language. This hybrid form of talk is used both to ease the discursive interaction while, at the same time, gathering forensic detail that may incriminate the interviewee. Ironically, a quite different form of hybrid talk has been noted by Mele and Bello (2007) in the talk of Nigerian security personnel when they encounter civilians at secu-

> **Hybrid discourse** episodes of talk or text in which different forms or registers of discourse are combined, e.g. the combination of conversational questioning and regulatory references observable in police interrogations.

rity roadblocks. Such roadblocks are set up by state officials such as police officers and soldiers in order to curb drug trafficking in Nigeria. Mele and Bello note the way that these officials interweave more everyday conversational talk with both official demands, such as inspection of documents, and with unofficial demands constituted by implicit invitations to the drivers involved that they provide bribes.

Moreover, such hybrid situations are made more complex because interviewers shift roles, for example, from the role of interrogator to the role of therapist, as they pursue their goals in establishing the evidential basis of claims made by witnesses and suspects. One of the ways in which this is accomplished (Johnson, 2008) is through the reformulation of what suspects say during the conduct of the police interview. Negotiations of 'the facts' which make up the suspect's initial story involve processes such as interrupting the suspect's production of this story and the use of questions at the end of the suspect's account which are designed to elicit the 'legal point' of the story, with the aim being to establish an evaluation of what is said that establishes features such as intent or state of mind. Of course, one of the interests that police officers have in mind here is a process which Johnson describes as the defendant leaving one identity, that of being an innocent person, and assuming another identity, that of being someone who admits some form of guilt. We can see this process unfold in the following extract, which is taken from an interview conducted in connection with a bar-room fight in which the suspect, while out drinking with a family group, allegedly fractured someone's skull. Prior to this extract, the suspect has maintained innocence, suggesting that the victim had been about to strike the suspect's brother, and so the suspect had struck the victim. At this point in the interaction, the police officer has asked the suspect to characterize the state that the suspect's family group was in.

Extract 6.9

SUS   we were all just having a laugh
      [Cough]
POL   'Cause speaking to the er- the people who work in the pub
      and said that a- as a group you were quite noisy and erm that

you were talking about the war-
SUS   (Yeah.)
POL   And the Germans and I think it would appear that this has
       been upsetting this fellow 'cause he's made some comment
       about it, about your brother talking about the war-
SUS   Yeah.
POL   Would you agree with that?
SUS   Now that I know that, yeah, I would that's- sounds like me.
                                              (Johnson, 2008, pp. 335–336)

In this extract, Johnson draws our attention to the way in which the interview process represents a negotiation over responsibility. The suspect begins by characterizing his family group's actions in a particular way, 'just having a laugh', which emphasizes the innocuous nature of their behaviour and, by implication, the unexpectedness of their activities being interrupted by someone outside the group. However, the police officer draws on the perspective of others who were present in the bar-room, the bar staff, to formulate a different version of events in which the outsider is presented as having had reasonable grounds for approaching the family group: the group's noisy behaviour and the controversial nature of what they were saying had caused upset to the person who approached them. Johnson notes that this represents a turning-point in the interaction since the suspect then presents himself, through the use of the present-tense formulation 'Now that I know that', as someone who now knows something that previously he did not. This move from the past to the present, says Johnson, marks out a transition of identity from someone who is completely innocent to someone who could be reasonably characterized as having some responsibility for the events that unfolded in the bar.

A major concern for the police officer in circumstances such as this is not just to establish that the defendant actually committed the crime, but that he or she did so knowingly. That is, the officer in some cases wishes to establish that the defendant had a 'guilty mind' in that he knew what he was doing constituted a crime. This admission is important in legal proceedings since it can determine the 'level' of the legal charge to be levied (e.g. such an admission may change a charge of recklessness into one of intentionally intending harm). Stokoe and Edwards (2008) point to one surprising means by which police officers seek to establish the 'guilty mind' of defendants. In their study of police interviews, they show that at a number of points police officers ask what they term 'silly questions' such as 'Did you have permission to smash your neighbour's door?'. The function of such questions is to allow the officer to appear interactionally affiliative with the suspect. Thus, such questions may be posed in an apparently friendly or joking manner. However, the institutional relevance of such questions is that they can lead the suspect to incriminate himself or herself by having them admit 'on the record' what their state of mind was during the commission of their crimes. Of course, as Kidwell (2009) has shown, those being interviewed by the police in such circumstances are well aware of the pitfalls that might arise and so when asked even an innocuous question like 'what happened' they are at pains to present their own versions of actions and events in terms that emphasize the ordinary nature of their activities.

In concluding, it is interesting to note that the defendant's concern with identity does not finish at the end of the trial. This is shown in an extreme form in a study of the last statements made by inmates on death row immediately prior to execution (Schuck and Ward, 2008). In this study, they utilize theoretical insights drawn from terror management theory. According to this theory, people seek to avoid thinking about their own death and the circumstances in which this may arise (Solomon, Greenberg and Pyszczynski, 2004). To accomplish this, they indulge in 'defence strategies' in which they reaffirm their own views of the world, in terms as varied as religion, ethnicity and politics, in order to bring about feelings of security. Schuck and Ward draw on these notions in a discursive analysis of the self-presentations which can be seen in the inmates' 'last words'. In particular, the theory predicts that people in this position will seek to reinforce their own identity through means such as 'immersing' themselves in their cultural beliefs and by seeking to represent their own identities as moral and worthy. They note that most of these statements began with a reference to the self in which they state an expression of active will or intention, before moving on to address the speaker's personal relationships which are usually expressed in positive terms.

Extract 6.10

(Sentence 1):   To my family and children, I love you very much. (…)
(Sentence 2):   To the (victim's) family (…) I know you may hate me for whatever reason.
(Sentence 3):   The Lord says hate no one. I hope you find peace in your heart. I know my words cannot help you, I truly mean what I say.
(Schuck and Ward, 2008, p. 53)

Schuck and Ward argue that in the first sentence, the speaker is trying to present a positive self-image. The second sentence introduces what might be thought of as a more negative theme, but this is dealt with in the way that the speaker treats the issue of hatred in his third sentence. In this way, last statements can be seen to be a means by which speakers both develop self-assurance and maintain connectedness with their social worlds.

Discussion

What this survey of recent discursive studies of the law shows, then, is that issues of identity are key concerns for all of those involved: lawyers, judges and lay people. We have seen that lawyers and judges draw upon the detail of the issue at hand in order to construct identities. But we also saw that the institutional nature of legal discourse provided other resources. For example, judges have the power to ask questions and so they have the opportunity, in asking those questions, to present versions of their own identities to the over-hearing legal audience. Police officers have legal rights and entitlements to ask questions of their suspects. And sometimes those questions are designed to establish a particular version of the suspect and his/her actions. We also saw that lay people display sensitivity to such processes. And so interactions between lawyers and witnesses, and between police officers and suspects often take the form of a complex negotiation of identities. Indeed, we even found that such concerns last with the lay person all the way to the door of the execution chamber.

In concluding this chapter, let us consider for a moment the ways in which institutional settings such as the courtroom provide a focus for theoretical tensions within discursive research. In one study, Hobbs (2008) used critical discourse analysis to examine the opening statement made by John Allen Muhammad, the 'Beltway Sniper', who presented himself in court as his own lawyer. Hobbs notes that Muhammad's identity as a criminal defendant invoked a negative reception of his claims by the press and other commentators. But in analysing the discursive properties of his opening statement, Hobbs concludes that in many respects it resembled statements made by seasoned lawyers who are highly regarded as experts in their field: Muhammad presented a theory of his case neatly encapsulated in an easily remembered thematic formulation, 'a theory is not evidence'; he used **analogy** designed to highlight family values; he deployed repetition, **irony** and poetic diction; he ensured his presentation had a vivid opening statement which encapsulated key facts in an impactful way. Since these are all techniques which are recommended by those skilled in the art of courtroom advocacy, it might seem as though Muhammad had performed well, and yet his presentation was poorly received. The solution to this puzzle, according to Hobbs, lies in part in the way that social power relations conditioned the reception of his statement by press and public. Hobbs argues that those assessing Muhammad's performance had internalized social ideologies which caused them to interpret what Muhammad said and how he said it in particular ways. One aspect of this is that, within the institutional setting of the courtroom, Muhammad had already acquired a specific identity: that of being the 'criminal defendant'. Being the criminal defendant meant, for Muhammad, that he did not possess what Bloom describes as the 'legal voice'. It is part of the social ideology which underpins the law that the law is an arcane and highly technical area from which lay persons are excluded. For this reason, it is a social expectation that the 'proper' procedure is one in which lay persons are represented by legal experts who give voice to the lay person's claims. So part of what makes a lawyer's statements successful

> **Analogy** using the properties of one subject of talk in producing a description of another and thereby indicating some general or abstract similarity.
> **Irony** a discursive device in which what is said differs from what is actually meant.

is the fact that they are being delivered by someone who has the appropriate 'lawyer' identity. In court, there is already an expectation, before anyone has spoken, that what lawyers say will be relatively skilful and appropriately professional, in comparison with what lay people may say, and these expectations condition how each person's talk is received. So even in cases where the 'formal' properties of the talk produced by a lawyer and a lay person are equivalent, the ways in which such talk is received are likely to differ.

This study seems to indicate that there are limitations to the discursive possibilities which are open to people in institutional settings such as the courtroom. But Hobbs's argument rests upon the critical discourse analytic notion that there are cognitive elements such as beliefs or expectations which can be drawn upon by the analyst in order to explain how talk is produced and received. It similarly relies upon the idea that these cognitive elements are associated with widespread social phenomena such as ideologies which condition our understanding of, or are even constitutive of, the social contexts in which such utterances are produced. And one consequence of the power of ideology is that we come to inhabit different identities: identities which represent extra-discursive analytic reference points by means of which discursive interactions can be explained. Within discursive research these are, of course, controversial claims. Other discursive researchers from outwith the critical discourse analysis domain emphasize the importance of restricting analytic comment to what is actually said by each participant, and to how other participants orient towards what is said in their subsequent talk. From this alternative perspective, the reliance upon extra-linguistic analytic devices such as cognitive beliefs, social ideologies or ideologically imposed identities is suspect. Now this does not mean that if an analyst refrains from appealing to cognitive or sociological phenomena, he or she is somehow committed to denying that the press and public evaluated Muhammad's presentation poorly. Rather, it is the claim that what is to count as a negative evaluation, and what it is for such evaluations to be made out in terms of institutional norms or social expectations, is itself a matter which is revealed through the analysis of talk or text. In this sense, then, the courtroom is akin to other institutional settings. It represents a discursive context in which one of the key debates in contemporary discursive research, the role of extra-linguistic context, is played out as different discursive researchers from competing paradigms offer up their understandings of the actions and events which arise in such a setting.

Chapter Summary

In this chapter, we looked at how identities are formulated in discourse within legal settings. The chapter begins by noting that in institutional settings of this sort, institutional roles provide lawyers, judges and police officers with rights and entitlements that lay people lack. It proceeds by looking at how lawyers use both talk and text to construct identities for those whom they or their legal adversaries represent. Lawyers produce particular 'versions' of clients, defendants and witnesses in order to achieve specific persuasive goals. These versions represent individuals in terms of their past and future actions, their relationships, their responsibilities, and their culpability. Next, the chapter shows that similar processes arise in the written texts which lawyers produce. It is noted that in constructing identities in this way, lawyers draw not only on their institutional entitlements, but also on the detail of the particular legal issue under consideration. Thus, as elsewhere, identity construction in legal contexts can be seen as a process which is interwoven with other aspects of talk such as the presentation of evidence or the description of actions and events. The chapter then moves on to consider evidence that the discourse of judges displays similar features. Notably, however, research also indicates that judges may utilize their institutional role to present versions of themselves, too. In turning to the discourse of lay people, the chapter reviews evidence that lawyers and police officers not only have institutional entitlements, but they may also make use of other discursive resources which enable them to portray defendants as guilty people. However, for the lay person, a relative lack of institutional lack of power may be addressed by a range of different discursive resources. Notable among these is the capacity of witnesses and defendants to provide answers to questions which incorporate extended justifications for their actions. Indeed this identity concern to maintain a version of themselves as in some sense innocent people could be seen to follow convicted felons all the way to the execution chamber. The chapter concluded with a brief discussion of the way in which legal contexts represent a useful case study in broader issues that arise in discursive research, especially those involving the role of local and distal discursive contexts.

Connections

One aspect of legal proceedings is often the negotiation of responsibility for violent crime. We saw some elements of this in Chapter 4 in the discussion of the relationship between violence and masculine identity. Issues of legality are also caught up with matters of nationality and ethnicity of the sort seen in Chapters 2 and 3, especially in relation to the status of immigrants and refugees. The discussion of the Waco tragedy in Chapter 3 shows that legal issues may also sometimes impinge on religion.

Further Reading

Galatolo, R. and Drew, P. (2006). Narrative expansions as defensive practices in courtroom testimony. *Text and Talk, 26*, 661–698.

'Yes but, no but, yes but ...': how witnesses deal with potential problems associated with giving a straight answer.

O'Byrne, R., Hansen, S. and Rapley, M. (2008). "If a girl doesn't say "no" ...': Young men, rape and claims of 'insufficient knowledge'. *Journal of Community and Applied Social Psychology, 18*, 168–193.

A potentially unsettling insight into contemporary discourse on rape.

Stokoe, E. and Edwards, D. (2008). 'Did you have permission to smash your neighbour's door?' Silly questions and their answers in police-suspect interrogations. *Discourse Studies, 10*, 89–111.

Activity Box

Accounts of legal cases are a fundamental staple of newspapers. Select a current or recent case which has received a lot of public attention, and examine the ways in which different newspapers have described the case and those involved. Do different newspapers represent the various actors in different ways? In the 'sound bite' quotations from police officers or lawyers, is there evidence that they are trying to construct identities for the accused or the victim?

7

Organizations, Work and Identities

Topics Covered in this Chapter

Key Terms

Diversity in employment

Genetic modification

Hedging statements

Marketization of higher education

Mentoring

Office hours

Identities in Context: Individuals and Discourse in Action, First Edition. Andrew McKinlay
and Chris McVittie.
© 2011 Andrew McKinlay and Chris McVittie. Published 2011 by Blackwell Publishing Ltd.

Bankers in the dock

Jérôme Kerviel, alleged to be the world's biggest rogue trader, will attempt to hide a
€5bn leaf in a multi-trillion euro forest when he goes on trial in Paris today. Mr
Kerviel's defence will be horrendously complex and very simple. His lawyers will
admit that what he did in 2007–8, to bet more than the value of France's second larg-
est bank on a series of trades on stock exchange futures, was insane. However, they
will also argue that his actions were rational, even tacitly approved, within a global
banking culture which had, itself, broken off relations with reality.

The Independent, Tuesday, 8 June 2010 (www.independent.co.uk/
news/world/europe/capitalism-in-the-dock-as-kerviel-
goes-on-trial-1994133.html)

If we needed a reminder of the central role that organizations play in our lives,
then recent events have provided just that. The global financial crisis of recent
years is commonly attributed to the actions of North American and European
banks in engaging in what are now regarded as risky and speculative financial decisions that ultimately resulted in substantial losses. Perhaps the most prominent
casualty of this period of corporate banking activities was the major United States
bank Lehman Brothers, the collapse of which in 2008 led to the largest bankruptcy
ever filed in US history. Even more recently we might think of the circumstances
surrounding BP plc, a company that is one of the world's largest oil and gas pro-
ducers and which is engaged in energy production in many areas across the globe.
The consequences of the explosion and subsequent fire on 20 April 2010, on the
Deepwater Horizon mobile offshore drilling unit owned by BP, have been well
documented in the world's media. The initial deaths of 11 workers on the unit,
together with the consequent major offshore oil spill in the Gulf of Mexico, have
led to BP being identified in ways that are less concerned with the production of
oil and gas than with the environmental and social impact of a major instance of
pollution that at the time of writing remains to be fully addressed.

Of course the effects of such corporate actions, and the ways in which corporations come to be identified, go well beyond the organizations themselves. Treating
BP as responsible for the outcomes of the Deepwater Horizon explosion will make
it accountable not just for the cleaning up of the oil that has been spilt but also for
the effects that this spill has had on the livelihoods and well-being of all affected,
whether employed in marine and fishing industries, tourism, or otherwise. On a
similar note, the effects of the actions of banks continue to be experienced by governments, taxpayers, borrowers, savers, shareholders, and individuals involved in a
diversity of other daily activities that are associated directly or indirectly with the
security and financial success of these organizations. Individuals thus have to make
sense of themselves and their own lives and activities in a context of changing
corporate identities.

Moreover, in these and other instances, the issue of identities becomes especially salient for those who work within organizations. The continuing impact of

the Deepwater Horizon spill increasingly became attributed not only to the initial explosion but also to the failure of BP as an organization to institute appropriate remedial action. Explaining BP's actions, past and ongoing, fell to Tony Hayward then Chief Executive of the company and the public face of the corporation. Over time, Hayward became identified as the individual face of BP's delay in stopping the spill and thus as individually accountable for corporate failure. In the extract above, describing the difficulties of France's Société Générale bank, we see the actions of another organizational employee come under close scrutiny. The question in that case is the extent to which the actions described (which are not disputed) should reasonably be attributed to one individual, or if instead they fall to be understood as reflecting and enacting an organizational culture that was itself flawed. The legal liability or non-liability of Jérôme Kerviel, of course, will in time be decided by courts of law. What this instance, that of Tony Hayward and BP, and other examples serve to highlight, however, are the issues of identity bound up with organizations, those who work within them, and their interactions with other social actors. It is to these matters that we turn in this chapter.

Organizations and Identities

For much of the time, organizations appear to us as recognizable elements of a stable social landscape. We are often unfamiliar with the detail of how organizational activities happen but treat this is being of little consequence unless things turn out unexpectedly. Certain forms of organizations of course do bring particular expectations. For example, we expect that health service providers will offer health care, and that transport operators will make available travel possibilities. Within organizations for which we work or with which we are involved in other ways, we will, however, be rather more familiar with the operations of the organization. In these cases, we and others involved in such contexts spend much of our daily lives negotiating how activities are carried out and making sense of ourselves, colleagues, others, and the organization itself in recognizable ways.

Understanding occupations and identities

In many instances, people who are not involved in an organization will have little understanding of how it works or the identities of the individuals with whom they interact. In such cases, those who are external to the organization will have rather less knowledge of organizational activities than is available to employees of the organization. Interactions between organizational employees and members of the public are thus often asymmetrical, in that the differences in knowledge and understanding between the parties can easily lead to misunderstanding or conflict.

Differences in available knowledge become all the more relevant when charges for organizational services are at issue (Prego-Vazquez, 2007). Nonetheless, for many organizations, negotiating good relations with members of the public is central to their activities and they will aim to ensure that dealings with those who seek to use their services proceed smoothly. Often, encounters of this sort proceed without difficulty, with the customer specifying what they require and the organization responding appropriately. Indeed as Robert Moore (2008) notes in a study of the operations in a quick print shop, many service encounters take more or less this form with customers describing what is sought and company employees demonstrating their recognition of these requests.

Extract 7.1

["Copies of this"]

05	Emp:	**How can we help you.**
06		(0.6)
07	Cus:	**I hope so.**
08	Cus:	(0.4) ((approaches counter))
09	Emp:	**{Oh yeah.}**
10	Cus:	{places stacks}
11	Cus:	**{We need}** (0.1) **three copies of this,**
12	Cus:	{places hands}
13	Cus:	{(0.3) **by:** (0.2) **three:}** **three thirty today?**
14	Emp:	{cranes neck to the left}
15		(0.1)
16	Emp:	**Three copies of this big hu:::ge stack.**
17	Emp:	(0.3) ((straightens body, maintains gaze))
18	Cus:	**Yeah, {there's two stacks?** (0.5)}
19	Cus:	{lifts top stack off to side}
20	Emp:	**N'kay.**

(Moore, 2008, p. 390)

Even in such interactions, however, difficulties can arise when the customer displays less knowledge than the company employee of what is required, as seen in Extract 7.2.

Extract 7.2

["Coated"]

14	Cus:	**Well let's do eleven by seventeen = and**
15		**then I need four of 'em?**
16		(0.6)
17	Emp:	**[Wha-]**
18	Cus:	**[An'I] need 'em coated.**
19		(0.9)

```
20   Emp:   >Wha' d' ya mean by coated.^
21          (0.4)
22   Cus:   {You know ya put 'em} {between the two plastic,(0.1)
23   Cus:   {drops pages in hand} {thrusts flat palms outward &
24   Cus:   [( deals )]}
25   Emp:   [You wan' it]} laminated?
26   Cus:   brings together}
27          (0.3)
28   Cus:   Laminated, thank you
```

(Moore, 2008, p. 395)

Unlike many service encounters, we see here the customer displaying some difficulty in describing what is sought. The term 'coated', although meaningful in
terms of customer needs, is treated as not being meaningful in organizational or
printing terms. This minor interactional difficulty, however, is relatively easily
resolved when the customer demonstrates through gesture and pointing what is
needed. After the customer needs are reformulated in printing terms as 'lami-
nated', the interaction can resume a smooth course and the participants agree the
provision of the appropriate services.

In other cases, certain forms of organizations and what they provide appear more
recognizable to us in that they are commonly associated with specific occupational
identities. The provision of health services, for example, is routinely delivered by
surgeons, doctors, nurses, and other healthcare professionals. All such identities are
routinely bound up with expectations of what a person so identified will do, that is,
that surgeons perform surgical operations, pharmacists dispense medications, and
so on. Yet, at the same time, occupational identities can also bring into play specific
social identifications of the individuals who will be found in these occupations.

Take, for example, the profession of nursing, an occupation that is associated
with a predisposition to care for others. Historically, in broad social terms, care-
giving has been primarily attributed to women, an understanding that has led to
nursing being constructed as an occupation that is largely relevant for women and
provided by women. Such understandings potentially make nursing a readily recognizable occupation for women to pursue, should they wish to do so, but at the same
time make less recognizable the identities of men who enter this profession. Male
nurses as a result have often been constructed as being gay or, in the specific context
of mental health nursing, as being 'macho' (Harding, 2007). These, however, are
not the only identities on offer for male nurses. Those who are not identified as gay
or 'macho' can instead be described as unwilling to engage in what are said to be the
mundane or unpleasant tasks involved in nursing of the 'housework' variety and
thus as deficient in carrying out many of the essential elements of nursing in practice (McKinlay *et al.*, 2010a). These identities of male nurses, although not relying
upon gendered understandings of gay and 'macho', instead proceed upon other
equally gendered understandings of nursing and related actions and continue to
construct nursing as an occupation that is primarily relevant for women.

Social understandings of gender can similarly be found in relation to other occupational identities. Let us consider the identity of an airline pilot. Typically over many years, in the cinema and elsewhere, a pilot has been presented as someone who is most likely male, white and middle class. These elements have combined to present the identity of an airline pilot as a sort of elite fatherly professional. This particular image of the airline pilot, moreover, has functioned not just to maintain a public image of the pilot but also to inform the ways in which current pilots make sense of their professional identities (Ashcraft, 2007). Pilots who describe them-selves in such traditional terms can negotiate their identities by drawing upon a readily available version of what a pilot is understood as being. At the same time of course, identity work of this sort reproduces social understandings of gender, in constructing a highly specific version of pilot as an occupational identity.

Identities then are not solely matters of negotiation between the parties immediately involved but have to be understood in a broader context of social practices. Often, the ways in which identities are constructed are relevant not just for those immediately involved but also for a wider audience and for their concerns. One example of such identity processes can be found in arguments surround-ing the use of **genetic modification** in the production of crops and foodstuffs. Genetic modification refers to the human manipulation of an organism's genetic structure in a way that does not occur naturally, through the transplantation of genetic material from other sources or deletion of existing material. Proponents of genetic mod-ification usually argue that such processes can improve the quality or availability of the crop in question, while opponents tend to argue that safety concerns or ecological issues have not been sufficiently considered. These argu-ments are found in relation to different industries, in claims either that the use of GM crops is necessary to improve production or that such use will impact negatively upon consumer confidence in the goods that are produced (Henderson, Weaver and Cheney, 2007). In her study of the arguments surrounding the introduction of genetically modi-fied cotton in India, Tomiko Yamaguchi (2007) notes that many of the arguments used there relied upon constructions of identities of Indian famers. In particular, by aligning themselves with certain versions of farmers' identities, combatants could advance their own arguments either for or against the use of GM cotton. For example:

> **Genetic modification**   the human manipulation of an organism's genetic structure in a way that does not occur naturally, through the transplantation of genetic material from other sources or deletion of existing material.

Extract 7.3

As I said earlier, we have 550 million farmers. Out of that, 70 percent are small and marginal farmers. What is important is the entire agreement [of the WTO] on agriculture – the way we have agreed upon – is going to break down barriers and open up markets. So we are now going to have cheaper imports coming into our country. When the cheaper imports start coming in, what will happen? The marginal farmer will be thrown out of agriculture. What will happen when he is made jobless?

(Yamaguchi, 2007, p. 97)

As seen in Extract 7.3, farmers were often identified as being vulnerable and in need of protection. This form of identity provided a basis upon which speakers could claim to be genuinely speaking in the interests of the (vulnerable) farmers.

Extract 7.4

Scientists used to be very happy if we could publish papers in the magazine *Nature*. We used to be on top of the world. We were not bothered by whether our findings reached farmers or not. But today, I feel that there should be no barriers, no walls, between the research laboratory and the farmer. I feel it is the responsibility of us scientists to take our message to farmers.

(Yamaguchi, 2007, p. 98)

This stance in turn allowed interested actors to present their own claims as genuinely representing the interests of the farmers, in contrast to others who claimed to speak on behalf of farmers but were not entitled to do so.

Extract 7.5

Now, right before the GEAC [Genetic Engineering Approval Committee] approved Bt cotton [GM cotton), the NGO, Central Institute convened a press conference. I was there with many other people, both from India and from abroad. Suddenly, how can the people who are not farmers enter into discussions like that? They are trying only to influence the decision-making processes. It is not ethical to try to represent farmers like that.

(Yamaguchi, 2007, p. 99)

Taken together, these constructions of farmers, of themselves, and of other groups in the debate, allowed speakers to argue for their own proposed outcomes, either by way of allowing or not allowing the use of GM cotton.

Extract 7.6

In the first instance, Indian people or Indian farmers are not only illiterate and poor, they are foolish also. If another farmer says it is a good idea, OK I will do it without caring what will happen. They are not concerned with the results. If he has done it, I will also do it. In that system, if one variety covers a large area, and if something happens to that one variety, maybe due to environmental conditions or weather conditions or rainfall ... maybe an area is not suitable for such a variety, an entire area will be just lost. A scenario like this will be hard for Indian farmers to bear.

(Yamaguchi, 2007, p. 100)

What all of this points to is that identities related to occupations are negotiated in particular contexts, such as the delivery of printing services, arguments surrounding the use of GM crops, or elsewhere. They are, however, at the same time interwoven with a wide and diverse range of social issues, for example those of social group memberships and of the identities of others within political debates. Occupational identities, or more specifically particular constructions of occupational identities, thus orient to a range of contexts in providing versions of individuals and their activities in an organizational realm.

Identities within organizations

Much of the everyday negotiation of identities of course occurs within organizations and is less immediately visible to the external world. In this, individual identities are inextricably bound up also with the identities of organizations themselves. Organizations can be understood as patterns of talk and interaction that perform the business of the organization and other functions also. For, while much of this talk is likely to be directed towards the business of the organization in terms of achieving goals, and liaising with work colleagues, other talk might well be concerned more with interaction in itself. Small talk, humour, politeness and similar elements are likely to feature to some extent in the interactions between workers and are perhaps less concerned with organizational business than with maintaining a flow of working relationships, although as we shall see even this distinction is problematic.

We might also think of work settings as providing opportunities for both formal and less formal interaction. The operation of many organizations is marked by meetings in which particular employees discuss matters relating to operation of the organization and how organizational goals should be achieved. In such interactions, specific identities come into play, including that of chair of the meeting. For meetings to function effectively as discussion or decision-making forums, it is important for the chair to ensure that items of business-at-hand are dealt with in an efficient time-limited way and that the meeting proceeds smoothly through the topics to be considered (Barnes, 2007). Similar processes can be seen in other forms of organizational talk. For example, organizations wishing to develop their practices in particular directions might seek the advice of consultants as to how such development might most usefully proceed. In such matters, changes in organizational practices have to be negotiated and the consultant has to present the outcomes of the consultation process as convincing to the employees of the organization (Kykyri, Puutio and Wahlstrom, 2007).

Often, however, the interactions occurring within organizations are less structured and less formal. Where issues arise in relation to the functioning of equipment such as IT equipment, the relevant expertise, work expectations and moral obligations of different people within the organization have to be negotiated in practice for the problem to be resolved satisfactorily (Quayle and Durrheim, 2008). One such example comes from a study by Alessandra Fasulo and Cristina Zucchermaglio (2008), of the interactions found within a Southern Italian clothing firm. In Extract 7.7, we see the firm owner Gino, a salesman Sal and a stylist

Claudia, discussing how some paper prints are to be imprinted onto clothing material using a high-temperature press.

Extract 7.7

[Claudia, stylist (Sty); Gino, firm owner (Own); salesman (Sal)]

```
 1   Sty:    But you have to:: stick them on yourself ?
 2           (1.2)
 3   Own:    I wanted to try [to do it myse::lf=
 4   Sty:                    [You must try=
 5   Own:    =Anyway.
 6           ↑yes- no:
 7   Sal:    ↑All right you put,
 8           the press at a hundred and seventy degrees,
 9           (0.7)
10           then you put paper, (1.5) material,
...
21   Own:    and you NEVER get
22           hundred and seventy-
23           I take the press to a hundred and sixty
24           so as to have a hundred and forty
25           inside
```
(Fasulo and Zuccermaglio, 2008, pp. 369–370)

Here, we see the exchange begin with Claudia querying whether Gino wishes to carry out the printing himself. Claudia and Sal then point out to Gino that the temperature for the press should be set at 170°. In so doing, they suggest that Gino is not familiar with the operation of the press. Gino responds by arguing that the temperature on the external display is not a reliable indication of how the press does actually operate, allowing him to display his own expertise and experience. More than this, however, it forestalls any interpersonal argument between the three people involved, in that their descriptions are based upon different forms of knowledge. Thus expertise is negotiated and working relations are maintained. As Fasulo and Zuccermaglio point out, talk of this sort allows all involved to negotiate identities associated with competence, while avoiding disagreements, and to ensure that problems arising are appropriately resolved to allow for the smooth functioning of the organization.

Exchanges such as that seen above thus facilitate the operations of an organization and the establishment of good working relationships. Over time, patterns of interaction that recur within any organization go to build up an organizational culture of the meanings that work practices have for all involved. In the development of organizational culture, much comes down to the ways in which managers and senior colleagues interact with others. Management can occur in overtly authoritarian ways but often is achieved through more subtle everyday communications with staff within the organization (Holmes, 2007). Janet Holmes and colleagues (Holmes, Schnurr and Marra, 2007) point to the ways in which the communicative style of a leader can both reflect and construct the understandings that subordinates have of how an organization operates and of their own identities within it. Below we see an extract from a meeting of employees in the IT section of a large organization in New Zealand, led by Tricia the Director of the section.

Extract 7.8

[*Tricia is informing her managers about the dates of an upcoming staff training event.*]

1.	Tricia:	now if people can't make it to that meeting
2.		then they've got to do the full one day training with
3.		on either the second third or fourth
4.	Carol:	well /that's a that's a good option\
5.	Evelyn:	/no it's the second fifth\ or sixth
6.	Tricia:	oh is it sheesh [laughs]
7.	Carol:	I think that's the good option the half day
8.		/+ or the one day\
9.	Noel:	/what are they what dates were they\ Evelyn
10.	Evelyn:	second fifth and sixth
11.	Noel:	fifth and sixth
12.	Evelyn:	cos the third and fourth are a weekend
13.	Tricia:	oh okay
14.	Evelyn:	hmm
15.	Tricia:	( ) check that
16.	Carol:	hey um the second fifth and sixth is that
17.		/saying\ our other staff are going to those one day ones?
18.	Tricia:	/mm\

(Holmes, Schnurr and Marra, 2007, p. 440)

Clearly evident in Extract 7.8 is the flexibility of the discussion, which comprises numerous turns from those present and on which Tricia as Director imposes relatively little direction. Tricia, although in charge of the meeting, adopts a democratic approach and exercises control in subtle ways allowing empowerment of all those present. This form of leadership can be contrasted with the style adopted by Kenneth, her successor as Director of the IT section, as seen in Extract 7.9.

Extract 7.9

[*This extract occurs immediately after Kenneth has officially opened the meeting*]

1.	Kenneth:	um we're still pursuing policy for secondment?
2.	Louisa:	um yes I've um had an update from Vijaya
3.		and he said um he'll talk to the HR staff (up)
4.		and he'll work something for us

5.		cos I've made a point that we need something
6.		in place pretty much you know ASAP
7.	Kenneth:	okay so we haven't um got a final um
8.	Louisa:	there there isn't anything in place
9.		/so he needs to go and talk to\
10.	Kenneth:	/okay + so there is\ no policy?
11.	Louisa:	yeah he needs to talk to Ted he needs to talk Ainsley
12.		he needs to talk to
13.	Ken:	okay
14.	Louisa:	so he told me this morning to just keep hounding him every week
15.	Kenneth:	okay
16.	Brent:	is it is it if there is no policy is it worth keeping it on the agenda
17.		I mean (/)\
18.	Kenneth:	/I think so\

(Holmes, Schnurr and Marra, 2007, p. 439)

In this extract, the members of the team take individual turns, each of which is met by a response from Kenneth of 'okay'. This interactional structure suggests that the team members are simply reporting to him as leader what has been happening, rather than engaging in any discussion of the issues being considered. The direction of the meeting consequently reflects a rather authoritarian style, in contrast to the democratic and empowering style of Tricia. As a consequence, the differences in leadership style, together with other differences (Schnurr, Marra and Holmes, 2007) provide very different patterns of team interactions as reflected in everyday working practices and the resulting organizational culture.

Given the ways in which individual organizations develop their own cultures, it is no surprise that those who have been longer in any organization will be more familiar with its patterns of working. By contrast, individuals coming new into any work environment might have difficulty in making sense of how an organization operates. One way for novices to deal with uncertainties that they have is to discuss these with others who have more experience of working in particular contexts (Vasquez, 2007; Vasquez and Urzua, 2009). Opportunities for discussions of this sort provide **mentoring**, a process whereby junior workers have the opportunity to receive guidance from more senior employees on their working practices and on developing working identities. The forms of mentoring available, however, will vary considerably according to the particular organization and anticipated outcomes of the mentoring process. Some organizations provide highly specific mentoring schemes that are primarily oriented to accomplishing specific goals while other organizations offer more flexible mentoring possibilities that can be negotiated to meet the needs of the individual mentee (Chiles, 2007). Thus, like other organizational interactions, mentoring too can function to empower or to disempower the employees who take part in the meetings. In many cases,

> **Mentoring**   a process whereby junior workers receive guidance from more senior employees on working practices and the development of working identities.

mentoring can all too easily come to reflect and to enact the very organizational culture that new employees are looking to the process to explain.

Organizations and Contexts

By now, you will have a sense of how organizations can be understood as flexible patterns of talk and interaction, reflecting and shaping the meanings of their activities for others. Of course, all of this discursive work takes place in contexts that are themselves continually in flux. In part, the changes in contexts that organizations face on a recurring basis are those that might be deemed conducive to conducting their businesses. The development of global markets provides opportunities for organizations to interact with more potential customers than ever before and to expand their activities. Alongside this expansion in markets, rapid developments in information and communication technologies facilitate the conducting of business on a global scale. Now-established mechanisms, such as foreign exchange markets, offer vast systems and possibilities for interaction through the exchange of transactions and information that is readily available (Knorr-Cetina, 2007). Advances in email communication similarly have made available an expanded range of possibilities, allowing organizations to distribute sales materials at a much lower cost than previously and to promote themselves in new ways (Cheung, 2008). Against this background, texts on business and management now commonly offer examples of the practices that are necessary for organizations to be successful in changing times (Lischinsky, 2008). Organizations thus have a range of ways to position themselves as suppliers of products or services to potential customers (Van de Mieroop, 2008) and to demonstrate their credentials as participants in competitive international markets (Hougaard, 2008).

Other ongoing changes might be less welcome, at least for certain organizations. The regulation of many organizations, in industries such as the supply of power and of communications, has led to increased accountability of these organizations. Thus, companies engaged in these markets might have to account for their activities not just to customers and shareholders, but also to regulators and broader interest groups. For example, in the UK, companies within the media and communications industry are required to have regard for people described as the 'citizen-consumer'. The interests of this group as citizens, as opposed to consumers, has to date been little specified but nonetheless they have become potentially relevant to the ways in which organizations operating within these markets are expected to deliver their services (Livingstone, Lunt and Miller, 2007). Another change in (relatively) recent years has come in the form of increased awareness of and attention to the impact of human activities (corporate and individual) on climate change. In response to widespread concern, a number of organizations have incorporated into their promotional literature images that associate them with due care towards the environment in order to establish their green credentials (Hansen and Machin, 2008). In changing times, it is not surprising that organizations are reluctant to make firm predictions about their future directions and success. Increasingly, they have come to rely in communications to shareholders and others on **hedging statements**. Hedging statements are those that describe future prospects in positive and reassuring terms but which in doing so rely upon belief or expectation rather than upon any firm prediction of future prospects. They thus do not commit the organization fully to the prediction on offer, allowing an organization to distance itself from the claim in the event that the suggested outcomes do not later materialize (McLaren-Hankin, 2008).

> **Hedging statements** statements that are offered in qualified terms and that do not fully commit the author of the statement to what is being claimed.

Here, in order to explore in more detail the effects that changes in contexts can have on the activities of organizations, we examine two examples of such changes. The first relates to organizations that provide helpline services, in which the context of what is being sought and the organization's response to any request can change turn by turn in the course of one or more telephone calls. The second example considers longer-term changes in contexts and the identities of organizations, taking the particular instance of educational providers.

Helpline services

In an era of global markets and rapidly developing communication technologies, many organizations have come to rely heavily on centralized telephone services to attempt to increase sales of their products or to provide customer assistance. Many of us will be familiar with receiving unceasing calls from companies looking to sell us double-glazing or with our attempts to obtain product guidance from call centres in distant parts of the globe. However, for many organizations the provision of help at a local level remains a central part of their activities, and helpline services are the most immediate and direct means of ascertaining what help is required and perhaps also providing that help. Typically, the help that helpline services of this sort provide relates either to personal difficulties of the individual caller to the helpline or to circumstances that the caller has witnessed and is reporting.

Where an individual calls to seek help in relation to personal difficulties, a first consideration is that the person making the call should demonstrate that he or she is entitled to the help that is requested. Part of this involves demonstrating that what is being asked for does come within what the service can and does provide. Contrary to popular myth, fire brigades do not ordinarily treat the rescue of cats from trees as a central part of their activities and a caller might well be encouraged to attempt rescue in ways other than asking for the intervention of emergency services! Nevertheless, people who take calls that seek help are expected to display empathy to a caller's problems and to offer reasonable support (Hepburn and Potter, 2007), and, where possible, to recognize the voices of those who have called them on previous occasions (Shaw and Kitzinger, 2007). For some helpline services, however, the common response to a call describing individual problems might be the act of listening to the caller's problems in itself. Michael Emmison and Susan Danby (2007), provide an example taken from a study of calls made to an Australian helpline, Kids Help Line. This helpline provides a counselling service for children and young persons aged between 5 and 18 but, unlike other services, it focuses on caring and listening rather than offering advice as to how to solve problems. We see in Extract 7.10 the early stages of one call made to the helpline.

Extract 7.10

[CT = call taker, c = caller]

```
1    CT:   Hello=Kids Help Line,
2    C:    Yeah=u:m. I've got a problem
3          (0.2)
4.         hh at scho:ol I'm always being tea:sed (.) about my weight=I'm
5          a very big girl and I don't know what to do
```
                                                (Emmison and Danby, 2007, p. 72)

We can see above at line 1 that the person taking the call begins by identifying the service but makes no offer of help, a standard initial response for Kids Help Line. The absence of such offer, however, places the onus on the caller to provide an account as to why he or she has made the call. The caller proceeds by describing a problem but this description in itself is not sufficient to make help relevant. It is only at line 5 when the caller states that 'I don't know what to do' that the request goes beyond the realm of caring and listening and indicates a need for more direct help from the service.

A particular point of note in the extract above is the precise formulation that the caller uses to elicit help, the statement at line 5 of being unable to deal with the problem that has been described. This form of statement is a common one in help-seeking situations in making explicit the need for help from others. Seeking help is an accountable matter, in that commonly people are expected to act on their own behalf so far as possible and to help themselves or to seek advice from family or friends in coping with problems. Thus, many helplines actively promote callers' own attempts to deal with any difficulties that might arise in their everyday lives (Pudlinski, 2008). Conversely, individuals are expected to seek help from external services only when there is reasonable warrant for them to do so. A good example of such expectations can be seen in a study by Derek Edwards and Liz Stokoe (2007) of calls made to a mediation service that is set up to deal with disputes that arise between neighbours. The mediation service aims to resolve neighbour disputes in cases where other attempts to resolve the disputes have failed and intervention by an external agency has become necessary. Below, we see an extract from one call made to the service.

Extract 7.11

[C = caller, M = mediator]

```
17   C    (…) Because I know as soon as they moved in our
18        um ca:r (.) *u- um car, they broke into our car,
19        an' I know it's ↓them as well.
20        (0.2)
21   M:   .hhh ↓Do you righ- an' you haven't spoken to
22        them at [↓a:ll about this. .hhhhh]
23   C:   [No: I 'av'nt spo:ken to] them I don't
24        kno:w what t'do::
25        (0.3)
26   M:   Ri::ght. Okay .hhh Sh- (.) so can *I- shall I
27        tell y'a little bit about what* we: ↓do an'=
28   C:   =[ R i : g h t. ]
29   M:   =[then you can dec ]ide wha- .hhh (…)
```

                                                    (Edwards and Stokoe, 2007, p. 27)

In the course of this exchange, the caller's first turn at lines 17 to 19 describes a specific problem that is attributed to the action of neighbours by way of breaking into a car. The mediator's initial response, at lines 21 to 22, does not take up the problem as described but instead questions whether the caller has attempted to deal with the complaint personally by speaking to the neighbours. The caller's response in turn denies having done so but at the same time offers a warrant for not attempting to deal with the problem personally. As Edwards and Stokoe note, questions by mediators of the sort seen here go beyond mere information-seeking as to the history of the complaint. Rather these questions also involve a normative element, in presenting discussion between neighbours as a preferred response and an expected course of action. Callers themselves treat mediators' questions in this way, in that those who have not discussed matters with their neighbours offer some account for not doing so, commonly in terms of inability or difficulty, the likelihood of failure, or fear of the consequences. It is only following these accounts, such as that seen in lines 23 and 24 in the extract above, that the mediator will describe the help that the mediation service can offer.

   There are of course many circumstances in which individual attempts to deal with reported problems would not be expected or would indeed be unwise. Members of the public are not expected to rush to put out fires in buildings, tackle people carrying guns, or deal with life-threatening situations. In such cases, callers to emergency services will be expected not to describe their own efforts to deal with the situation that is reported but instead to provide the information that is necessary for the emergency service to respond. Thus, where callers report incidents that warrant action by emergency services they are required to provide sufficient detail of what they are reporting. Call-takers in such circumstances respond to callers who do not provide enough initial information by seeking further information until sufficient detail is available to determine the help that is necessary (Cromdal, Osvaldsson and Persson-Thunqvist, 2008). Often, however, calls to emergency services take the form seen below. Extract 7.12 comes from a study by Geoffrey Raymond and Don Zimmerman (2007) of calls made to a 911 (i.e. a 999) emergency call line in response to a single event, the 1990 Mountain Glade Fire which occurred in a coastal community on the Pacific Coast of the USA. This extract details the initial report of the fire.

Extract 7.12

```
01   CT:   Nine one one emergency- May I help you
02   C:    Ah yes there's a fire just starting at thuh corner of
03         ( uh ) Two Thirty Five and Mountain Gla:de Roa::d, (uh)
04         brush fire.
05         (2.0)
06   CT:   Which side sir
07   C:    Ah it'd be on thuh downhill side.
08         (1.0)
09   CT:   See anybody around th- See anybody around it
...        ((12 lines omitted))
22   CT:   An you went up what thuh top tuh call: or are you in:
23         uh car phone
24   C:    I'm on a car phone I was jus' passin' by.
25   CT:   Uhkay we'll get someone there.
26   C:    Thank you=
27   CT:   Unhuh=bye=
28   C:    Bye.
```
                              (Raymond and Zimmerman, 2007, p. 37)

What we see in the extract above is the call-taker's identification of the service at line 1 being immediately followed by the caller's description of the event that has occurred, namely the fire. As is clearly evident, this description is immediately treated as sufficient grounds for the call and for the request for help from the emergency services. Acceptance of this description and the action taken in response to it established the event as necessary warrant for help. Subsequent calls made to the helpline therefore were less concerned with reporting the details of the fire than with ensuring that the service was aware of it, as seen below.

Extract 7.13

```
01      CT:   Nine one one emergency.
02            (.)
03 →    C:    Does thuh fire department know that there's uh big fire
```

```
04 →             ((noise)) on San Pedro Pass,
05 →    CT:    Yes, we're on our way to that thank you
```
                                        (Raymond and Zimmerman, 2007, p. 44)

As, over time, it became established that the fire had been reported and that the emergency services were responding to it, subsequent callers treated this as established knowledge and were more concerned with seeking guidance and advice from the service:

Extract 7.14

```
01      CT:    Nine one one
02 →    C:     Um I live on San Miguel Ridge Road: (.) Can you
03 →           tell me where thuh fire is that's above me.=
04      CT:    =There's two fires::
05             (.)
06      C:     The one above me.
07      CT:    I've no idea=There's one at one fifty four and Old
08             San Pedro, .hh an' there's one at uh: started on (.)
09             forty four hundred block: you know where the dump is
10      C:     Yeah I-
11      CT:    'an it's moving over toward Bel Canto.
12      C:     >Okay< Thanks.
```
                                    (Raymond and Zimmerman, 2007, pp. 49–50)

What these extracts demonstrate are the differences occurring in calls made to the fire services and differences in their responses over time as the fire continued and spread. In a quickly changing context, the orientations and expectations of callers altered markedly, necessitating different responses from the fire service in ways that oriented both to the callers' requests and to the shifting context within which these requests were made. Not all contexts, of course, change just as rapidly as this one did; nonetheless these extracts point clearly to the need for helpline services, and indeed other organizations, to be able to respond to the ever-changing social events around them and the meanings that these events have for the individuals and other social actors that they encounter in their daily organizational practices.

Organizations in education

Traditionally, schools and universities have been associated with a range of familiar activities. Educational organizations have in large part been understood to be centres of learning and teaching with rather less emphasis, if any, being given to the commercial elements of providing education. Certainly, to some extent, education continues to work in these ways. Schools continue to award grades for pupils' learning and to use these in determining pupils' future progress through the school system (Mazeland and Berenst, 2008). Universities continue to involve interactions between teaching staff and students, whether by way of structured lectures and tutorials or in less formal ways such as **office hours** meetings that allow students to address questions, solve problems, and discuss matters relevant to their studies with their teachers (Limberg, 2007). Even where such contact occurs in less traditional forms, such as telephone tutorial conferences, the interactions between staff and students remain recognizably familiar and display patterns of student participation similar to those found in more traditional face-to-face settings (Horton-Salway *et al.*, 2008).

> **Office hours**   informal meetings that allow students to address questions, solve problems, and discuss matters relevant to their studies with their teachers.

The provision of education, however, has always been understood and negotiated within a wider social arena. For example, in the United States, unlike most Western countries, local school boards have for some time been responsible for overseeing and determining the ways in which schools are run. Meetings of school boards are held in public, and almost always allow time for contributions from local citizens. These contributions allow board members to hear the views of community residents on matters relating to the schools, but are often regarded as simply 'gripes' from local citizens on any matters that they dislike. In a study of local citizens' talk at school board meetings, Karen Tracy and Margaret Durfy (2007) note that contributors often do express negative comments about the running of the schools. For example:

Extract 7.15

My name is Annette Crawford. Ladies and gentlemen of the board I am here tonight to represent the Baobab Community high school parent council. The termination of the Baobab charter contract is very distressing.

(Tracy and Durfy, 2007, p. 232)

Above we see the form in which many citizens framed complaints that they wished to make about aspects of how the schools were run. The speaker identifies herself as a representative of a parent council, positioning her not just as someone with a personal complaint but as a representative of another body. Identifications such as this worked to emphasize the broad local interests involved in the matter being discussed and to establish the speaker's right to be heard at the meeting. Following such identifications, speakers would frame their complaints in ways that suggested broad rather than personal interests, as seen in the extracts below.

Extract 7.16

Why would the decision of a highly qualified, very competent superintendent, be changed? Is it politics or is it protecting one's own friend?

(Tracy and Durfy, 2007, p. 239)

Extract 7.17

Okay then I just have one other thing to say and I won't add anymore to it. I just wanted to say this. And this is kind of my summation of- of the of the school thing. I heard about the coach and everything else. And I just, I just would like to ask you guys this question tonight. And that is, *will the children you were yesterday, would they be proud of the decision you're gonna make tonight?* Thank you.

(Tracy and Durfy, 2007, p. 241)

As well as grounding their complaints in broad concerns, speakers phrased these in terms that indicated disagreement with the running of the schools but which did so in ways that avoided outright conflict. In this, the use of rhetorical questions as seen above provided one useful means by which the speakers could put their points across. Their contributions thereby displayed what was termed 'reasonable hostility', in voicing complaints as to how the schools were run in terms that were apparently representative of the broader interests of the local community.

While the above example points to how schools can have to negotiate their practices within the context of a local community, educational providers increasingly have had to negotiate the meanings of their practices in somewhat broader contexts. Earlier in this chapter, we noted that the contexts within which organizations now operate have taken on international and global elements. In this, education has been no exception. As Saarinen (2008) notes, higher educational policy documents, in particular those devised by the Organization for Economic Co-operation and Development (OECD) and the European Union (EU), have come to promote principles that are not grounded solely in the delivery of learning and teaching. Instead, policy documents such as these have foregrounded the issue of quality in higher education and set alongside this an emphasis on consumer choice and competitiveness. These policy documents have in turn shaped how individual governments and states, and indeed how much of the wider population, make sense of universities in changing times.

The reframing of higher education, in terms of quality of services, consumer choice and competitiveness instead of learning and teaching, have functioned to construct universities as organizations that in most respects are little different from commercial organizations. Moreover, regardless of how one might respond to this change, the **marketization of higher education** has had particular consequences both for those who enter into university and for universities themselves as providers of education. To identify the recipients of higher education as consumers who make choices in a competitive world is markedly different from identifying them as students. Universities, for their part, have responded by acting in ways that often closely resemble the marketing practices of commercial

Marketization of higher education   framing of higher education, in commercial terms of quality of services, consumer choice and competitiveness instead of learning and teaching.

corporations. For example, in a study of Malaysian universities, Hajibah Osman (2008) notes that these universities have used careful branding and marketing to establish their corporate identities. These corporate practices are especially evident in the prospectuses that the universities issue to prospective students, as seen below.

Extract 7.18

USM campus with its tropical setting of lush greenery exudes an atmosphere most conducive to learning and yet is located within easy reach of the state capital ... which has all the trappings and amenities of a modern city.

(Osman, 2008, p. 67)

Extract 7.19

This campus houses all the facilities that a modern community is worthy of ... a state-of-the-art sports complex complete with an Olympic-size swimming pool and stadium, a fully-equipped library, a 24-hour medical clinic ... (IIUM)

(Osman, 2008, p. 68)

Extract 7.20

Over the years, UM has received an accolade of awards and achievements ...

(Osman, 2008, p. 70)

Although these descriptions are designed in part to be informative, we can see that they all provide opportunities for the universities to promote themselves within different parts of their prospectuses. These descriptions, along with numerous others found elsewhere, such as in mission statements and details of academic programmes, all serve to identify the universities issuing them as organizations with particular credentials in respect of the services they can offer to potential consumers. If successful in identifying the universities in these terms, such descriptions can confer a competitive advantage on the university issuing the prospectus.

The marketization of higher education in times of global competition is of course by no means limited to Malaysia or indeed to any country or countries. Corporate documents, such as a university's international student prospectus, have on a global scale come to reflect the values and forces of a free competitive international market. At least as much attention now is focused on providing an innovative product in the form of the best possible 'university experience' as it is on highlighting the education available to students (Askehave, 2007). Similarly to other organizations, universities have responded to broader social changes by marketing what they offer as effectively as possible and demonstrating their business credentials in an ever-changing and competitive context.

Identity Challenges

In this chapter so far we have examined how individuals, both within organizations and as people who seek organizational products and services, and organizations themselves negotiate identities in local and social contexts. Negotiation of individual and corporate identities present a range of challenges, whether gaining the services or help that is being sought, in making sense of organizational practices and culture, or in being successful in an always changing world. In this final section we consider two specific forms of challenge to identity that can arise within the realm of work and organizations. The first of these arises most visibly for the individual. We have noted that organizations over time develop their own cultures and that those arriving new to an organization might experience difficulties in becoming familiar with its practices. These difficulties, and the challenges that they present for identity, become all the more salient for people who are unable to gain employment within organizations, in other words job-seekers. The second challenge arises at the corporate level. We examined above how organizations seek to make sense of what they do in changing contexts, some of these changes being potentially beneficial to an organization. Other changes in contexts can be rather more challenging for organizations, especially when the changes are not anticipated and are highly damaging to the corporate identities that organizations might claim for themselves.

Seeking employment

The usual course of seeking employment is for organizations to advertise vacancies that occur and for individuals to apply for these vacancies. Being successful in an application, however, is not necessarily a straightforward process, especially in difficult economic times. Also, those who apply for work will often be wholly unfamiliar with the established patterns and practices of an organization to which they apply. Interviewing panels look to candidates to demonstrate their aptitude for the employment that is sought, and a candidate's failure to do so will reduce the chances of gaining that employment (Lipovsky, 2008). For individual candidates, one way of increasing the prospects of success is through interactional training that will increase their understanding of employers' expectations and the attributes generally associated with the work that they seek (Sniad, 2007).

Often, however, the problems experienced by individuals in obtaining employment arise not through difficulties in demonstrating their attributes to prospective employers but through being ascribed particular identities on grounds of belonging to specific social groups. As we saw earlier, certain occupations can easily be associated with members of specific social groups based on gender, ethnicity or other factors. More than this, the ascription of certain group identities can make available inferences that are highly negative in terms of abilities to engage meaningfully in employment. One such example is that of older jobseekers. The under-representation of older workers in the workplace has become a matter of concern in many countries across the globe, all the more so as changing demographics lead to increasing numbers of people potentially belonging to this group and as times of economic difficulty are likely to require individuals to extend their working lives further than previously was the case. Yet, the problems faced by older people who seek employment have been well documented and numerous studies point to the continuing difficulties faced by people who are identified as older jobseekers. It is interesting to note that even initiatives designed to identify and highlight these difficulties have had little outcome in terms of facilitating the employment of older workers. For example, certain identifications of older (non-) workers can function to make individuals themselves primarily responsible for gaining the attributes that they require to return to the workplace (Ainsworth and Hardy, 2007). Other initiatives, such as the advocacy of equal opportunities in employment, while acknowledging the social contexts of the identities of older workers have similarly failed to change employers' understandings of particular jobs and thus equally have produced few if any benefits for older workers as a group (McVittie, McKinlay and Widdicombe, 2003).

More recent moves to promote employment opportunities for older workers have sought to engage with organizations' own understandings of their practices and of the identities of employees and customers. Initiatives such as the promotion of **diversity in employment** have been framed largely in terms of a business case that seeks to persuade organizations of the benefits of including people from all social groups, older job-seekers included, within their workplaces.

> **Diversity in employment** the principle of including people from all social groups within the workplace.

Thus, the idea of diversity might appear consistent with organizations' own identities and the meanings that they give to their practices. It appears, however, that even attempts such as this have had little impact upon the employment difficulties experienced by many older people and indeed that such moves can mask rather than address the problems that older people can face in seeking work (McVittie, McKinlay and Widdicombe, 2008a).

The problem of being unable to obtain employment on grounds of age thus presents a challenge to the identities of those who find themselves in such circumstances. Similarly to other identities, however, the meanings of experience are open to negotiation. As Chris McVittie and colleagues (McVittie, McKinlay and Widdicombe, 2008b) note, individuals in such contexts have available to them different ways in which they can make sense of themselves and their difficulties in gaining employment. One such way is for older jobseekers to describe themselves as the victims of age discrimination, as seen below.

Extract 7.21

CM: Have you found age to be a factor in looking for employment?

JN: I think it must be because…when I first came up here ten years ago I (.) study and I used to do temporary work in summer and I could pick up work like that (snaps fingers) I could pick up a newspaper, I could just walk in to an agency or as I did (.) I rang up Edinburgh University after a while and sort of would always get (.) And then maybe about five years ago it began to get difficult (.) both in London and here … So there was nothing (.) in me that I could see you know was inadequate to (.) sort of (.) and I could only think it had to be age.

                              (McVittie, McKinlay and Widdicombe, 2008b, p. 250)

In the extract above, we see JN describing herself as someone who is actively seeking work but is unsuccessful through no fault of her own part or efforts. Her current lack of success is contrasted with a record of previous success in finding work, leaving her age and employers' responses to it as the candidate explanation as to why she is unable now to find employment. A rather different identity, however, is equally available in such circumstances:

Extract 7.22

CM: Have you found age as a factor in looking for employment?

PO: I think (.) well (.) I haven't had that many interviews… but (.) I keep trying. Not so hard as I used to actually (.) (laughing) I've been kept very busy lately (.) e:m that's another thing, better not say too much on the tape (laughing) No, it's just that e:m (.) my sons (.) e:m have all got houses, They've just bought new houses or changed houses and such like and (.) there's such a lot to do when you do move from house to house (.) One of them's a complete rewire and (.) knocking down walls, building up walls and such like and what have you. Lucky enough, I did that as well in my life (.) e:m having had many different houses myself. I always bought old ones, did them up (.) sold them then and carried on and such like.

                              (McVittie, McKinlay and Widdicombe, 2008b, p. 252)

Instead of describing himself as unemployed due to employers' practices, PO here describes himself as actively engaged in other projects and as being less committed to seeking work than previously. Clearly this is not an identity that he would necessarily share or attempt to negotiate with a benefits adviser, workplace co-ordinator or other in similar position, as the interviewee himself notes!

As McVittie and colleagues point out, these two identities invoke very different versions of work and the interviewee's relationship to the world of employment. They demonstrate clearly that the identity of older jobseeker is not a unitary one but can be negotiated differently according to the demands of the local context and the goals of the speaker. More than this, however, they also draw upon social understandings of individuals, of employment, and of organizational practices in presenting identities that are meaningful both in individual and social terms.

Negative corporate identities

The examples with which we began this chapter, drawn from banking and oil and gas production, described organizations and particular individuals within them that had been ascribed highly problematic identities following their involvement in negatively evaluated actions. In considering the consequences of negatively evaluated actions for corporate and individual identities, it is useful at this point to examine a previous instance of an organization and its chairman that found itself in very similar circumstances to those described earlier.

Let us consider the case of PowderJect Pharmaceuticals plc, a former British biotechnology company. In early 2002, the company was awarded by the UK Government a contract worth £32 million for the supply of smallpox vaccine. As a result of this success, and its previous acquisition of a competitor business, PowderJect was widely identified in the financial and popular press as a successful organization that was expanding its activities in growing markets. In April 2002, however, news emerged that in the 12 months prior to the award of this contract the company had made donations of £100,000 to the Labour Party that at that time formed the UK Government. This revelation provoked a 'cash-for-contracts' scandal, with allegations being made that the company had been awarded the contract as a result of these donations.

Yvonne McLaren-Hankin (2007) examines the ways in which PowderJect in its press releases, and the media in newspaper reports, identified the company and its officers both prior to and following the allegations. Before April 2002, press releases issued by the company described its progress in highly positive terms. The descriptions below, for example, come from a company press release issued in September 2000 following its acquisition of a competitor vaccine business.

Extract 7.23

(1) PowderJect has the opportunity to create an enviable range of high value products.

(2) Combining Medeva's range of existing vaccines with PowderJect's innovative vaccine R&D pipeline will create a significant vaccines business, which is ideally situated to capture a significant share of the rapidly transforming vaccine market.

(McLaren-Hankin, 2007, p. 1095)

The positive identity projected by the company's press releases was at this time reflected in press descriptions of the company. Below we see the descriptions of PowderJect found in a report by the *Guardian* UK newspaper published on 8 September 2000 under the heading 'PowderJect gains vaccine booster'.

Extract 7.24

(3) The deal sharply increases the scale of Oxford-based PowderJect, which employs just 250 people. It will be funded by a placing of shares at 600p to raise £35m.

(4) The division, which employs 800 people in Speke, Merseyside, is one of the biggest suppliers of vaccines to the national health service. It manufactures flu vaccines, which are distributed to the elderly each winter, yellow fever antidotes for travellers and BCG inoculations against tuberculosis.

(McLaren-Hankin, 2007, p. 1096)

After April 2002, however, the company's own descriptions and those found in the popular press diverged markedly. Company press releases made no reference to the 'cash-for-contracts' scandal and instead continued to highlight the financial performance of the organization. The following descriptions come from a press release issued on 14 May 2002, after the news of the donations and contract had come to light.

Extract 7.25

(9) PowderJect's flu franchise achieved a number of additional milestones during the year …

(10) PowderJect is at the beginning of an exciting new chapter as a major force in vaccination.

(11) PowderJect now has the financial strength to extend its R&D into other commercially attractive areas of immunology.

(McLaren-Hankin, 2007, p. 1098)

Although these press releases continued the positive tone of those issued before April 2002, subsequent press reports did not take up the company's own descriptions of its activities. Instead, press coverage turned to the issue of the company's donations to the Labour Party and to the company's response to the allegations made.

Extract 7.26

(12) Paul Drayson, the chairman of PowderJect, vowed to continue giving money to the Labour Party despite the controversy that erupted when his company won a £32m Government contract to supply smallpox vaccine.

(The Independent, 15 May 2002)

(13) Mr Drayson, the chairman and chief executive of PowderJect, insisted his firm had won the contract because it had put in 'the best bid' of the five competitive tenders and that two donations of £50,000 to the party were irrelevant. (The Guardian, 15 May 2002)

(McLaren-Hankin, 2007, p. 1099)

Although the financial press continued to report company activities largely in terms of financial indicators, the reports such as these in the general press made little mention of financial success. Instead, they cast doubt on the actions of the organization and its chairman, suggesting a failure to learn from previous mistakes. At the same time, the reports distanced themselves from any positive views that were expressed and attributed these directly to the company and its chairman. In these ways, the press reports of PowderJect constructed the organization in highly negative ways and as tainted by its past actions and ongoing failures. Needless to say, these identities were somewhat at odds with the efforts of the company itself and of Paul Drayson as an individual to identify themselves with organizational success! It may come as no surprise to discover that organizational attempts to rework the company's identity in response to such press constructions were unsuccessful, with PowderJect in 2003 being taken over by a competitor pharmaceutical company, leading to the ultimate loss of corporate identity.

Discussion

Over the course of this chapter, we have examined how organizations can be understood as recurring patterns of talk and interaction that over time develop their own organizational logics. Certainly, the interactions that occur are those of individuals, as employees, leaders and customers, all of which go to make up what we recognize as organizations. This discourse does not take place in a vacuum but against a backdrop of social understandings of what occupations can and should be, of how services are negotiated and of social practices that are continually in flux. All of these negotiations point to the range of discursive work that is every day caught up in the ways that organizations make sense of themselves and that we, as employees, customers, recipients of services, and otherwise, come to understand them. It is within these ongoing patterns of interactions that organizations appear to us in recognizable forms. What we come to recognize is of course another matter: organizations and those who work within them can be understood in a diversity of ways. It remains to be seen if organizations that once were identified in largely favourable ways suffer similar identity problems and failures to those of PowderJect, or if they are able to renegotiate identities that are accepted in ways similar to those that they previously enjoyed.

Chapter Summary

Organizations play a major role for all of us in our everyday lives, whether as employees, customers, shareholders, taxpayers, or in other social capacities. Although organizations are commonly presented to us as being autonomous entities, on closer inspection we can recognize them as recurring patterns of talk and interaction within work, relationships, and other social outcomes are accomplished.

The identities of those who work for particular organizations are negotiated on a daily basis in interactions with customers who seek organizational services. Particular occupational identities, however, can become bound up with social expectations of gender and other group memberships. In addition, a range of social actors will offer particular versions of occupational identities in order to make their own arguments.

Organizations over time develop their logics and cultures through the patterns of interaction that recur within them. In this, leaders can be more powerful than junior employees in influencing the organizational cultures that emerge. Mentoring of junior employees can be useful but often simply reflects existing cultures rather than assisting employees who are new to an organization.

Organizations and those who work for them are continually orienting to changing contexts of operation. In some cases, contexts can change rapidly; in other cases, such as the provision of education, contexts change markedly and necessitate broad organizational changes in response.

Particular identity challenges arise for individuals who are unable to gain employment within organizations and for organizations that are ascribed negative corporate identities following negatively evaluated actions. Individuals and organizations can rework their identities in response to such difficulties but might have to do in very different ways for these to be meaningful.

Connections

The gendered construction of particular occupations is inextricably linked to gender identities more generally, as discussed in Chapter 4.

The legal consequences of specific ascriptions of identity and accountability are discussed in more detail in Chapter 6.

See also Chapter 8 for further discussion of the identities found in forms of communications such as emails, web links, and other virtual media.

Further Reading

McLaren-Hankin, Y. (2007). Conflicting representations in business and media texts: The case of PowderJect Pharmaceuticals plc. *Journal of Pragmatics, 39*, 1088–1104.

A good example of how corporate and individual organizational identities can readily become negatively evaluated.

Moore, R. J. (2008). When names fail: Referential practice in face-to-face service encounters. *Language in Society, 37*, 385–413.

Useful examples of how differences in organizational and customer knowledge can be overcome in everyday practices.

Yamaguchi, T. (2007). Controversy over genetically modified crops in India: Discursive strategies and social identities of farmers. *Discourse Studies, 9*, 87–107.

This study shows how political actors and others can deploy versions of occupational identities for their purposes.

Activity Box

Many of you reading this chapter will find yourselves within a higher education organization, looking to make sense of itself and those within it in ever-changing contexts. How do you make sense of your own identity within that organization? In what ways and to what extent do you understand this identity in terms of education, learning and teaching, or alternatively in terms of quality and consumer choice? How do you understand your own identity as linked to that of the organization within which you find yourself?

8

Virtual Identities

Topics Covered in this Chapter

Key Terms

'419' emails

Avatar

Blogs

Emoticon

Marked

Online community

SMS text messaging

Social networking

Identities in Context: Individuals and Discourse in Action, First Edition. Andrew McKinlay
and Chris McVittie.

The killing of an avatar

A 43-year-old Japanese piano teacher could face five years of jail or a fine of up to $5,000 for, essentially, the murder of her online husband from the game 'Maple Story.' The woman was enraged after the man, who was married to her in the game but not in real life, abruptly broke off the online relationship, so she signed on to his profile with his identification and password and terminated his avatar ..177.

Her online husband, a 33-year-old office worker from Sapporo, Japan, had reported the crime and death of his avatar to police.

Virtual 'Maple Story' murder reveals online lives gone too far, 24 October 2008 (www.findingdulcinea.com/news/technology/September-October-08/Virtual–Maple-Story–Murder-Reveals-Online-Lives-Gone-Too-Far.html)

Maple Story, the game referred to in the extract above, provides a virtual environment that is designed in many respects to mimic real life experiences. Within the game, participants can purchase items, engage in virtual relationships with other players, and even 'earn' a wedding. As with similar games, such as Second Life and World of Warcraft, Maple Life has proved to be extremely popular among users, providing an online world that has attracted more than 50 million subscribers. What we see in the extract above, however, are the consequences of these forms of online participation being taken up offline in real world events. An **avatar**, such as that described above, is a visual or textual representation of an individual within an online game, discussion or community. Here, the avatar being discussed in effect comprised the identity of the online husband within the environment of Maple Life: the termination of this avatar ended his identity in the game. The importance of this identity to the online husband, a 33-year-old office worker from Sapporo, Japan, is evidenced by the description of its loss as 'death of his avatar'. In his statement reporting the 'crime' to police, he stated that he had 'raised' the avatar for more than a year. For her part, the Japanese piano teacher who was his online wife told police on her arrest 'I was suddenly divorced, without a word of warning. That made me so angry'. She was subsequently charged with illegal access to a computer and with the manipulation of electronic data.

> **Avatar**   an online representation of an individual, taking the form of a visual or textual representation of that individual within an online game, discussion, or community.

The circumstances described here clearly demonstrate how strongly the two people involved identified with their online presences. By explaining her actions as resulting from the termination of an online relationship, the piano teacher makes relevant a range of inferences about her understandings of that relationship and of its meanings for her. On a similar note, the online husband's description of the time that he spent in 'raising' the avatar points to a very particular form of identification with this online representation. From descriptions such as these, and indeed descriptions found in other instances of unauthorized computer access, we get a sense of how easily offline and online identities can become blurred. Far from being constructions that have little impact elsewhere, virtual identities can be understood as often bound up with concerns that have considerable meanings across many aspects of everyday lives. In this chapter we explore how people negotiate identities in virtual environments, the meanings that these identities can have, and the extent to which these identity practices resemble those found in other contexts.

Communications Technologies and Identities

Technological contexts of communication, such as the virtual world of Maple Life, obviously differ from face-to-face contexts in one highly important respect: they are produced by human designers. The ways in which communications technologies operate reflect the understandings of those who design them and the technological possibilities that are available to them (Alby and Zuccermaglio, 2007). Furthermore, these understandings and the contexts that result from them are oriented to facilitating forms of interaction that will vary from one context to another. For example, the advent and rise of teleshopping whether by way of single programmes or entire television channels is oriented towards producing action outcomes, rather than communicative exchanges between the presenters on the one hand and the viewing audience on the other. Presenters will seek to construct identities that make themselves appear trustworthy and to describe products in ways that make them attractive to viewers; whether viewers take up or resist these efforts, however, is not designed to be included within a broadcast itself (Kline, 2005). In a similar way, web sites are often designed to facilitate specific forms of discussions and to allow participation only by named individuals. Educational web sites thus can be produced to promote discussions around a specified topic, such as literature, and to allow access only to students and teachers who are to take part in these discussions (Love, 2006). Other web sites also are designed to reflect and enable certain forms of user involvement and interaction. Take, for example, web sites that are set up to promote **social networking**, the practices through which individual users develop and enter into social relations with others who share their interests and activities. By definition, all social networking web sites allow users to provide information about themselves and to interact with other users. Specific web sites, however, vary in terms of the profiles

Social networking   the practices through which individual users develop and enter into social relations with others who share their interests and activities.

that individual users can build and the forms of networks that are generated. For example, web sites such as LinkedIn and ASmallWorld are relatively tightly structured by way of the information that users can enter and the networks that result.

By contrast Facebook, as many readers will be aware, is somewhat more flexible in the information that users can post and in the interactions that they have with other users (Papacharissi, 2009).

Of course, contexts such as these vary in more respects than their design features. Designers might well develop contexts to operate in certain ways, but there is the question also of how users do actually make use of them. Well, evidence suggests that many people often do not make use of the full range of possibilities that are technologically available to them and that instead they come to rely upon the elements that become familiar in their initial interactions with the technology. Other possibilities are not taken up and thus play little part in subsequent user interactions (Geer and Barnes, 2007). Consequently, the identities that individuals pursue in technologically mediated contexts in many instances are bound up with the identities that they negotiate or are ascribed elsewhere. In this section, we examine these practices in two forms, first by way of interactions and identity consequences found in SMS text messaging and, second, in terms of the social group memberships that people bring to virtual contexts.

Text messaging and turns

In some respects, textual communications sent via electronic means, such as email and text messaging, reflect features found in everyday face-to-face interactions. For example, senders in framing their messages commonly orient to issues of politeness in considering how the message will be taken up by the intended recipients (Graham, 2007; Hatipoglu, 2007). In other ways, however, communications sent by electronic messaging differ markedly from those occurring in everyday face-to-face settings. One of the most popular, and perhaps most accessible, forms of electronic textual communication is that of **SMS (Short Message Service) text messaging**. SMS text messaging comprises the transmission of short text messages, of up to 160 characters, between users of mobile phones and sometimes between users of mobile phones and users of fixed line phones. Usually SMS text messages will convey some information to the recipient about the sender, such as the phone number from which the message was sent, the person associated with that phone number, or both. The textual nature of this form of communication, however, inevitably means that texts will not convey other information surrounding the message, such as visual cues, or the tone of voice or pace of delivery of the sender.

> **SMS (short message service) text messaging** the transmission of short text messages, of up to 160 characters, between users of mobile phones and sometimes between users of mobile phones and users of fixed line phones.

Senders of text messages often include in their messages elements that are designed to address in part the absence of contextual information about the content of the message. We are all familiar with the inclusion in such communications

Emoticon   a symbol included in a message that is intended to display to the recipients the feelings or emotions of the sender.

of features such as **emoticons**, symbols intended to display to recipients the feelings or emotions of the sender and to provide guidance as to the tone of the written text. Notwithstanding such efforts, however, interactions that occur via text messaging inevitably vary from face-to-face interactions. Consider the following extracts taken from a study of SMS text messaging by Ian Hutchby and Vanita Tanna (2008).

Extract 8.1

Sender: B
11:10
05-09-2003
1 →→   morning u, hows the
2   pampering going?:-)
3 →   stu's tryin 2 organise
4   something next
5 →   friday..can u come
6   out?

(Hutchby and Tanna, 2008, p. 153)

Extract 8.2

Sender: D
17:11
05-09-2003
1 →→   Hi and, didnt go 2
2   health club, had 2 pic
3   up elise cos she wz
4   ill, mum got her nw,
5   been in hairdresas 4
6 →   2hrs. Dnt think i cn
7   get a sita 4 fri

(Hutchby and Tanna, 2008, pp. 154–155)

The two extracts above comprise an initial message sent by SMS text messaging and the response received. At line 2 of the initial message we see a smiley emoticon indicating the tone and emotions of the sender at that point. This, together with the informal language and abbreviated words used throughout the message and response, indicates informality and an ease and familiarity between those involved in the exchange. The message contains multiple units, in this case a greeting, an inquiry, an announcement and a question/invitation. It thereby constitutes what Hutchby and Tanna term a 'package-text' in that it performs various actions within the same turn.

Turns that incorporate multiple elements are not specific to text messaging as a form of communication and are often found also in naturally occurring conversations. When multiple-unit turns occur in everyday conversation, a recipient will ordinarily respond to the units in the reverse order of presentation. Thus, the recipient treats the final unit as being most topically relevant and responds to it first and thereafter to the remaining units in reverse order of receipt. This form of response reflects the relative proximities of the various units to the topic currently under discussion. What is noteworthy in the exchange of texts seen above is that the response adopts a format that differs somewhat from responses to multiple-unit turns found in everyday talk. Here, the recipient's response maintains the same order of units found in the initial message: the first unit of the response addresses the first unit of the message and continues in that order.

The difference is clear but one question that we might reasonably ask is whether this matters; that is, how important is the order of units in this context? The answer, according to Hutchby and Tanna, is that this specific feature of SMS text messaging tells us much about how it works as a form of communication. What it indicates is that recipients of text messages treat these texts as packages of information rather than as combinations of different elements. These forms of exchange show how individuals orient to the limitations of the technology as a medium for meaningful interaction.

Treating SMS text messages as 'packages' is certainly consistent with the capacity of the technology that allows only communications of up to 160 characters at a time. Within this limited capacity, there is little scope for extended negotiation of identities, unless of course such negotiations take place across a number of turns. It is unsurprising therefore that identities that begin in text environments are developed further through everyday contact and that those that are worked out in face-to-face exchanges provide the basis for abbreviated text-based communication (Aarsand, 2008). In these ways, the communications occurring through SMS text messaging can in large part be seen as adjuncts to or continuations of communications in other settings that allow greater scope for interaction and for the negotiation of identities.

Social groups in virtual worlds

The identities produced in SMS text messages, then, are bound up with the identities that individuals negotiate in other contexts. We might ask at this point whether and to what extent the same is true of other forms of electronic communication: do people reproduce in virtual worlds the identities that they claim or are ascribed elsewhere?

Many interactions occurring in virtual contexts on the internet do appear to involve the development of identities that resemble those of offline contexts. In such instances, individuals are less oriented to the development of different forms of identity than with working out identities that are relevant in face-to-face

Blog a web site or part of a web site associated with an individual, which comprises regular entries describing that individual, and his or her experiences, feelings and actions.

contexts. For example web logs, commonly known as **blogs,** are web sites or parts of web sites that are associated with specific individuals and comprise regular entries describing those individuals, and their experiences, feelings and actions. Usually these entries are displayed in reverse chronological order. Blogs are not entirely individual accomplishments, in that most blogs incorporate interactive elements that allow visitors to the web site to post comments on the entries that are displayed. Nonetheless, the focus on the blogger as the primary author of the web site postings provides the opportunity for him or her to foreground identity concerns and to develop these over time. As such, blogs offer possibilities for people to present versions of themselves and their interactions with others and to direct these versions towards a particular anticipated audience. Antonio Garcia-Gómez (2010) provides some examples of these practices from a study of the blogs of female teenagers in Spain and in the UK. We see one blog posting below.

Extract 8.3

Once upon a time there was a poor girl who lived in a small town. She had never ever dreamt of being popular or going out with the most handsome guys in high school. One day she was going out with her friends when they saw a bunch of cool guys. She didn't dare to go up to them but then one guy came and asked her if she had any dope. She couldn't believe it. Almost without realising they had a lay in the park [...] They have been inseparable since then.

(Garcia-Gómez, 2010, p. 145)

In such postings, the teenage bloggers presented versions of themselves and of their relationships to an anticipated audience of other teenagers. Often, their descriptions of relationships, although available to all who visited the web site, were specifically directed at particular individuals that included current boyfriends or ex-boyfriends. The versions of identities and of relationships found on these web sites commonly drew upon prevailing social understandings of heterosexuality and of femininity, applying them to the bloggers' own personal experiences. By recirculating and making relevant these understandings, however, the bloggers could develop versions of their own feminine identities to share with those who visited their web sites.

Similar practices of identity negotiation are found in numerous internet contexts. In a study of postings to the bulletin boards of online support groups for victims of domestic violence, Anna Hurley and colleagues (Hurley, Sullivan and McCarthy, 2007) point to the ways in which contributors described themselves and their experiences. Again, many postings describe, in ways designed to be meaningful to other contributors, the individuals' experiences and their relationships with their abusers. In addition, however, contributors often compared their current selves to their previous selves.

Extract 8.4

In 1981 I joined Alanon and AA, this is where I got the knowledge and POWER to begin to fight back. This was the beginning of the end. In 1985 I kicked my husband to the curb, I started heavy therapy, next thing was in 1987 I confronted my uncle on the sexual abuse that I was subjected to as a child, I took back my life! I now control my own destiny . . .

   'Survival is just existing-Victory is Total Control!'

   'I will not call myself a survivor, I am a victor. (I succeeded in defeating my evil-doers)'.

(Hurley, Sullivan and McCarthy, 2007, p. 869)

As Hurley and colleagues note, such juxtapositions of past selves with current selves serve to emphasize the contributors' descriptions of who they are now. Taken together with descriptions of experiences and of relationships with abusers, these descriptions provide powerful strategies for constructing current identities that have overcome experiences of abuse.

As we have seen, internet contexts provide spaces for individuals to develop identities that build upon their descriptions of experiences occurring in face-to-face contexts. Equally, however, these contexts offer possibilities for people to construct identities that are somewhat different from those that are commonly ascribed to them. Consider being ascribed the identity of being a disabled person. Such an identity makes available inferences of difference and deficit in not having the abilities that are routinely attributed to others. The identity of being disabled consequently often meets with negative evaluations in face-to-face social encounters. Virtual contexts, by contrast, present opportunities for people who might be ascribed these identities to work up different versions of themselves that do not carry negative associations, all the more so on web sites that are specifically oriented to their concerns. Giving these opportunities, individuals who post to such a web site construct identities of disabled people in positive terms as members of an active and multi-dimensional group, and do not reproduce the attributes of disabled identities that are negatively evaluated elsewhere (Thoreau, 2006).

Online Communities

In the preceding section, we looked at some of the possibilities available in virtual contexts for people to work up versions of themselves that orient to identity issues arising in offline interactions. These instances, however, are but a few of the opportunities for identity that virtual contexts make available. Sherry Turkle, writing in 1995, noted that even then 'the Internet has become a significant social laboratory for experimenting with the constructions and reconstructions of self that characterize postmodern life. In its virtual reality, we self-fashion and self-create' (Turkle, 1995, p. 180).

What this means is that, in virtual contexts, there is no requirement for people to interact in ways that reproduce or rework identities that are similar to those of other settings. Certainly, individuals on the internet might orient to such attributes of identity, but it is equally open to them to experiment with other versions of identity that differ markedly from those that might occur in face-to-face encounters. Of course, most internet users are well aware of these possibilities for producing identities that bear little relationship to other versions of identity. For those who seek to work up different versions of themselves, virtual contexts offer scope for identity work that might be rather more difficult to bring off elsewhere. Equally, however, in the absence of other information relating to identities, it becomes more difficult for users to convince those with whom they interact that they are who they claim to be. In this section, we explore some consequences of these opportunities for experimenting with versions of the self. We start by looking at some possibilities for playing with identities and thereafter turn to the potentially problematic issue of authenticating identities in virtual contexts.

Playing with identities

When discussing SMS text messaging above, we noted that written communications lack many of the features that are found in everyday talk, such as tone of voice and rate of delivery of speech of the sender. Other elements of speech are equally absent. Speakers in everyday contexts do not necessarily produce grammatical sentences or continuous speech, rather talk generally is punctuated by features such as pauses, hesitations and speech particles. Take for example the particle 'um'. This particle occurs frequently in everyday talk and is usually taken to be an unintended utterance that signals some uncertainty in the description that is being produced. It is unlikely, however, to occur naturally in written communications, especially as an internet user would have to type it into a communication. When therefore we do see the particle 'um' in such communications, this would suggest that it is part of the design of these communications, quite possibly being put to a use that differs from its use in everyday talk. Patricia Lange (2008) provides some examples of the use of 'um' in communications within online contexts. Consider the two examples below.

Extract 8.5

1   Graham says, "Well, we're waiting, who got pissy drunk, who fell out of a
    second
2   story window onto the hard concrete below, etc?"
3   . . .
4   **Margaret says, "That would be Fred . . . Fred . . . Fred and . . . um Fred".**

Extract 8.6

1   [Dennis] If no one else enters, can I just make a little dot, call
2   it a logo and win since it's the 'best' one in the contest? (laughs)

3   [**Walter**] **Um ... no.**
4   [Pete] Uhm contest?
5   [Dennis] Fine, I'll make a real one ...

(Lange, 2008, pp. 202–203)

It is immediately apparent from these examples that 'um' cannot be taken to indicate hesitation on the part of the contributor. We see at line 4 in Extract 8.5 the repetition of the name Fred with the 'um' being produced immediately prior to the last occurrence of the name. Given that Margaret has by that point of her statement already referred to 'Fred' three times, it is highly unlikely that she is uncertain as to the name that is to be produced. In Extract 8.6, the 'um' at line 3 precedes a definite rejection of the suggestion contained in the preceding question. Again, there seems to be little uncertainty on the part of Walter that Dennis's suggestion should be rejected. In these examples, 'um' works to parody its function in everyday talk, mimicking uncertainty where none exists. In doing so, it serves to emphasize the response and to do so in a way that promotes the social nature of the interaction. The affiliation among the contributors to the discussion, resulting from these and other uses of 'um', thus points to the ways in which internet users can play with elements of naturally occurring language to achieve somewhat different effects.

Just as internet users can play with their communications to each other, constructing teasing versions of who they are within discussions, so too they can seek to play with identities in more far-reaching ways. In a study of Swiss internet relay chats (IRCs), Daniel Rellstab (2007) observes that those taking part in the chats do on occasions seek to negotiate gendered identities that are at odds with other apparent aspects of identity. The extract below comes from an IRC channel called 'chatlounge', and comprises an exchange between two contributors who identify themselves as 'changes' and 'werner'. 'Changes' appears to be female, in that her previous postings are consistent with this identity and she has been appointed by the telecommunications company as operator of another chat channel known as 'ladiesonly'. As its name suggests, 'ladiesonly' is designed to be used only be female chatters. The gender of 'werner' is unknown, although in a Swiss context this online name suggests that he (or she) is male. Immediately prior to the exchange below, 'changes' and other chatters on 'chatlounge' have been discussing occasions when men have tried to chat in the 'ladiesonly' channel. Werner then makes a first contribution to the discussion.

Extract 8.7

[12:00:30 a.m.:] werner: i love the ladies, it's so harmlessly hot.
[12:00:57 a.m.:] changes: hm ... you seem to be totally a lady ... smile
[12:01:06 a.m.:] werner: i'm there every day, the experiences are incredible

(Rellstab, 2007, p. 772)

Here, 'werner's' claim to be a regular chatter in the 'ladiesonly' channel meets with some scepticism from 'changes' in her response to the posting. We have already seen how speech particles can be used ironically, to mimic uncertainty where there is none. Here, 'changes'' use of 'hm' together with her final description 'smile' suggest that she is unconvinced by 'werner's' claim. Following this exchange and some further chat, 'changes' and 'werner' both move to the 'ladiesonly' channel. This move can be seen by all chatters then using the channel, and leads to some problems for 'werner' given the choice of user name.

Extract 8.8

[12:10:15 a.m.:] werner: ohh!!
[12:10:37 a.m.:] changes: werner, your nick is probably not so ideal..
[12:10:57 a.m.:] changes: how about rosi?

(Rellstab, 2007, p. 774)

As 'changes' comments, the name 'werner' is unlikely to be well received by chatters on 'ladiesonly'. Shortly after this exchange, 'werner' is kicked off the channel by another user, 'cati'. On re-entering 'ladiesonly' werner announces a change of name.

Extract 8.9

[12:16:14 a.m.:] ***: werner is now known as werner_f.

(Rellstab, 2007, p. 774)

However, as the chat in 'ladiesonly' progresses, it quickly becomes apparent that 'werner' does not seek to claim that this apparent switch of gender is authentic, as we see below.

Extract 8.10

[12:18:30 a.m.:] werner_f: wow what this_f provoked hey!!
[12:18:40 a.m.:] changes: hm, werner?
[12:18:48 a.m.:] werner_f: i am a coveted man!!
[12:18:57 a.m.:] cleopatra7: yeye changes, and honestly, 4 opened windows are enough, I don't need a 5th, gg
[12:18:58 a.m.:] werner_f::-(unfortunately only by men
[12:19:19 a.m.:] changes: smile cleo, rather you than me
[12:19:24 a.m.:] werner_f: i am compassionate with you cleopatra 7
[12:19:34 a.m.:] changes: grins werner.
[12:19:41 a.m.:] werner_f: but it is flattering isn't it:-))

(Rellstab, 2007, p. 775)

Following the initial expression of surprise, 'werner_f's' subsequent turns reflect a range of possibilities of gender and sexuality. The postings above in turn make available highly diverging identities of being male (notwithstanding the change of chat name), being homosexual, and being heterosexual. These postings point to ambiguity in identity and suggest that 'werner_f' is happy to play with the identity possibilities now available in 'ladiesonly'. Werner_f's next two turns, however, indicate that he (or she) has had enough of playing with different identities and is leaving the chatroom.

Extract 8.11

[12:21:19 a.m.:] werner_f: so but now I am leaving, it's getting uncanny … I am
    getting uncannily/incredibly fucked here
[12:21:43 a.m.:] ***: werner_f is now known as werner.

(Rellstab, 2007, p. 775)

As Rellstab observes, these and similar exchanges seen in other IRCs, all point to ways in which identity attributes of gender and sexuality are potentially available for reworking within the virtual world of internet relay chat. What is perhaps most interesting, however, is that all attempts at reworking identities are clearly **marked** as attempts and are recognized as such by other chatters. On the conclusion of these attempts, prevailing understandings again come into play and the IRC exchanges take on more familiar patterns.

> **Marked** a feature of an utterance, designed to draw the hearer's attention in some way.

Findings such as these suggest that virtual contexts can indeed make available possibilities for experimenting with different versions of the self. In these cases, however, identity experiments are easily recognizable as attempts rather than as plausible new versions of identity. Playing with identities of course is one thing; gaining acceptance as being the identity that is claimed is another.

Doing authenticity

Over time the interactions that occur in any context can become patterned, leading to the establishment of shared meanings of those who participate in the ongoing context. In this, virtual contexts are no exception: the interactions and discussions on web sites can be just as complex and coherent as those that occur in face-to-face settings (Stromer-Galley and Martinson, 2009; von Münchow and Rakotonoelina, 2010). These ongoing patterns of interaction can lead to web sites taking on their own identities for those involved. Commonly in their postings to a web site, users display to each other their shared understandings of that web site, for example treating it not just as a medium of communication but as a particular place for interaction (Goodings, Locke and Brown, 2009). Interactions such as these lead to the development of **online communities** in which users make sense of themselves and those with whom they interact in relation to that place.

> **Online community** a group of users who make sense of themselves in terms of shared understandings, such as attributions of spatial organization, that are associated with a particular web site.

The meanings located within online communities, moreover, have implications not just for established members of a community but also for newcomers who might wish to join that community. In order to gain acceptance, a newcomer will have to demonstrate to other users that he or she has the attributes that are understood as relevant to the community. One example of such identity negotiations comes from a study by Marisol Del-Teso-Craviotto (2008) of gender and sexual identities in chatrooms. Within these particular chatrooms, newcomers have to demonstrate to other users that they are authentic participants who are entitled to engage in the ongoing discussions. Three overarching attributes of identity in these contexts, as Del-Teso-Craviotto observes, are age, gender and sexuality, and it is to these elements of identities that newcomers orient in their postings. One way for them to do so is by making quickly available to other users details of age, sex and location. Below we see an extract containing postings from a chatroom designated as 'Thirties Love'.

Extract 8.12

Infilm919:	< 34/m/Virginia/pic
	'34, male, Virginia, picture'
SmrtMenComeHithr:	How are ya?
SingleMDgrl:	33/f/Maryland
	'33, female, Maryland'

(Del-Teso-Craviotto, 2008, p. 257)

As in the examples above, the initial postings of many newcomers adopted a formulaic form to identify themselves as candidate participants in the ongoing chat. Other users made information relating to age, gender or sexuality available even more quickly, choosing user names that reflect the relevant attributes, such as 'MALE4SALE30, LVNVCowboy, Diamondboy02, sirenita1 "mermaid 1", ELHO-MBRE157 "the man 157", MsGaPeach35 "Ms Georgia Peach35", TiO18Mad, [or] "guy 18 Madrid"' (Del-Teso-Craviotto, 2008, pp. 257–258). Often, however, contributors sought to establish their online credentials by describing themselves in more emphasized ways, as seen in the extract below taken from the 'Lesbian 30s' chatroom.

Extract 8.13

HOTAZHEAT88:	COME HERE I GOT TITS (@) (@)
. . .	
Xboigyrlx2227:	OOOOOOO NICE AND PERKY AND FIRM
Da1nonlyteas:	my god look at the size of Hots nips
. . .	
Xboigyrlx2227:	SEND THEM THIS WAY

(Del-Teso-Craviotto, 2008, p. 258)

In Extract 8.13, the user name adopted, the symbols used to reflect physical attributes and the use of uppercase letters all work to warrant the identity of the initial contributor. We see subsequent contributors taking up this posting as reflecting an authentic identity and responding in relevant terms. At the same time, however, descriptions such as this can be seen to draw upon widely available understandings of gender and there were few attempts across the chatrooms to subvert or rework identities that prevail in other contexts. For newcomers to the chatrooms, however, the construction of identities in recognizable social terms proved to be an advantage. As Del-Teso-Craviotto (2008) notes, by describing themselves in terms consistent with broader understandings of identities, newcomers came to be treated as authentic participants who were entitled to take part in the chatrooms.

Authenticity of identity, then, is a discursive accomplishment. In this, virtual contexts are little different from face-to-face ones in which participants seek to display the attributes that are associated with being an identity and not just knowing about it (see e.g. Widdicombe and Wooffitt, 1995). Virtual contexts, however, offer greater scope for doing authenticity than do face-to-face settings, in that there usually is no visual information that can be inspected for consistency with the identity being proposed. Consider the following extract that comes from a study by Miriam Locher and Sebastian Hoffman (2006) of interactions on an internet advice column that provides health advice to students in an American university. Below we see one response given by the advice-giver, 'Lucy' to a question seeking guidance in relation to panic attacks experienced by the questioner's partner.

Extract 8.14

Panic attacks are periods of heightened anxiety often coupled with an extreme fear of being in crowded or closed places . . . Accompanying symptoms include a sense of chest pain, shallow breathing, lightheadedness, dizziness, sweating, a pounding heart, chills or flushes, nausea, and even tingling or numbness in the hands . . . Panic attacks are common, frequently linked to feelings of loss. . . . While your support may be comforting to your partner, it would be wise for her to get professional counseling, especially since her panic is affecting your relationship . . .

Lucy

(Locher and Hoffman, 2006)

The question that led to this response was presented in a commonly recurring format that included some background context, formulated the query as a problem, and sought advice in relation to the health problem as described. 'Lucy's' response that we see above provides general information, describing how the problem is caused, gives a summary of symptoms, and sets out patterns of occurrence. The response concludes by advising what intervention would be appropriate for the person experiencing the problem, the partner of the questioner. We might note also how the response is framed. The response addresses the questioner in the second person 'you', personalizing the advice that is provided. The advice-giver, however, does not adopt the first person pronoun but instead frames the response throughout in the third person. All statements are presented in objective terms and presented as descriptions of established knowledge. Together these elements suggest medical expertise, identifying the advice-giver as someone who can speak authoritatively about the topics being discussed.

What is interesting here, however, is that 'Lucy' does not exist as a person. The advice column under consideration is run by a team of professional health educators, any of whom at different times might respond to questions posted. Responses from any members or members of the team are designed to be received as coming from one person, the fictional 'Lucy', making the web site more personal and user-friendly than might otherwise be the case. Thus, although having no identity other than that found in these sequences, 'Lucy' in this context acquires an authentic identity as someone who is appropriately qualified and knowledgeable to provide the advice that students seek from 'her'.

Illness and Support Groups

One form of online community that has become increasingly common in recent times is that of the support group. Support groups can potentially offer a range of identity benefits that are not as readily available in face-to-face settings. Consider, for example, people who identify themselves as experiencing illnesses for which no objective evidence is available and which rely upon the acceptance of their subjective claims. As we have noted elsewhere, conditions of this sort, such as that of ME (myalgic encephalomyelitis), are commonly contested and those who identify themselves as sufferers often meet with scepticism from health professionals and others. Online groups for those who identify themselves as ME sufferers allow opportunities for them to share their experiences with others who report similar experiences. In these contexts, their reports of illness and attendant identities are more likely to meet with acceptance from other users than with challenge. At the same time, through the negotiation of experience, users can develop community understandings of their condition and use these shared understandings to negotiate identities as genuine sufferers (Guise, Widdicombe and McKinlay, 2007). Alternatively, users of online communities can develop identities that are wholly inconsistent with those that would be ascribed to them in other contexts by medical professionals or by other people. Thus, for example, contributors to a self-injury discussion forum can construct self-injury as positive rather than negative, allowing themselves to identify themselves in positive terms by engaging in this behaviour (McVittie, Goodall and McFarlane, 2009).

Of course, as we have seen, individual communities over time develop their own logics and meanings for members of those communities. Thus, web sites that focus on potentially similar topics can construct illness and identities in highly divergent ways. One example of divergence can be seen in web sites that focus on anorexia nervosa. Many of these web sites are centred on the principle of recovery, consistent with medical practices surrounding the condition, and therefore look to promote users' efforts to recover from anorexia nervosa. Other web sites, by contrast, take the form of 'pro-ana' web sites that promote anorexia nervosa as a valued form of identity and encourage users' descriptions of actions that maintain the condition, for instance in providing tips on how to hide the condition from family or friends. Sarah Riley and colleagues (Riley, Rodham and Gavin, 2009) note that the topics of discussion found on recovery and pro-ana web sites are remarkably similar, with users in each case describing themselves, their actions and their experiences. The differences between these two forms of online community lie not in the topics of discussion but in the forms that the users' descriptions take. Below we see an example from each form of web site of a description of body size.

Extract 8.15

I weigh 114 right now, at 50400, and I want to weigh 104 or something like that ... I'm actually proud of myself because I've gotten down to the bottom weight for my height on the FDA chart (Extract 1, Pro-Ana).

Physically wise my mom is pushing for me to gain back my muscle mass (apparently I have lost quite a bit) and some lbs. this seems bizarre to me. I am working on eating more and better. My blood pressure seems to be much more stable, I am not orthostatic now, meaning when I stand up I don't feel like passing out. Yay! (Extract 2, Recovery).

(Riley, Rodham and Gavin, 2009, p. 353)

Differences can be seen also in the users' descriptions of their actions with the body:

Extract 8.16

the last three or four months have seen me sliding backwards ... Fortunately I still eat pretty well. I am an athlete and I enjoy working out so much, so that keeps me eating. But then I started binging ... All these foods I had denied myself for so long. (Extract 4, Recovery)

Have been eating like hell today again and feel crap. While I was planning to fast again today. I had a very nice chocolate chip cookie and after that THREE sandwiches of at least 150 cals each!!!! I drank loads of water with it, but I still couldn't purge!!! I feel so bad!!!!! I am going to try to get it out again ... (Extract 6, Pro-Ana)

(Riley, Rodham and Gavin, 2009, pp. 354–355)

And again in users' descriptions of their experiences:

Extract 8.17

Thing is iv been really tired and if I go for a little walk then I feel really faint. Iv always thought that as I havnt fainted for awhile now that im ok (Extract 8, Recovery).

My hair is starting to thin out A LOT!! Its really scarey!! Has this happened to anyone else?? Any advice on how to stop this? Im so tempted to go buy that Rogain for Women shampoo!! LoL!!! (Extract 9, Pro-Ana).

(Riley, Rodham and Gavin, 2009, pp. 355–356)

As we see in the three sets of extracts above, users' postings to the recovery web sites and the pro-ana web sites diverge markedly in the content of the descriptions that they give of themselves, what they do and what they experience. Most noticeably, the differences lie in how they evaluate these various elements and what is constructed as positive in terms of their own identities. It is this divergence in preferred forms of self, actions and experiences and the ways in which the users evaluate their own versions that mark out as relevant the identity of being on the road to recovery on the one hand, and the identity of being pro-anorexic on the other hand.

Moreover these preferred forms of identities and the established logics of the online communities in each case have consequences for others who might seek to take part in discussions as new users of a particular web site. For example, newcomers to web sites that orient to recovery from anorexia nervosa will be expected in their postings to present identities that are consistent with the accepted aims of the community. A newcomer might well initially be welcomed but will thereafter be expected to claim an intention to recover. Any postings that suggest uncertainty as to the meaning of anorexia nervosa, or that potentially evaluate the condition positively, will meet with resistance and possibly rejection from other users (Stommel and Koole, 2010).

One part, then, of joining an online support group is to identify oneself in a way that is consistent with the identities of other group members. This in itself, however, might not be sufficient to gain acceptance as a member of the group. For often newcomers have not just to reproduce understandings that are meaningful to the group but also to do so in ways that demonstrate the authenticity of the identity in question. Identity work of this sort requires individuals to display that they live the identity that is claimed and have not simply gained knowledge about that identity. In a study of an internet forum for 'suicidal thoughts', Judith Horne and Sally Wiggins (Horne and Wiggins, 2009) show that forum users display their authenticity as people who have suicidal thoughts through the ways in which they post to the forum. Below we see one example, by way of a posting from Caroline and the response that it receives from Martina.

Extract 8.18

1   Caroline, Posts: 628; 12:03 p.m.
2   Almost did it yesterday. Will do it today. Have nothing left keeping me here.
3   It's worse than its ever been and those i love have abandoned. Its not worth
4   it anymore. i'll miss you. i'll always love you.
5   this is somebody's fault.

(Horne and Wiggins, 2009, p. 176)

Extract 8.19

1   Martina, Posts: 1313; 12:54pm
2   (((((Caroline)))))NO hon – hang on! It will get better. We love
3   you and don't want to see you go … we need you hon! Please get some
4   help, please!
5   Its someone's fault you say – write it out here. Let 'er loose –
6   maybe we can help.
7   Take care of yourself please hon – I don't want to see you
8   hurting this badly.
9   (((((((((hugs)))))))))))

(Horne and Wiggins, 2009, p. 177)

What we see in Caroline's posting is a narrative of her experiences and a description of these experiences as comprising a state of being that goes beyond depression. The description is built up with a series of extreme case formulations that emphasize the extent of the problems that Caroline is experiencing and suggests that she is on the verge of committing suicide. Suicide is thereby presented as potentially being a rational response to her situation. The ending, however, that 'this is somebody's fault' opens the possibility for responses. What perhaps is particularly noteworthy here is that Caroline does not express any need for help or support. This posting received a number of responses in the forum, one of which we see from Martina. We see Martina, in responding, take up the issue made relevant by Caroline of someone else being to blame for the circumstances in which Caroline finds herself and using this to frame her response. The response, through the use of expressive symbols, emphasizes Martina's wish to help Caroline and can be treated as a strong expression of support. This posting and response can be contrasted with another posting made to the web site, seen in the extract below.

Extract 8.20

1   Christine, Posts: 3; 12:06am
2   My story is as follows: I'm an 18 year old female who suffers
3   from depression, cutting (self-injury), social anxiety disorder,
4   obsessive compulsive disorder, extreme stress, and insomnia. [7
5   sentences missing] Please write back if you can at least share
6   your experience or relate. Thanks!

(Horne and Wiggins, 2009, p. 181)

Like Caroline's posting seen above, this posting by Christine opens with a description of her problems. Here, however, the manner in which Christine lists these problems suggests a medical rather than personal basis for the descriptions and suggests that she has researched the problems rather than having experienced them. Nor does the posting convey any particular sense of urgency. All of these elements lead to a failure to communicate an authentic identity of being suicidal. Unlike Caroline's posting above, Christine here does explicitly seek help. She does so, however, in a manner that trivializes the identities of other members of the forum in suggesting that they are there for reasons other than feeling suicidal. Thus, Christine's descriptions fail to identify her as authentically suicidal and also trouble the identities of other users. Perhaps unsurprisingly, Christine received no responses to her posting on this forum.

Identity Challenges

Many of us who use email on a regular basis will be all too familiar with receiving unsolicited emails from senders with whom we have had no previous contact. Of such emails, a considerable number attempt to engage our interest in products that the senders wish to advertise or sell and we respond to these, ignore them or delete them as we choose. Other unexpected emails, however, take a rather different form. Imagine that you log on to your email account one day to learn that, as an outcome of a prize draw of which you were previously unaware, you have been selected to be the lucky recipient of a vast sum of money. For you to receive this amount, all that you are required to do is to provide the necessary identity details to allow payment to be made to you. Or, alternatively, you receive what is framed as a heartfelt request from an unfortunate individual living overseas who desperately requires your help. All that this help involves is your assistance in transferring a considerable sum of money from the sender's country to yours and you will be handsomely rewarded for providing this assistance. Again, all that is needed for this to happen is for you to provide some details of yourself and your bank. Some examples of such emails can be seen below.

Extract 8.21

From: Mrs.Kate Watters < mrskate_watters11@yahoo.com >
Reply-To: barrali_ibrahim56@yahoo.com.hk
Sent: Wednesday, February 28, 2007 9:39 PM
To: undisclosed-recipients:
Subject: Your E-Mail Address Have Won $600,000.00
GLOBAL ONLINE SWEEPSTAKE LOTTERY,
Hochstr.76 -56112
Lahnstein, Germany.
WINNING NOTIFICATION

We happily announce to you the draw of the Global Online Sweetstake Lottery International programs held on the 27th of February 2007 in Amsterdam Holland. Your e-mail address attached to ticket number: 564 75600545–188 with serial number 5388/02 drew the lucky numbers: 31-6-26-13-35-7,which subsequently won you the lottery in the 2nd category.

You have therefore been approved to claim a total sum of $600,000.00(Six hundred Thousand United States Dollars) in cash credited to file RPC/9080118308/04 made available from a total cash prize of US $11 Million dollars, shared amongst the first SIX (6) lucky winners in this category. All participants were selected randomly from world wide web sites through a computer drawn system and extracted from over 100,000 companies. This promotion takes place annually.

Please note that your lucky winning number falls within our Africabooklet representative in Abuja Nigeria as indicated in your play coupon, In view of this, your $600,000.00 (Six hundred Thousand Dollars)would be released to you by our affiliate bank in Abuja Nigeria as soon as you establish contact, Please be warned. To file for your claim, please contact by email first our fiduciary agent: Barrister Ali Ibrahim, Abuja Nigeria, Email Address is: (barrali_ibrahim56@yahoo.com.hk)

Telephone numbers:+2348027447360.

To avoid unnecessary delays and complications, you are to contact the fiduciary agent in Nigeria with the followings details above. Your full names, contact address, age, private telephone/fax number and occupation. Quote your Ticket number reference/batch numbers in any correspondences with us or our designated agent.

Faithfully,
Mrs Kate Watters
GLOBAL SWEEPSTAKE LOTTERY.
      (from http://www.consumerfraudreporting.org/lotteryscam_Global.php)

Extract 8.22

From: suzanavy@web-mail.com.ar
Subject: LOOKING FORWARD TO HEARING FROM YOU URGENTLY
Date: February 23, 2005 6:20:37 AM PST
MRS.SUZANA NUHAN VAYE
%BARR.OMENKA.P. WILLIAMS
TEL/FAX:27–11–507–6559
EMAIL:omenwilliams@web-mail.com.ar
ATTN: MD/CEO

Kindly accept my apology for sending my mail to you. I Am a true God fearing person, and I want you to trust me and help me out in this my condition. I believe you are a highly respected personality, considering the fact that I sourced your profile from a human resource profile database on your country in the Internet.

Though, I do not know to what extent you are familiar with events and fragile political situation in Liberia but it has formed consistent headlines in the CNN, BBC news bulletins.

My Name is MRS.SUZANA NUHAN VAYE from Liberia, a Country in West Africa. My late Husband is Issac Nuhan Vaye, Deputy Minister of Public Works in Liberia. My Husband was falsely accused of plotting to remove the then PRESIDENT OF LIBERIA CHARLES TAYLOR) from office. Without trial, Charles Taylor killed him. You can verify this from some of the international newspapers posted in the web sites below:

(i) http://www.usatoday.com/news/world/2003–07–15-liberia_x.htm
(ii) http://www.unwire.org/UNWire/20030716/449_66 21.asp

Before my husband was killed, he moved out the sum of $21.5 million and large quantities of Diamonds through a diplomatic means, and deposited it with a Security Company Abroad.

All that is needed is for my lawyer to instruct the company to transfer the funds/ diamonds to your account, I will remunerate you with 20% at the end, but most of all is that I solicit your trust in this transaction. I have been confined only to our country home and all my calls are monitored, So I will advise you contact my private Attorney on his contact stated below for onward proceedings: -

NAME:BARR.OMENKA.P. WILLIAMS (ATTORNEY)
TEL/FAX:27–11–507–6559
EMAIL:omenwilliams@web-mail.com.ar

Kindly include your Full Name, Private Telephone and Fax Numbers where you can always be reached, your Residential or Company Address to enable him send detail information/documents that will enable you receive the fund without any problem either now or in future as all modalities as been perfected.

Please your urgent response is needed.
Best Regards.
MRS.SUZANA NUHAN VAYE (WIDOW)
    (from http://www.vaughns-1-pagers.com/internet/nigerian-fraud-emails.htm)

Now, in other circumstances, learning that we are to come into sums of money that often run into millions of pounds might indeed be considered good fortune. Equally, we might be willing and able to assist strangers who approach us for assistance that we can easily provide. In the context of email, however, instances such as these we routinely treat with suspicion and rightly so. For emails that take the forms above, or similar forms, have come to be known as **'419' emails**, '419' being the term for online financial fraud in terms of the penal code of Nigeria where many of these emails originate. Recipients who do respond to '419' emails in the ways that are requested will almost invariably discover later that, not only have the promised sums of money failed to materialize, but also that any monies lying in the accounts for which they provided personal details have quickly disappeared and cannot be recovered.

'419' emails emails that attempt to commit financial fraud by eliciting the bank details of the recipient in response to inauthentic announcements of lottery successes or requests for assistance.

Most people who receive '419' emails, however, are wary of what is proposed by these senders and do not respond to requests of this sort. It is interesting, therefore, to consider more precisely what it is about these emails that leads us to treat with suspicion the identities that they propose. As Blommaert (2005) points out, the senders appear to be familiar with sophisticated computer technologies and with the use of the English language as a marker of particular identities in a global context. Often, however, the names given in the emails do not appear consistent with the proposed countries of residence, or the forms of English used do not display appropriate knowledge of what is being described. In addition, '419' emails are commonly framed in very particular discursive ways. Chiluwa (2009) notes that these messages usually include greetings, self-identifications, attempts at confidence-building, narratives and proposed action outcomes. Failure to convince a reader in any of the elements will lead to the message being treated as inauthentic. For example, informal greetings included in formally worded notifications serve to give rise to suspicion, as do narratives that rest on doubtful information that cannot be verified. As a result, the majority of '419' emails simply fail to convince readers of the authenticity of the identities that are claimed.

As Chiluwa (2009) observes, however, '419' emails are designed to be persuasive and minor lapses in detail might not be sufficient to alert all readers to the potential dangers of what appears. Indeed the very persistence of such messages, and media reports of the consequences for unlucky recipients who do respond to them, suggests that these emails can be effective constructions in some instances. It appears unlikely, therefore ,that such messages will disappear entirely in the near future. Thus, '419' emails present identity challenges to all involved as senders and recipients. Those who send such messages still have much discursive work to do if they are to achieve greater acceptance of their identifications than happens at present. For all who receive these unsolicited communications, however, the challenge remains of examining the identities that are available in this and other forms of virtual media and of responding in appropriate ways to the identifications that we encounter now and in the future.

Discussion

In this chapter, we have examined a range of the identity possibilities available in contexts that are made available by various forms of communications technologies. In a number of ways, the more precise forms of technology impact upon the sorts of identity work that individuals can do. Thus, to construct and maintain meaningful identities solely through SMS text messages that are restricted to 160 characters each is likely to require a considerable amount of texting! This perhaps is of little consequence if we use these forms of interaction to continue from or to reflect identities that are negotiated elsewhere. Many virtual contexts, by contrast, open up a wide and diverse range of identity possibilities.

For our part, we can take up these possibilities or at least some of them in ways of our choice, whether in working out identity concerns, playing with different forms of identity or sharing our experiences with others. One thing that we might take from all such work is that although virtual worlds inevitably differ in many respects from face-to-face encounters and other everyday forms of talk, in other ways they differ little, if at all, from these contexts. Issues of working out who we and other people are, the extent to which others share our interests and activities, and the authenticity of the identities that people claim for themselves are all issues that surface in human interaction wherever arising. Given these possibilities and similarities with offline settings, it is perhaps easier to understand how easily any distinction between identities in virtual settings and those in face-to-face settings can become blurred. The identities that individuals negotiate in virtual worlds can be no less meaningful than those they claim in other contexts. Thus, when the identity implications of life in virtual games such as Maple Life, spill over into other interactions, it is perhaps not surprising. By contrast, it perhaps indicates to us just how real and meaningful virtual identities can become, whether in the form of virtual games or in emails from those who claim to bring us good fortune or who seek our assistance. It is all too easy to see how the identities produced in contexts such as these can lead to real-world consequences!

Chapter Summary

Contexts for interactions made available through communications technologies differ from face-to-face contexts in that they are produced by human designers and reflect the understandings of those designers. Social networking web sites, for example, vary in the possibilities that they provide for development of individual profiles and networks.

People who interact using communications technologies often do not use the full range of options that are available. In order to understand virtual identities, we need to examine how individuals make use of the available possibilities. SMS text messaging is often used to begin or continue interactions from face-to-face contexts. Many web sites, including blogs and online groups allow people to work out identity concerns that arise from face-to-face contexts.

Online communities provide opportunities for people to play with different identities. In many instances, however, it is important for users to display authenticity in the identities that they claim, sometimes even when those identities are fictional.

Online support groups develop their own logics and meanings of health and illness. Newcomers to these groups are expected to identify themselves in recognizable ways and to be authentic in their descriptions of experience.

Communications technologies also open up possibilities for individuals to claim fraudulent identities, particularly those found in '419' emails. These emails, however, display features that cast doubt on the authenticity of the sender. The challenge remains for recipients to treat the identities on offer as inauthentic and not to respond in ways proposed by the senders.

Connections

The interactions occurring in virtual contexts frequently include negotiations of gender identities, and potentially attempts to play with gender identities. For a more detailed discussion of gender identities, see Chapter 4.

Health and illness are relevant to many internet contexts, especially web sites that provide health advice, the negotiation of medical expertise and how individuals make sense of health and illness identities within support groups. See Chapter 5 for more detail of these topics.

Issues of how designers make sense of their working practices, the ways in which groups develop their own patterns and meanings, and the difficulties potentially encountered by newcomers to existing groups are all relevant to organizational contexts. For further discussion see Chapter 7.

Further Reading

Chiluwa, I. (2009). The discourse of digital deceptions and '419' emails. *Discourse Studies, 11*, 635–660.

A salutary warning of some of the dangers of electronic forms of communication. Perhaps also some useful guidance on how to spot and avoid them!

Horne, J. and Wiggins, S. (2009). Doing being 'on the edge': Managing the dilemma of being authentically suicidal in an online forum. *Sociology of Health and Illness, 31*, 170–184.

This study provides a useful example of how people seek to gain support from others in online groups and of the contextual importance of being authentic in identity claims.

Rellstab, D. H. (2007). Staging gender online: Gender plays in Swiss internet relay chats. *Discourse and Society, 18*, 765–787.

Some interesting examples of how individuals play with different identities online and of the ways that other users respond to them.

Activity Box

Think of a web site (online group, social networking web site, or other) to which you regularly contribute. To what extent do you understand the identities of other users of that web site? Do you have other forms of interaction with them and, if so, how consistent are the identities online with those in other settings? How do you convince other users of who you are and make sense of this to yourself when not using the web site?

Afterword
Identities and Contexts

In this book, we have examined a range of issues relating to identities and contexts. One way of approaching this text is to treat the topics covered as in effect being split between broad issues of identities and the more detailed concerns of specific contexts. Certainly, the first half of the book does focus on what we might take to be the most common and most dominant ways of identifying people, in terms of national identities, ethnic and religious identities, and gender identities. In contrast to other approaches to identity, we do not treat these identities as being in any way self-evident or available to be 'read off'. Rather, the prevailing occurrence of these identities means all the more that they have to be negotiated across a wide diversity of settings within which people make sense of themselves as they live their daily lives and are to be understood as discursive accomplishments in these settings. The second half of the book is organized around examination of contexts. Here, contexts involving health and illness, the law and legal system, organizations and work, and the virtual worlds made available by technologies, all provide opportunities within which individuals work out who they are in relation to emerging and established practices and understandings. These are but some of the contexts that recur in our lives, albeit perhaps some of the more marked ones.

Yet, as we begin to examine issues of identities on the one hand, and those of contexts on the other hand, it quickly becomes apparent that any attempted distinction between these topics is problematic. Identities that invoke gender, for example, are found across numerous contexts on a recurring basis. But it is not the case that gender *is* gender *is* gender. The meanings of gender identities are somewhat different in discussions of interpersonal relationships than they are in the negotiation of occupational identities or in the virtual worlds of internet relay chatrooms. Claims to ethnic identities that rely upon shared understandings will

Identities in Context: Individuals and Discourse in Action, First Edition. Andrew McKinlay and Chris McVittie.

take on somewhat different meanings in contexts of prejudice and discrimination than they do in contexts of commonality and cultural practices. Conversely, we can see contexts to be bound up with broad issues of identities in all forms. Discussions of health and illness, for example, can include issues that range broadly from gender to morality to agency. In a similar vein, organizational contexts provide for work-based identities but can also make relevant elements of collaborative activities, interpersonal relations, and broad social issues of politics and climate change. The interactions occurring in these and other contexts therefore orient to a diverse range of identity possibilities. Moreover, as we have noted, contexts themselves require to be interpreted. What makes small talk within a doctor's surgery, for instance, part of a health consultation rather than part of a social exchange between acquaintances who have known each other over a period of time? In some cases, contexts might appear to us to be relatively fixed: legal settings are legal settings because they have come to be understood in particular ways and we orient to them as particular forms of interaction. In other cases, however, the ways in which contexts are constructed in certain ways are more immediately evident, such as the meanings that support groups (offline or online) come to have for their users. Sometimes we have to work out who we are in relation to circumstances that are clearly changing, either quickly following a specific event or more slowly in response to social changes that include globalization and climate change. The constant flux of social practices inevitably impacts upon how we make sense of the circumstances within which we find ourselves.

What all of this demonstrates is the inherently problematic quality of attempting to draw any meaningful distinction between identities and contexts. In this book we have used one organizing principle to consider these matters. This principle, however, also falls to be understood in context; the context of a particular book that is oriented to the discussion of social topics in certain ways. Other forms of organizing the materials would be possible. We hope that the version produced here has been of interest to you and has served to highlight many of the issues of identities and contexts in ways that will stimulate further enquiry. For, identities and contexts are the features that come to define our understandings of the world in which we live and interact with others. As we negotiate who we are and who we take other people to be, we are at the very same time making sense of our social worlds and of what goes on within them, in our everyday face-to-face encounters with others, in our dealings with established forms of social practices, or in the virtual realms of the internet. These contexts are what we make them, as we identify ourselves within social worlds.

Glossary

'419' emails   emails that attempt to commit financial fraud by eliciting the bank details of the recipient in response to inauthentic announcements of lottery successes or requests for assistance.

Accountability   responsibility, especially in relation to the speaker's responsibility in providing a particular account.

Acculturation   a process in which the different cultural aspects of two groups are combined, usually indicating a more reciprocal arrangement than that found in integration.

Action orientation   the property of talk which directs it towards accomplishing specific outcomes or goals.

Affiliative stance   a position adopted in which one displays support for someone else.

Agency   the property of being the source or cause of action or events.

Analogy   using the properties of one subject of talk in producing a description of another and thereby indicating some general or abstract similarity.

Apartheid   a political and legal system of social separation based on race.

Asylum-seekers   people seeking to effect international migration by claiming entry into a host country as a result of dangers they face in their home countries.

Attributions   explaining actions and events by ascribing causes to them.

Authority to speak   acceptance that a speaker is suitably qualified to make definitive comments on a topic.

Avatar   an online representation of an individual, taking the form of a visual or textual representation of that individual within an online game, discussion or community.

Banal nationalism   nationalistic talk which relies upon everyday, commonplace forms of expression and which can be contrasted with extreme or overtly xenophobic forms of nationalism.

Blog   a web site or part of a web site associated with an individual, which comprises regular entries describing that individual, and his or her experiences, feelings and actions.

Identities in Context: Individuals and Discourse in Action, First Edition. Andrew McKinlay and Chris McVittie.
© 2011 Andrew McKinlay and Chris McVittie. Published 2011 by Blackwell Publishing Ltd.

Categorization   organizing experience by using terms which denote sorts or kinds of phenomena.

Category incumbent activities   a set of activities that are presented as being normatively related to membership of a specific category.

Code-switching   the use of more than one language in a single discursive episode usually associated with some attempt to mark this switch in language as significant.

Concessions   items of discourse in which someone apparently gives way on a particular point of argument.

Conversation analysis   the collection and analysis of naturally occurring talk emphasizing its sequential properties and the actions performed.

Couple identity   a sense of self that is grounded in a relationship with someone else rather than in oneself as an individual.

Critical discourse analysis   the analysis of discourse with an emphasis on the way it is affected by power and ideology.

Cross-examination   the questioning of witnesses by the lawyer not representing the party who has called the witness.

Cultural specificity   the property that some aspects of social arrangements or normative ways of thinking possess such that these aspects and ways of thinking are unique to a particular culture.

Direct examination   the questioning of witnesses by the lawyer representing the party who has called the witness.

Disavowals   utterances designed to inoculate the speaker against negative inferences.

Disclaimer   a phrase that is designed to prevent hearers from drawing otherwise potentially available inferences.

Discourse analysis   the collection and analysis of verbal material, spoken or written, which emphasizes properties such as structure and variability and focuses on action.

Discourses   extended elements of talk and/or text that represent routinized ways of formulating a broad topic such as masculinity or oppression (see 'repertoires').

Discrimination   unfair behaviour directed at others as a result of prejudice.

Discursive psychology   the use of discursive techniques to analyse talk of psychological states and the application of those analyses to real world settings.

Disempowerment   the removal of the ability to be a competent social actor with agentic status.

Display talk   talk that is designed not only to further an ongoing interaction but to present a particular perspective on what is said to an overhearing audience.

Dispreferred responses   conversational turns, designed as responses to a prior turn, in which what is said is taken to be potentially problematic for the recipient, e.g. turning down a request.

Diversity in employment   the principle of including people from all social groups within the workplace.

Emoticon a symbol included in a message that is intended to display to the recipients the feelings or emotions of the sender.

Empowerment   giving people power to make appropriate decisions about their own lives and experiences.

Evaluation   talk which situates the relevant topic in a comparative frame indicating features such as levels of goodness or worth.

Expert witness   a witness whose testimony is produced on the basis of his or her skills or knowledge.

Expertise   specialized understanding of, and practice within, a particular field of activity.

Extreme case formulation   a discursive construction which uses the strongest version of comparative terms or phrases.

Face   a representation of self that reflects socially approved attributes.

Facework   Goffman's term for the negotiation of matters of face in everyday interactions.

Feminism   the view that men and women should be treated equally.

Flexibility   a property of discourse that allows for similar discursive constructions to be employed for different ends.

Foucauldian discourse analysis   a form of discourse analysis which relies on the work of Foucault and emphasizes the historical and ideological aspects of discourse.

Framing a term deriving initially from Goffman to indicate participants' organization of their experiences into recognizable activities.

Gender-blind   a property of processes such as formal organizational equality policies in which individuals are to be considered while ignoring their gender.

Gender-specific   understood as being relevant only for men or for women.

Genetic modification   the human manipulation of an organism's genetic structure in a way that does not occur naturally, through the transplantation of genetic material from other sources or deletion of existing material.

Globalization   a reference to international processes in which facets of life such as economic prosperity or legal frameworks are said to have taken on characteristics that transcend national boundaries.

Hedging statements   statements that are offered in qualified terms and that do not fully commit the author of the statement to what is being claimed.

Hegemony   a social arrangement in which particular views are treated as being normal or unremarkable, viewed as problematic where such views favour social elites in some way.

Heterosexism   a form of thinking that views heterosexuality as normative.

Hybrid discourse   episodes of talk or text in which different forms or registers of discourse are combined, e.g. the combination of conversational questioning and regulatory references observable in police interrogations.

Hybrid identities   identities that can be viewed as a mixture of more than one nationality or ethnicity.

Hyphenated identities   similar to hybrid identities, these mixed identities are so-called because of the nomenclature, e.g. Spanish-American.

Ideology   an organized set of ideas which typifies the thinking of a group or society.

Idiomatic expressions   commonplace phrases or sayings that are found in everyday language and are difficult to challenge.

Imagined community   a phrase that highlights the way in which political and social entities are perceived by their members as having an underlying sameness even if such similarities are difficult to establish on an objective level.

Immigrants   people who have left their place of origin and have settled in another place, such as those who have left one nation state and settled in another.

Individual pathology   disorder or problem that is treated as located within the individual person.

Institutional norms   sets of expectations or beliefs that are taken to be rules of interaction associated with particular contexts, such as those observable in law courts or other organizational settings, and which differ from expectations associated with everyday conversation.

Integration   a process in which the different cultural aspects of two groups are combined, usually indicating that a minority culture has been subsumed within the majority culture.

Interactional context   the background or setting within which two or more people engage in social action.

Interest   a concern held by someone that is relevant to the discursive actions that are being produced.

Irony   a discursive device in which what is said differs from what is actually meant.

Lay constructions   descriptions or accounts of practices and procedures that do not require expertise, often described as such in a context where professional discourse on the same topic is also available.

Macho identities   masculine identities in which 'traditional' views of men associated with power and control are highlighted.

Macro-analyses   analyses of analytic terms such as 'nationality' that draw upon large-scale features such as economic histories or socio-political developments.

Marginalization   a process in which an individual or group faces social arrangements in which they lack the normal rights and entitlements of others.

Marked   a feature of an utterance, designed to draw the hearer's attention in some way.

Marketization of higher education   framing of higher education, in commercial terms of quality of services, consumer choice and competitiveness instead of learning and teaching.

Mediation   service that aims to resolve disputes where other attempts have failed and intervention by an external agency is necessary.

Membership categories   discursive labels indicating that an individual can be classified as belonging to a particular group.

Membership categorization analysis   analysis of discourse that proceeds by examining the ways in which people are characterized as belonging to particular social groups.

Mentoring   a process whereby junior workers receive guidance from more senior employees on working practices and the development of working identities.

Metaphors   figures of speech used to refer to something not literally identified by means of similarities between it and the thing which is explicitly mentioned.

Minimal response   a conversational turn, produced in response to a prior turn, which is noticeably brief.

Mitigation   the description of extenuating circumstances designed to reduce possible responsibility for otherwise blameworthy actions.

Moral imperative   an obligation to act in certain accepted ways.

Narrative   an episode of talk or text that displays recognizably story-like features.

Narrative analysis   the analysis of talk in terms of its story-like elements.

Narrative expansions   the provision of extended items of talk (or text) in which an initial response is followed by other discourse which is either presented as being relevant to that initial response or is concatenated to it by some discursive device (e.g. the use of terms such as 'on the other hand …').

Nationalism   the view that peoples across the world can be thought of in terms of the nation states to which they belong and that in consequence members of a particular nation state should give due consideration to their own nation's best interests.

Natural language generation   the production by an intelligent system of linguistic output that is designed to resemble human language.

Nature   the influence of innate factors in human behaviour.

New racism   the expression of prejudice in talk or text in a manner which attends to potential inferences of appearing to be prejudiced.

Norm   a standard or rule which applies to human behaviour.

Nurture   the influence of social and environmental factors on human behaviour.

Objective   pertaining to aspects of the world independently of any individual's view or perspective.

Objective evidence   evidence such as measurements or readings that is not treated as dependent upon any individual view.

Office hours   informal meetings that allow students to address questions, solve problems, and discuss matters relevant to their studies with their teachers.

Online community   a group of users who make sense of themselves in terms of shared understandings, such as attributions of spatial organization, that are associated with a particular web site.

Oral argument   within legal contexts, that form of discourse that arises in court in which lawyers present accounts of actions and events through speech rather than by the presentation of written argument.

Orienting   interpreting what is said in a specific way and displaying this interpretation in how one responds.

Patient information leaflets   leaflets issued with medications to provide patients with details of the products and how to use them.

Patient journey   the course of an individual's various experiences of dealing with health professionals in, for example, a hospital.

Performative   a description of particular actions that emphasizes their role-like properties over suggestions that such actions arise from objective or natural causes.

Place-identities   constructions of people in relationship to particular formulations of location.

Positioning   adopting or being placed in a particular role through discursive means with the assumption that what is said will be heard as influenced by this perspective.

Pre-analytic categories   typologies produced by an analyst before the analysis has been performed.

Prejudice   dislike of others who are described as different from oneself, e.g. in terms of category membership.

Primordialism   the reductive view that ethnic categories are grounded in more basic or natural categories.

Rapport   sensitivity to and empathy with a conversational partner.

Reformulation   talk in which a partial or complete word or phrase is followed by a restatement in other words of what was just said.

Reframing   adopting a position in which a particular discursive framework of explanation is challenged.

Repertoires   extended elements of talk and/or text that represent routinized ways of formulating a broad topic such as masculinity or oppression (see 'discourses').

Rhetorical psychology   the application of discursive techniques to the study of persuasive language and, more broadly, the view that talk is inherently argumentative.

Scepticism   the expression of disbelief in a claim or set of claims.

Self-processes   analytically derived descriptions of psychological forms of thought that are directed towards the self.

Sex   the biological distinction between men and women.

Sexism   prejudice against others in respect of their gender.

Situated accomplishments   a term used to describe social actions whose full meaning can only be understood by relating them to their context of production.

Small talk   talk that relates to commonplace topics and which is not directly relevant to the main topic at hand.

SMS (short message service) text messaging   the transmission of short text messages, of up to 160 characters, between users of mobile phones and sometimes between users of mobile phones and users of fixed line phones.

Social constructionism   the view that social phenomena are best understood as the outcome of discursive interaction rather than as extra-discursive phenomena in their own right.

Social networking   the practices through which individual users develop and enter into social relations with others who share their interests and activities.

Stake   an interest in or concern with how what is said is interpreted by hearers.

Subject positions   a social role or standpoint that is made available to the individual as a result of social action being embedded with a large-scale or framing discourse.

Subjective accounts   descriptions provided on the basis of an individual's own view or perspective.

Subjectivities   forms of discourse in which actions and events are described in a way which highlights the partial or interested nature of what is said about them.

Supra-national   a term used to refer to elements of interaction or organizational forms which arise at levels beyond that of the nation state, such as international bodies like the European Union.

Swinging   a practice in which couples exchange partners with one another for sexual reasons.

Talk-in-interaction   discourse which reflects and is constitutive of the local context of a particular social interaction.

Temporal discourse   talk or text which employs referents to time such as historical accounts or descriptions of the future.

The other a term   whose usage has grown in the social scientific domain as a catch-all expression denoting one or more sets of individuals who are classified as not belonging to one's own category.

Troubles telling   talk that is designed to be heard as a report of recent or current difficulties.

Undermining   weakening or countering an argumentative position.

Variability   a property of discourse that allows for different discursive constructions to be employed for similar ends.

Variationism   the view that different categories of people such as men and women produce language that varies categorically.

Women's liberation   a social and political movement begun in the 1960s that strove for equality for women.

References

Aarsand, P. A. (2008). Frame switches and identity performances: Alternating between online and offline. *Text and Talk, 28*, 147–165.

Achugar, M. (2007). Between remembering and forgetting: Uruguayan military discourse about human rights (1976–2004). *Discourse and Society, 18*, 521–547.

Agne, R. R. (2007). Reframing practices in moral conflict: Interaction problems in the negotiation standoff at Waco. *Discourse and Society, 18*, 549–578.

Ainsworth, S. and Hardy, C. (2007). The construction of the older worker: Privilege, paradox and policy. *Discourse and Communication, 1*, 267–285.

Alby, F. and Zucchermaglio, C. (2007). Embodiment at the interface: Materialization practices in Web design. *Research on Language and Social Interaction, 40*, 255–277.

Amer, M. M. (2009). 'Telling-it-like-it-is': The delegitimation of the second Palestinian Intifada in Thomas Friedman's discourse. *Discourse and Society, 20*, 5–31.

Anderson, B. (1983). *Imagined Communities: Reflections on the Origin and Spread of Nationalism.* London: Verso.

Andersson, M. (2008). Constructing young masculinity: A case study of heroic discourse on violence. *Discourse and Society, 19*, 139–161.

Anspach, W., Coe, K. and Thurlow, C. (2007). The other closet? Atheists, homosexuals and the lateral appropriation of discursive capital. *Critical Discourse Studies, 4*, 95–119.

Antaki, C. (2007). Mental-health practitioners' use of idiomatic expressions in summarising clients' accounts. *Journal of Pragmatics, 39*, 527–541.

Antaki, C., Finlay, W. M. L. and Walton, C. (2007). The staff are your friends: Intellectually disabled identities in official discourse and interactional practice. *British Journal of Social Psychology, 46*, 1–18.

Antaki, C., Walton, C. and Finlay, W. M. L. (2007). How proposing an activity to a person with an intellectual disability can imply a limited identity. *Discourse and Society, 18*, 393–410.

Ashcraft, K. L. (2007). Appreciating the 'work' of discourse: Occupational identity and difference as organizing mechanisms in the case of commercial airline pilots. *Discourse and Communication, 1*, 9–36.

Identities in Context: Individuals and Discourse in Action, First Edition. Andrew McKinlay and Chris McVittie.

Askehave, I. (2007). The impact of marketization on higher education genres – the international student prospectus as a case in point. *Discourse Studies, 9,* 723–742.

Atton, C. (2006). Far-right media on the internet: culture, discourse and power. *New Media and Society, 8,* 573–587.

Augoustinos, M. and Every, D. (2007). The language of 'race' and prejudice – a discourse of denial, reason and liberal-practical politics. *Journal of Language and Social Psychology, 26,* 123–141.

Bamberg, M., De Fina, A. and Schiffrin, D. (2007). Introduction. In M.Bamberg, A. De Fina and D. Schiffrin (Eds.), *Selves and identities in narrative and discourse* (pp. 1–8). Amsterdam: John Bejamins.

Banks, M. (1996). *Ethnicity: Anthropological Constructions.* London: Routledge.

Barnes, R. (2007). Formulations and the facilitation of common agreement in meetings talk. *Text and Talk, 27,* 273–296.

Bartesaghi, M. (2009). Conversation and psychotherapy: How questioning reveals institutional answers. *Discourse Studies, 11,* 153–177.

Barth, F. (1969). Introduction. In F. Barth (Ed.), *Ethnic Groups and Boundaries* (pp. 9–37). London: Allen & Unwin.

Baruh, L. and Popescu, M. (2008). Guiding metaphors of nationalism: The Cyprus issue and the construction of Turkish national identity in online discussions. *Discourse and Communication, 2,* 79–96.

Belanger, E. and Verkuyten, M. (2010). Hyphenated identities and acculturation: Second-generation Chinese of Canada and the Netherlands. *Identity, 10,* 141–163.

Bercelli, F., Rossano, F. and Viaro, M. (2008). Different place, different action: Clients' personal narratives in psychotherapy. *Text and Talk, 28,* 283–305.

Bilic, B. and Georgaca, E. (2007). Representations of 'mental illness' in Serbian Newspapers: A critical discourse analysis. *Qualitative Research in Psychology, 4,* 167–186.

Billig, M. (1987). *Arguing and Thinking: A Rhetorical Approach to Social Psychology.* Cambridge: Cambridge University Press.

Billig, M. (1995). *Banal Nationalism.* London: Sage.

Blackledge, A. (2006). The racialization of language in British political discourse. *Critical Discourse Studies, 3,* 61–79.

Blommaert, J. (2005). Making millions: English, indexicality and fraud. *Working Papers in Urban Language and Literacies, 29,* 1–24.

Bowskill, M., Lyons, E. and Coyle, A. (2007). The rhetoric of acculturation: When integration means assimilation. *British Journal of Social Psychology, 46,* 793–813.

Branaman, A. (1997). Goffman's social theory. In C. Lemert and A. Branaman (Eds.), *The Goffman Reader* (pp. xlv–lxxii). Oxford: Blackwell.

Brenner, A. (2009). Speaking of 'respect for women': Gender and politics in U.S. foreign policy discourse, 2001–2004. *Journal of International Women's Studies, 10,* 18–32.

Brooks, S. (2009). Radio food disorder: The conversational constitution of eating disorders in radio phone-ins. *Journal of Community and Applied Social Psychology, 19,* 360–373.

Brown, P. and Levinson, S. C. (1987). *Universals in Language Usage: Politeness Phenomena.* Cambridge: Cambridge University Press.

Burdsey, D. (2007). Role with the punches: The construction and representation of Amir Khan as a role model for multiethnic Britain. *Sociological Review, 55,* 611–631.

Burman, E. and Parker, I. (1993). Introduction – discourse analysis: The turn to the text. In E. Burman and I. Parker (Eds.), *Discourse Analytic Research: Repertoires and Readings of Texts in Action* (pp. 1–13). London: Routledge.

Buttny, R. (2004). *Talking Problems: Studies of Discursive Construction*. Albany: State University of New York Press.

Buttny, R. and Ellis, D. G. (2007). Accounts of violence from Arabs and Israelis on night-line. *Discourse and Society, 18*, 139–161.

Campbell, S. and Roberts, C. (2007). Migration, ethnicity and competing discourses in the job interview: Synthesizing the institutional and personal. *Discourse and Society, 18*, 243–271.

Capdevila, R. and Callaghan, J. E. M. (2008). 'It's not racist. It's common sense': A critical analysis of political discourse around asylum and immigration in the UK. *Journal of Community and Applied Social Psychology, 18*, 1–16.

Carless, D. (2008). Narrative, identity and recovery from serious mental illness: A life history of a runner. *Qualitative Research in Psychology, 5*, 233–248.

Cashman, H. R. (2005). Identities at play: Language preference and group membership in bilingual talk in interaction. *Journal of Pragmatics, 37*, 301–315.

Chang, G. C. and Mehan, H. B. (2006). Discourse in a religious mode: The Bush adminis-tration's discourse in the war on terrorism and its challenges. *Pragmatics, 16*, 1–23.

Chatwin, J. (2008). Pre-empting 'trouble' in the homoeopathic consultation. *Journal of Pragmatics, 40*, 244–256.

Cheung, M. (2008). 'Click here': The impact of new media on the encoding of persuasive messages in direct marketing. *Discourse Studies, 10*, 161–189.

Chiles, T. (2007). The construction of an identity as 'mentor' in white collar and academic workplaces: A preliminary analysis. *Journal of Pragmatics, 39*, 730–741.

Chiluwa, I. (2008). Religious vehicle stickers in Nigeria: A discourse of identity, faith and social vision. *Discourse and Communication, 2*, 371–387.

Chiluwa, I. (2009). The discourse of digital deceptions and '419' emails. *Discourse Studies, 11*, 635–660.

Coates, J. (1996). *Women Talk*. Oxford: Blackwell.

Condor, S. (2000). Pride and prejudice: Identity management in English people's talk about 'this country'. *Discourse Studies, 11*, 175–205.

Condor, S. (2006a). Public prejudice as collaborative accomplishment: Towards a dialogic social psychology of racism. *Journal of Community and Applied Social Psychology, 16*, 1–18.

Condor, S. (2006b). Temporality and collectivity: Diversity, history and the rhetorical con-struction of national entitativity. *British Journal of Social Psychology, 45*, 657–682.

Croghan, R. and Miell, D. (1998). Strategies of resistance: 'Bad' mothers dispute the evi-dence. *Feminism and Psychology, 8*, 445–465.

Cromdal, J., Osvaldsson, K. and Persson-Thunqvist, D. (2008). Context that matters: Producing 'thick-enough descriptions' in initial emergency reports. *Journal of Pragmatics, 40*, 927–959.

Curl, T. S. and Drew, P. (2008). Contingency and action: A comparison of two forms of requesting. *Research on Language and Social Interaction, 41*, 129–153.

Daiute, C. and Lightfoot, C. G. (2003). *Narrative Analysis: Studying the Development of Individuals in Society*. London: Sage.

Das, R. (2008). Nation, gender and representations of (in)securities in Indian politics: Secular-modernity and Hindutva ideology. *European Journal of Women's Studies, 15*, 203–221.

de Cillia, R., Reisigl, M. and Wodak, R. (1999). The discursive construction of national identities. *Discourse Studies, 10,* 149–173.

de Visser, R. and McDonald, D. (2007). Swings and roundabouts: Management of jealousy in heterosexual 'swinging' couples. *British Journal of Social Psychology, 46,* 459–476.

Del-Teso-Craviotto, M. (2008). Gender and sexual identity authentication in language use: The case of chat rooms. *Discourse Studies, 10,* 251–270.

Dixon, J. and Durrheim, K. (2000). Displacing place-identity: A discursive approach to locating self and other. *British Journal of Social Psychology, 39,* 27–44.

Dixon, J. and Durrheim, K. (2004). Dislocating identity: Desegregation and the transformation of place. *Journal of Environmental Psychology, 24,* 455–473.

Durkheim, E. (1912). *The Elementary Forms of Religious Life.* New York: The Free Press.

Eckert, P. and McConnell-Ginet, S. (2003). *Language and Gender.* Cambridge: Cambridge University Press.

Edley, N. and Wetherell, M. (1999). Imagined futures: Young men's talk about fatherhood and domestic life. *British Journal of Social Psychology, 38,* 181–194.

Edwards, D. (1997). *Discourse and Cognition.* London: Sage.

Edwards, D. (2005). Discursive psychology. In K. L. Fitch and R. E. Sanders (Eds.), *Handbook of Language and Social Interaction* (pp. 257–273). Mahwah, NJ: Lawrence Erlbaum.

Edwards, D. and Potter, J. (2005). Discursive psychology, mental states and descriptions. In H. te Mulder and J. Potter (Eds.), *Conversation and Cognition* (pp. 241–278). Cambridge: Cambridge University Press.

Edwards, D. and Stokoe, E. (2007). Self-help in calls for help with problem neighbors. *Research on Language and Social Interaction, 40,* 9–32.

Ehrlich, S. (2002). Legal institutions, nonspeaking recipiency and participants' orientations. *Discourse and Society, 13,* 731–747.

Emmison, M. and Danby, S. (2007). Troubles announcements and reasons for calling: Initial actions in opening sequences in calls to a national children's helpline. *Research on Language and Social Interaction, 40,* 63–87.

Eriksen, T. (2010). Ethnicity, race and nation. In M. Guibernau and J. Rex (Eds.), *The Ethnicity Reader: Nationalism, Multiculturalism and Migration* (pp. 46–53). Cambridge: Polity Press.

Erikson, E. H. (1968). *Identity: Youth and Crisis.* New York: Norton.

Every, D. and Augoustinos, M. (2007). Constructions of racism in the Australian parliamentary debates on asylum seekers. *Discourse and Society, 18,* 411–436.

Every, D. and Augoustinos, M. (2008a). 'Taking advantage' or fleeing persecution? Opposing accounts of asylum seeking. *Journal of Sociolinguistics, 12,* 648–667.

Every, D. and Augoustinos, M. (2008b). Constructions of Australia in pro- and anti-asylum seeker political discourse. *Nations and Nationalism, 14,* 562–580.

Fairclough, N. L. (1995). *Critical Discourse Analysis: The Critical Study of Language.* Harlow: Longman.

Fasulo, A. and Zucchermaglio, C. (2008). Narratives in the workplace: Facts, fictions and canonicity. *Text and Talk, 28,* 351–376.

Fearon, J. D. and Laitin, D. D. (2000). Violence and the social construction of ethnic identity. *International Organization, 54,* 845–877.

Figgou, L. and Condor, S. (2007). Categorising category labels in interview accounts about the 'Muslim minority' in Greece. *Journal of Ethnic and Migration Studies, 33,* 439–459.

Finlay, W. M. L. (2007). The propaganda of extreme hostility: Denunciation and the regulation of the group. *British Journal of Social Psychology, 46,* 323–341.

Finn, M. and Malson, H. (2008). Speaking of home truth: (Re)productions of dyadic-containment in non-monogamous relationships. *British Journal of Social Psychology, 47*, 519–533.

Flowerdew, J. and Leong, S. (2007). Metaphors in the discursive construction of patriotism: The case of Hong Kong's constitutional reform debate. *Discourse and Society, 18*, 273–294.

Foucault, M. (1980). *Power / Knowledge*. Brighton: Harvester.

Foucault, M. (2002). *The Archaeology of Knowledge*. London: Routledge.

Fozdar, F. (2008). Duelling discourses, shared weapons: Rhetorical techniques used to challenge racist arguments. *Discourse and Society, 19*, 529–547.

Frers, L. (2009). Space, materiality and the contingency of action: A sequential analysis of the patient's file in doctor–patient interactions. *Discourse Studies, 11*, 285–303.

Galatolo, R. and Drew, P. (2006). Narrative expansions as defensive practices in courtroom testimony. *Text and Talk, 26*, 661–698.

Garcia, A. C. (2000). Negotiating negotiation: The collaborative production of resolution in small claims mediation hearings. *Discourse and Society, 11*, 315–343.

Garcia-Gómez, A. G. (2010). Disembodiment and cyberspace: Gendered discourses in female teenagers' personal information disclosure. *Discourse and Society, 21*, 135–160.

Geer, R. and Barnes, A. (2007). Beyond media stickiness and cognitive imprinting: Rethinking creativity in cooperative work and learning with ICTs. *Education and Information Technologies, 12*, 123–136.

Giddens, A. (1991). *Self and Society in the Late Modern Age*. Cambridge: Polity Press.

Giroux, H. A. (1995). National identity and the politics of multiculturalism. *College Literature, 22*, 42–57.

Gnisci, A. and Pontecorvo, C. (2004). The organization of questions and answers in the thematic phases of hostile examination: Turn-by-turn manipulation of meaning. *Journal of Pragmatics, 36*, 965–995.

Goffman, E. (1959). *The Presentation of Self in Everyday Life*. New York: Doubleday.

Goffman, E. (1967). *Interaction Ritual: Essays in Face-to-Face Behavior*. Chicago, IL: Aldine.

Goodings, L., Locke, A. and Brown, S. D. (2009). Social networking technology: Place and identity in mediated communities. *Journal of Community and Applied Social Psychology, 17*, 463–476.

Gough, B. (2006). Try to be healthy, but don't forgo your masculinity: Deconstructing men's health discourse in the media. *Social Science and Medicine, 63*, 2476–2488.

Graham, S. L. (2007). Disagreeing to agree: Conflict, (im)politeness and identity in a computer-mediated community. *Journal of Pragmatics, 39*, 742–759.

Guise, J., McKinlay, A. and Widdicombe, S. (2010). The impact of early stroke on identity: A discourse analytic study. *Health, 14*, 75–90.

Guise, J., McVittie, C. and McKinlay, A. (2010). A discourse analytic study of ME/CFS (Chronic Fatigue Syndrome) sufferers' experiences of interactions with doctors. *Journal of Health Psychology, 15*, 426–435.

Guise, J., Widdicombe, S. and McKinlay, A. (2007). 'What's it like to have ME?' The discursive construction of ME in computer-mediated communication and face-to-face interaction. *Health, 11*, 87–108.

Gumperz, J. J. (1982). *Discourse Strategies*. Cambridge: Cambridge University Press.

Hansen, A. and Machin, D. (2008). Visually branding the environment: Climate change as a marketing opportunity. *Discourse Studies, 10*, 777–794.

Hansen, M. B. M. (2008). On the availability of 'literal' meaning: Evidence from courtroom interaction. *Journal of Pragmatics, 40*, 1392–1410.

Harding, T. (2007). The construction of men who are nurses as gay. *Journal of Advanced Nursing, 60,* 636–644.

Hatipoglu, C. (2007). (Im)politeness, national and professional identities and context: Some evidence from e-mailed 'Call for Papers'. *Journal of Pragmatics, 39,* 760–773.

Heisterkamp, B. L. (2006). Conversational displays of mediator neutrality in a court-based program. *Journal of Pragmatics, 38,* 2051–2064.

Henderson, A., Weaver, C. K. and Cheney, G. (2007). Talking 'facts': Identity and rationality in industry perspectives on genetic modification. *Discourse Studies, 9,* 9–41.

Hepburn, A. and Potter, J. (2007). Crying receipts: Time, empathy and institutional practice. *Research on Language and Social Interaction, 40,* 89–116.

Hepworth, J. (1999). *The Social Construction of Anorexia Nervosa.* London: Sage.

Heritage, J. (1984). *Garfinkel and Ethnomethodology.* Cambridge: Polity Press.

Ho, E. Y. (2006). Behold the power of Qi: The importance of Qi in the discourse of acupuncture. *Research on Language and Social Interaction, 39,* 411–440.

Hobbs, P. (2007a). Extraterritoriality and extralegality: The United States Supreme Court and Guantanamo Bay. *Text and Talk, 27,* 171–200.

Hobbs, P. (2007b). Judges' use of humor as a social corrective. *Journal of Pragmatics, 39,* 50–68.

Hobbs, P. (2007c). Lawyers' use of humor as persuasion. *Humor, 20,* 123–156.

Hobbs, P. (2008). It's not what you say but how you say it: The role of personality and identity in trial success. *Critical Discourse Studies, 5,* 231–248.

Holmes, J. (2007). Monitoring organisational boundaries: Diverse discourse strategies used in gatekeeping. *Journal of Pragmatics, 39,* 1993–2016.

Holmes, J. and Meyerhoff, M. (2003). *The Handbook of Language and Gender (Blackwell Handbooks in Linguistics).* Oxford: Blackwell.

Holmes, J., Schnurr, S. and Marra, M. (2007). Leadership and communication: Discursive evidence of a workplace culture change. *Discourse and Communication, 1,* 433–451.

Horne, J. and Wiggins, S. (2009). Doing being 'on the edge': Managing the dilemma of being authentically suicidal in an online forum. *Sociology of Health and Illness, 31,* 170–184.

Horton-Salway, M. (2007). The 'ME bandwagon' and other labels: Constructing the genuine case in talk about a controversial illness. *British Journal of Social Psychology, 46,* 895–914.

Horton-Salway, M., Montague, J., Wiggins, S. and Seymour-Smith, S. (2008). Mapping the components of the telephone conference: An analysis of tutorial talk at a distance learning institution. *Discourse Studies, 10,* 737–758.

Hougaard, G. R. (2008). Membership categorization in international business phonecalls – the importance of 'being international'. *Journal of Pragmatics, 40,* 307–332.

Hurley, A. L., Sullivan, P. and McCarthy, J. (2007). The construction of self in online support groups for victims of domestic violence. *British Journal of Social Psychology, 46,* 859–874.

Hutchby, I. and Tanna, V. (2008). Aspects of sequential organization in text message exchange. *Discourse and Communication, 2,* 143–164.

Hutchby, I. and Wooffitt, R. (1998). *Conversation Analysis: Principles, Practices and Applications.* Oxford: Polity Press.

Innes, B. (2007). 'Everything happened so quickly?' – HRT intonation in New Zealand courtrooms. *Research on Language and Social Interaction, 40,* 227–254.

James, W. (1890). *The Principles of Psychology – Volume 1*. New York: Holt & Co.

Jaspal, R. and Cinnirella, M. (2010). Coping with potentially incompatible identities: Accounts of religious, ethnic and sexual identities from British Pakistani men who identify as Muslim and gay. *British Journal of Social Psychology, 49*, 1–22.

Jefferson, G. (2004). A note on laughter in 'male-female' interaction. *Discourse Studies, 6,* 117–133.

Jenkings, K. N. and Barber, N. (2006). Same evidence, different meanings: Transformation of textual evidence in hospital new drugs committees. *Text and Talk, 26*, 169–189.

Jingree, T. and Finlay, W. M. L. (2008). 'You can't do it... it's theory rather than practice': Staff use of the practice/principle rhetorical device in talk on empowering people with learning disabilities. *Discourse and Society, 19*, 705–726.

Johnson, A. (2005). Police questioning. In K. Brown (Ed.), *The Encyclopedia of Language and Linguistics* (2nd edn, pp. 661–672). Oxford: Elsevier.

Johnson, A. (2008). 'From where we're sat ...': Negotiating narrative transformation through interaction in police interviews with suspects. *Text and Talk, 28*, 327–349.

Johnston, A. M. (2008). Co-membership in immigration gatekeeping interviews: Construction, ratification and refutation. *Discourse and Society, 19*, 21–41.

Juan, L. (2009). Intertextuality and national identity: Discourse of national conflicts in daily newspapers in the United States and China. *Discourse and Society, 20*, 85–121.

Kendall, S. (2008). The balancing act: Framing gendered parental identities at dinnertime. *Language in Society, 37*, 539–568.

Kidwell, M. (2009). What happened? An epistemics of before and after in 'at-the-scene' police questioning. *Research on Language and Social Interaction, 42*, 20–41.

Kitzinger, C. (2000). Doing feminist conversation analysis. *Feminism and Psychology, 10,* 163–193.

Kjaer, A. L. and Palsbro, L. (2008). National identity and law in the context of European integration: The case of Denmark. *Discourse and Society, 19*, 599–627.

Kline, S. L. (2005). Interactive media systems: Influence strategies in television home shopping. *Text, 25*, 201–231.

Knorr-Cetina, K. (2007). Global markets as global conversations. *Text and Talk, 27,* 705–734.

Korteweg, A. C. (2008). The Sharia debate in Ontario: Gender, Islam and representations of Muslim women's agency. *Gender and Society, 22*, 434–454.

Kuo, S. H. (2007). Social change and discursive change: Analyzing conversationalization of media discourse in Taiwan. *Discourse Studies, 9*, 743–765.

Kurri, K. and Wahlstrom, J. (2007). Reformulations of agentless talk in psychotherapy. *Text and Talk, 27*, 315–338.

Kuzar, R. (2008). The term return in the Palestinian discourse on the right of return. *Discourse and Society, 19*, 629–644.

Kykyri, V. L., Puutio, R. and Wahlstrom, J. (2007). Calling in a witness: Negotiating and factualizing preferred outcomes in management consultation. *Text and Talk, 27*, 201–224.

Labov, W. (1972). *Language and the Inner City: Studies in the Black English Vernacular*. Oxford: Blackwell.

Lamont, P., Coelho, C. and McKinlay, A. (2009) Explaining the unexplained: Warranting disbelief in the paranormal. *Discourse Studies, 11*, 543–559.

Lange, P. G. (2008). An implicature for um: Signaling relative expertise. *Discourse Studies, 10,* 191–204.

Lawes, R. (1999). Marriage: An analysis of discourse. *British Journal of Social Psychology, 38,* 1–20.

Lazar, M. M. (2005). Politicizing gender in discourse: Feminist critical discourse analysis as political perspective and praxis. In M. M. Lazar (Ed.), *Feminist Critical Discourse Analysis* (pp. 1–30). Basingstoke: Palgrave Macmillan.

Leary, M. R. (2004). Editorial: What is the self? A plea for clarity. *Self and Identity, 3,* 1–3.

Lederer, R. (1996). *Disorder in the Court: Legal Laughs, Court Jests and Just Jokes Culled from the Nation's Justice System.* Vienna, VA: NCRA Press.

Lehtinen, E. (2007). Merging doctor and client knowledge: On doctors' ways of dealing with clients' potentially discrepant information in genetic counseling. *Journal of Pragmatics, 39,* 389–427.

Lesser, J. (1999). *Negotiating National Identity: Immigrants, Minorities and the Struggle for Ethnicity in Brazil.* Durham, NC: Duke University Press.

Leudar, I., Hayes, J., Nekvapil, J. and Baker, J. T. (2008a). Hostility themes in media, community and refugee narratives. *Discourse and Society, 19,* 187–221.

Leudar, I., Sharrock, W., Hayes, J. and Truckle, S. (2008b). Psychotherapy as a 'structured immediacy'. *Journal of Pragmatics, 40,* 863–885.

Licoppe, C. and Dumoulin, L. (2010). The 'curious case' of an unspoken opening speech act: A video-ethnography of the use of video communication in courtroom activities. *Research on Language and Social Interaction, 43,* 211–231.

Lillian, D. L. (2007). A thorn by any other name: Sexist discourse as hate speech. *Discourse and Society, 18,* 719–740.

Limberg, H. (2007). Discourse structure of academic talk in university office hour interactions. *Discourse Studies, 9,* 176–193.

Lindgren, S. (2009). Representing otherness in youth crime discourse: youth robberies and racism in the Swedish Press 1998–2002. *Critical Discourse Studies, 6,* 65–77.

Lipovsky, C. (2008). Constructing affiliation and solidarity in job interviews. *Discourse and Communication, 2,* 411–432.

Lischinsky, A. (2008). Examples as persuasive argument in popular management literature. *Discourse and Communication, 2,* 243–269.

Livingstone, S., Lunt, P. and Miller, L. (2007). Citizens, consumers and the citizen-consumer: articulating the citizen interest in media and communications regulation. *Discourse and Communication, 1,* 63–89.

Locher, M. A. and Hoffmann, S. (2006). The emergence of the identity of a fictional expert advice-giver in an American Internet advice column. *Text and Talk, 26,* 69–106.

Locke, A. (2009). 'Natural versus taught': Competing discourses in antenatal breastfeeding workshops. *Journal of Health Psychology, 14,* 435–446.

Love, K. (2006). APPRAISAL in online discussions of literary texts. *Text and Talk, 26,* 217–244.

Lu, L. W. L. and Ahrens, K. (2008). Ideological influence on BUILDING metaphors in Taiwanese presidential speeches. *Discourse and Society, 19,* 383–408.

Luchjenbroers, J. and Aldridge, M. (2007). Conceptual manipulation by metaphors and frames: Dealing with rape victims in legal discourse. *Text and Talk, 27,* 339–359.

Lynn, N. and Lea, S. (2003). 'A phantom menace and the new Apartheid': The social construction of asylum-seekers in the United Kingdom. *Discourse and Society, 14,* 425–452.

Macaulay, R. K. S. (2005). *Talk that Counts: Age, Gender and Social Class Differences in Gender.* Oxford: Oxford University Press.

Machin, D. and Mayr, A. (2007). Antiracism in the British government's model regional newspaper: The 'talking cure'. *Discourse and Society, 18,* 453–478.

MacMartin, C. (2002). (Un)reasonable doubt? The invocation of children's consent in sexual abuse trial judgments. *Discourse and Society, 13,* 9–40.

Marley, C. (2008). Assuming identities: The workings of intertextual metaphors in a corpus of dating ads. *Journal of Pragmatics, 40,* 559–576.

Marra, M. and Holmes, J. (2008). Constructing ethnicity in New Zealand workplace stories. *Text and Talk, 28,* 397–419.

Martinez, E. G. (2006). The interweaving of talk and text in a French criminal prehearing trial. *Research on Language and Social Interaction, 39,* 229–261.

Martinovski, B. (2006). A framework for the analysis of mitigation in courts: Toward a theory of mitigation. *Journal of Pragmatics, 38,* 2065–2086.

Maseide, P. (2007). Discourses of collaborative medical work. *Text and Talk, 27,* 611–632.

Matoesian, G. M. (1999). The grammaticalization of participant roles in the constitution of expert identity. *Language in Society, 28,* 491–521.

Matoesian, G. M. (2001). *Law and the Language of Identity: Discourse in the William Kennedy Smith Rape Trial.* Oxford: Oxford University Press.

Maynard, D. W. and Hudak, P. L. (2008). Small talk, high stakes: Interactional disattentiveness in the context of prosocial doctor–patient interaction. *Language in Society, 37,* 661–688.

Mazeland, H. and Berenst, J. (2008). Sorting pupils in a report-card meeting: Categorization in a situated activity system. *Text and Talk, 28,* 55–78.

McKinlay, A. and McVittie, C. (2007). Locals, incomers and intra-national migration: Place-identities and a Scottish island. *British Journal of Social Psychology, 46,* 171–190.

McKinlay, A. and McVittie, C. (2008). *Social Psychology and Discourse.* Oxford: Wiley-Blackwell.

McKinlay, A. and McVittie, C. (2011). 'This is jist my life noo': Marriage, children and choice in a Scottish fishing community. *Discourse and Society, 22,* 1–15.

McKinlay, A., Cowan, S., McVittie, C. and Ion, R. (2010a). Student nurses' gender-based accounts of men in nursing. *Procedia: Social and Behavioral Sciences, 5,* 345–349.

McKinlay, A., McVittie, C. and Della Sala, S. (2010). Imaging the future: Does a qualitative analysis add to the picture? *Journal of Neuropsychology, 4,* 1–13.

McKinlay, A., McVittie, C., Reiter, E., Freer, Y., Sykes, C. and Logie, R. (2010b). Design issues for socially intelligent user-interfaces: A qualitative analysis of a data-to-text system for summarizing clinical data. *Methods of Information in Medicine, 49,* 379–387.

McKinlay, A., McVittie, C. and Sambaraju, R. (In press). 'This is ordinary behaviour': Categorization and culpability in Hamas leaders' accounts of the Palestinian / Israeli conflict. *British Journal of Social Psychology.*

McLaren-Hankin, Y. (2007). Conflicting representations in business and media texts: The case of PowderJect Pharmaceuticals plc. *Journal of Pragmatics, 39,* 1088–1104.

McLaren-Hankin, Y. (2008). 'We expect to report on significant progress in our product pipeline in the coming year': Hedging forward-looking statements in corporate press releases. *Discourse Studies, 10,* 635–654.

McManus, J. (2009). The ideology of patient information leaflets: A diachronic study. *Discourse and Communication, 3,* 27–56.

McVittie, C. (2006). Critical health psychology, pluralism and dilemmas: The importance of being critical. *Journal of Health Psychology, 11,* 373–377.

McVittie, C., Cavers, D. and Hepworth, J. (2005). Femininity, mental weakness and difference: Male students account for anorexia nervosa in men. *Sex Roles: A Journal of Research, 53,* 413–418.

McVittie, C. and Goodall, K. (2009). Harry, Paul and the Filipino maid: Racial and sexual abuse in local contexts. *Journal of Health Psychology, 14,* 651–654.

McVittie, C., Goodall, K. and McFarlane, S. (2009). 'Your cuts are just as important as anyone else's': Individuals' online discussions of self-injury. *Health Psychology Update, 18,* 3–7.

McVittie, C., Goodall, K. and McKinlay, A. (2008). Resisting having learning disabilities by managing relative abilities. *British Journal of Learning Disabilities, 36,* 256–262.

McVittie, C., McKinlay, A. and Widdicombe, S. (2003). Committed to (un)equal opportunities: New ageism and the older worker. *British Journal of Social Psychology, 42,* 595–612.

McVittie, C., McKinlay, A. and Widdicombe, S. (2008a). Organizational knowledge and discourse of diversity in employment. *Journal of Organizational Change Management, 21,* 348–366.

McVittie, C., McKinlay, A. and Widdicombe, S. (2008b). Passive and active non-employment: Age, employment and the identities of older non-working people. *Journal of Aging Studies, 22,* 248–255.

McVittie, C. and Tiliopoulos, N. (2007). When 2–3% really matters: The (un)importance of religiosity in psychotherapy. *Mental Health, Religion and Culture, 10,* 515–526.

McVittie, C. and Willock, J. (2006). 'You can't fight windmills': How older men do health, ill-health and masculinities. *Qualitative Health Research, 16,* 788–801.

Mead, G. H. (1913). The social self. *Journal of Philosophy, Psychology and Scientific Methods, 10,* 374–380.

Mele, M. L. and Bello, B. M. (2007). Coaxing and coercion in roadblock encounters on Nigerian highways. *Discourse and Society, 18,* 437–452.

Meyer, M. (2001). Between theory, method and politics: Positioning of the approaches to CDA. In R. Wodak and M. Meyer (Eds.), *Methods of Critical Discourse Analysis.* (pp. 14–31). London: Sage.

Moore, R. J. (2008). When names fail: Referential practice in face-to-face service encounters. *Language in Society, 37,* 385–413.

Ng, S. H. (2007). Language-based discrimination – blatant and subtle forms. *Journal of Language and Social Psychology, 26,* 106–122.

Norris, S. (2007). The micropolitics of personal national and ethnicity identity. *Discourse and Society, 18,* 653–674.

O'Byrne, R., Hansen, S. and Rapley, M. (2008). 'If a girl doesn't say "no"...': Young men, rape and claims of 'insufficient knowledge'. *Journal of Community and Applied Social Psychology, 18,* 168–193.

Osman, H. (2008). Re-branding academic institutions with corporate advertising: A genre perspective. *Discourse and Communication, 2,* 57–77.

Oteiza, T. and Pinto, D. (2008). Agency, responsibility and silence in the construction of contemporary history in Chile and Spain. *Discourse and Society, 19,* 333–358.

Owens, T. (2006). Self and identity. In J. Delamater (Ed.), *Handbook of Social Psychology* (pp. 205–232). New York: Kluwer Academic/Plenum Publishers.

Papacharissi, Z. (2009). The virtual geographies of social networks: A comparative analysis of Facebook, LinkedIn and ASmallWorld. *New Media and Society, 11*, 199–220.

Parker, I. (1992). *Discourse Dynamics: Critical Analysis for Social and Individual Psychology.* London: Routledge.

Pascual, E. (2006). Questions in legal monologues: Fictive interaction as argumentative strategy in a murder trial. *Text and Talk, 26*, 383–402.

Pichler, P. (2007). Talking traditions of marriage – negotiating young British Bangladeshi femininities. *Women's Studies International Forum, 30*, 201–216.

Pond, R. (2008). Protection, manipulation or interference with relationships? Discourse analysis of New Zealand lawyers' talk about supervised access and partner violence. *Journal of Community and Applied Social Psychology, 18*, 458–473.

Potter, J. (1997). Discourse analysis as a way of analysing naturally occurring talk. In D. Silverman (Eds.), *Handbook for Qualitative Research Methods for Psychology and the Social Sciences* (pp. 144–160). London: Sage.

Potter, J. (2003). Discursive psychology: Between method and paradigm. *Discourse and Society, 14*, 783–794.

Potter, J. and Wetherell, M. (1987). *Discourse and Social Psychology: Beyond Attitudes and Behaviour.* London and Thousand Oaks, CA: Sage.

Prego-Vazquez, G. (2007). Frame conflict and social inequality in the workplace: Professional and local discourse struggles in employee / customer interactions. *Discourse and Society, 18*, 295–335.

Pudlinski, C. (2008). Encouraging responses to good news on a peer support line. *Discourse Studies, 10*, 795–812.

Quayle, M. and Durrheim, K. (2008). Producing expertise and achieving attribution in the context of computer support. *British Journal of Social Psychology, 47*, 727–762.

Raymond, G. and Zimmerman, D. H. (2007). Rights and responsibilities in calls for help: The case of the mountain glade fire. *Research on Language and Social Interaction, 40*, 33–61.

Reicher, S. and Hopkins, N. (2001). *Self and Nation: Categorization, Contestation and Mobilization.* London: Sage.

Reisigl, M. and Wodak, R. (2001). *Discourse and Discrimination: Rhetorics of Racism and Anti-Semitism.* London: Routledge.

Rellstab, D. H. (2007). Staging gender online: Gender plays in Swiss internet relay chats. *Discourse and Society, 18*, 765–787.

Reynolds, J. and Wetherell, M. (2003). The discursive climate of singleness: The consequences for women's negotiation of a single identity. *Feminism and Psychology, 13*, 489–510.

Richardson, E. (2007). She was workin like foreal': Critical literacy and discourse practices of African American females in the age of hip hop. *Discourse and Society, 18*, 789–809.

Riley, S., Rodham, K. and Gavin, J. (2009). Doing weight: Pro-ana and recovery identities in cyberspace. *Journal of Community and Applied Social Psychology, 19*, 348–359.

Roca-Cuberes, C. (2008). Membership categorization and professional insanity ascription. *Discourse Studies, 10*, 543–570.

Rosulek, L. F. (2008). Manipulative silence and social representation in the closing arguments of a child sexual abuse case. *Text and Talk, 28*, 529–550.

Ruusuvuori, J. (2007). Managing affect: Integration of empathy and problem-solving in health care encounters. *Discourse Studies, 9*, 597–622.

Ryan, E. B. (2006). Finding a new voice – writing through health adversity. *Journal of Language and Social Psychology, 25,* 423–436.

Saarinen, T. (2008). Persuasive presuppositions in OECD and EU higher education policy documents. *Discourse Studies, 10,* 341–359.

Sacks, H. (1992). *Lectures on Conversation.* Oxford: Blackwell.

Sala, E., Dandy, J. and Rapley, M. (2010). 'Real Italians and Wogs': The discursive construction of Italian identity among first generation Italian immigrants in Western Australia. *Journal of Community and Applied Social Psychology, 20,* 110–124.

Sandfield, A. and Percy, C. (2003). Accounting for single status: Heterosexism and ageism in heterosexual women's talk about marriage. *Feminism and Psychology, 13,* 475–488.

Scheffer, T. (2006). The microformation of criminal defense: On the lawyer's notes, speech production and a field of presence. *Research on Language and Social Interaction, 39,* 303–342.

Schnurr, S., Marra, M. and Holmes, J. (2007). Being (im)polite in New Zealand workplaces: Maori and Pakeha leaders. *Journal of Pragmatics, 39,* 712–729.

Schryer, C. F., Gladkova, O., Spafford, M. M. and Lingard, L. (2007). Co-management in healthcare: negotiating professional boundaries. *Discourse and Communication, 1,* 452–479.

Schubert, S. J., Hansen, S., Dyer, K. R. and Rapley, M. (2009). 'ADHD patient' or 'illicit drug user'? Managing medico-moral membership categories in drug dependence services. *Discourse and Society, 20,* 499–516.

Schuck, A. R. T. and Ward, J. (2008). Dealing with the inevitable: Strategies of self-presentation and meaning construction in the final statements of inmates on Texas death row. *Discourse and Society, 19,* 43–62.

Seymour-Smith, S. (2008). 'Blokes don't like that sort of thing': Men's negotiation of a 'troubled' self-help group identity. *Journal of Health Psychology, 13,* 785–797.

Shaw, R. and Kitzinger, C. (2007). Memory in interaction: An analysis of repeat calls to a home birth helpline. *Research on Language and Social Interaction, 40,* 117–144.

Shepherd, L. J. (2006). Veiled references: Constructions of gender in the Bush Administration discourse on the attacks on Afghanistan post 9/11. *International Feminist Journal of Politics, 8,* 19–41.

Sheriff, M. and Weatherall, A. (2009). A feminist discourse analysis of popular-press accounts of postmaternity. *Feminism and Psychology, 19,* 89–108.

Shin, S. and Milroy, L. (2010). Conversational codeswitching among Korean-English bilingual children. *International Journal of Bilingualism, 4,* 351–383.

Simmons, K. and Lecouteur, A. (2008). Modern racism in the media: Constructions of 'the possibility of change' in accounts of two Australian 'riots'. *Discourse and Society, 19,* 667–687.

Simon, B. (2004). *Identity in Modern Society: A Social Psychological Perspective.* Oxford: Blackwell.

Slade, D., Scheeres, H., Manidis, M. *et al.* (2008). Emergency communication: The discursive challenges facing emergency clinicians and patients in hospital emergency departments. *Discourse and Communication, 2,* 271–298.

Smith, A. D. (2008). The shifting landscapes of 'nationalism'. *Studies in Ethnicity and Nationalism, 8,* 317–330.

Smithson, J. and Stokoe, E. H. (2005). Discourses of work-life balance: Negotiating 'genderblind' terms in organizations. *Gender Work and Organization, 12,* 147–168.

Sniad, T. (2007). 'It's not necessarily the words you say … it's your presentation': Teaching the interactional text of the job interview. *Journal of Pragmatics, 39,* 1974–1992.

Solomon, S., Greenberg, J. and Pyszczynski, T. (2004). The cultural animal: Twenty years of terror management theory and research. In J. Greenberg, S. L. Koole and T. Pyszczynski (Eds.), *Handbook of Experimental Existential Psychology* (pp. 13–34). New York: Guilford Press.

Stets, J. E. and Burke, P. J. (2005). A sociological approach to self and identity. In M. R. Leary and J. P. Tangney (Eds.), *Handbook of Self and Identity* (pp. 128–152). New York: Guilford Press.

Stokoe, E. H. (2005). Analysing gender and language. *Journal of Sociolinguistics, 9,* 118–133.

Stokoe, E. H. (2006). On ethnomethodology, feminism and the analysis of categorial reference to gender in talk-in-interaction. *Sociological Review, 54,* 467–494.

Stokoe, E. and Edwards, D. (2008). 'Did you have permission to smash your neighbour's door?' Silly questions and their answers in police-suspect interrogations. *Discourse Studies, 10,* 89–111.

Stommel, W. and Koole, T. (2010). The online support group as a community: A micro-analysis of the interaction with a new member. *Discourse Studies, 12,* 357–378.

Stromer-Galley, J. and Martinson, A. M. (2009). Coherence in political computer-mediated communication: Analyzing topic relevance and drift in chat. *Discourse and Communication, 3,* 195–216.

Stygall, G. (2001). A different class of witnesses: Experts in the courtroom. *Discourse Studies, 3,* 327–349.

Su, H.-Y. (2009). Code-switching in managing a face-threatening communicative task: Footing and ambiguity in conversational interaction in Taiwan. *Journal of Pragmatics, 41,* 372–392.

Swann, J. (2002). Yes but is it gender? In L. Litoselliti and J. Sunderland (Eds.), *Gender Identity and Discourse Analysis.* (pp. 43–68). Amsterdam: John Benjamins.

Tannen, D. (1999). The display of (gendered) identities in talk at work. In A. C. Bucholtz, L. C. Liang and L. A. Sutton (Eds.), *Reinventing Identities: The Gendered Self in Discourse.* (pp. 221–240). Oxford: Oxford University Press.

Taylor, C. (2002). *Varieties of Religion Today.* Cambridge, MA: Harvard University Press.

Tekin, B. C. (2008). The construction of Turkey's possible EU membership in French political discourse. *Discourse and Society, 19,* 727–763.

ten Have, P. (1999). *Doing Conversation Analysis: A Practical Guide.* London: Sage.

Thoreau, E. (2006). Ouch! An examination of the self-representation of disabled people on the Internet. *Journal of Computer-Mediated Communication, 11,* 442–468.

Thornborrow, J. (2002). *Power Talk: Language and Interaction in Institutional Discourse.* Harlow: Longman.

Tracy, K. (2009). How questioning constructs judge identities: Oral argument about same-sex marriage. *Discourse Studies, 11,* 199–221.

Tracy, K. and Durfy, M. (2007). Speaking out in public: Citizen participation in contentious school board meetings. *Discourse and Communication, 1,* 223–249.

Triandafyllidou, A. (2001). *Immigrants and National Identity in Europe.* London: Routledge.

Trosborg, A. (1995). Introduction. *Journal of Pragmatics, 23,* 1–5.

Tuffin, K. and Frewin, K. (2008). Constructing the law: Discourses and social practices. *Journal of Community and Applied Social Psychology, 18,* 68–82.

Turkle, S. (1995). *Life on the Screen: Identity in the Age of the Internet.* New York: Simon and Schuster.

Turner, J. C. and Onorato, R. S. (1999). Social identity, personality and the self concept: A self-categorization perspective. In T. R. Tyler, R. M. Kramer and O. P. John (Eds.), *The Psychology of the Social Self* (pp. 11–46). Mahwah, NJ: Lawrence Erlbaum.

Ulrich, M. and Weatherall, A. (2000). Motherhood and infertility: Viewing motherhood through the lens of infertility. *Feminism and Psychology, 10,* 323–336.

Van de Mieroop, D. (2008). Co-constructing identities in speeches: How the construction of an 'other' identity is defining for the 'self' identity and vice versa. *Pragmatics, 18,* 491–509.

Van de Mieroop, D. and van der Haar, M. (2008). Negotiating identities in the context of social work goals: The case of an intercultural institutional interaction. *Research on Language and Social Interaction, 41,* 364–386.

Van Dijk, T. A. (2001). Principles of critical discourse analysis. In M. Wetherell, S. Taylor and S. J. Yates (Eds.), *Discourse Theory and Practice: A Reader* (pp. 300–317). London: Sage.

Van Dijk, T. A. (2005). *Racism and Discourses in Spain and Latin America.* Amsterdam: John Benjamins.

Van Dijk, T. A. (2006). Ideology and discourse analysis. *Journal of Political Ideologies, 11,* 115–140.

Vasquez, C. (2007). Moral stance in the workplace narratives of novices. *Discourse Studies, 9,* 653–675.

Vasquez, C. and Urzua, A. (2009). Reported speech and reported mental states in mentoring meetings: Exploring novice teacher identities. *Research on Language and Social Interaction, 42,* 1–19.

Verkuyten, M. (2001). 'Abnormalization' of ethnic minorities in conversation. *British Journal of Social Psychology, 40,* 257–278.

Verkuyten, M. (2005a). Accounting for ethnic discrimination – A discursive study among minority and majority group members. *Journal of Language and Social Psychology, 24,* 66–92.

Verkuyten, M. (2005b). *The social psychology of ethnic identity.* London: Routledge.

Vincent, D., Laforest, M. and Bergeron, A. (2007). Lies, rebukes and social norms: On the unspeakable in interactions with health-care professionals. *Discourse Studies, 9,* 226–245.

von Münchow, P. and Rakotonoelina, F. (2010). Questions and explanations in French and Anglo-American Usenet newsgroups. *Discourse Studies, 12,* 311–329.

Wallwork, J. and Dixon, J. A. (2004). Foxes, green fields and Britishness: On the rhetorical construction of place and national identity. *British Journal of Social Psychology, 43,* 21–39.

Weatherall, A. (1998). Women and men in language – an analysis of seminaturalistic person descriptions. *Human Communication Research, 25,* 275–292.

Weber, M. (1978). *Economics and Society.* Berkeley, CA: University of California.

Weigert, A. J., Smith Teitge, J. and Teitge, D. W. (1986). *Society and Identity.* Cambridge: Cambridge University Press.

Wetherell, M. (2003). Racism and the analysis of cultural resources in interviews. In M. Wetherell and H. Houtkoop-Steenstra (Eds.), *Analysing Race Talk: Multidisciplinary Perspectives on the Research Interview* (pp. 11–30). Cambridge: Cambridge University Press.

Wetherell, M. and Edley, N. (1999). Negotiating hegemonic masculinity: Imaginary positions and psycho-discursive practices. *Feminism and Psychology, 9,* 335–356.

Wetherell, M. and Potter, J. (1998). Discourse and social psychology – silencing binaries. *Theory and Psychology, 8,* 377–388.

Wharton, S. (2006). Divide and rule: The power of adversarial subjectivities in the discourse of divorce. *Text and Talk, 26,* 791–814.

Whitehead, K. and Kurz, T. (2009). 'Empowerment' and the pole: A discursive investigation of the reinvention of pole dancing as a recreational activity. *Feminism and Psychology, 19*, 224–244.

Widdicombe, S. and Wooffitt, R. (1995). *The Language of Youth Subcultures: Social Identity in Action*. Hemel Hempstead: Harvester Wheatsheaf.

Wiggins, S. (2009). Managing blame in NHS weight management treatment: Psychologizing weight and 'obesity'. *Journal of Community and Applied Social Psychology, 19*, 374–387.

Wilkinson, R. (2007). Managing linguistic incompetence as a delicate issue in aphasic talk-in-interaction: On the use of laughter in prolonged repair sequences. *Journal of Pragmatics, 39*, 542–569.

Williams Camus, J. T. (2009). Metaphors of cancer in scientific popularization articles in the British press. *Discourse Studies, 11*, 465–495.

Williams, V., Ponting, L., Ford, K. and Rudge, P. (2009). 'A bit of common ground': Personalisation and the use of shared knowledge in interactions between people with learning disabilities and their personal assistants. *Discourse Studies, 11*, 611–624.

Willott, S. and Griffin, C. (1999). Building your own lifeboat: Working-class male offenders talk about economic crime. *British Journal of Social Psychology, 38*, 445–460.

Winiecki, D. (2008). The expert witnesses and courtroom discourse: Applying micro and macro forms of discourse analysis to study process and the 'doings of doings' for individuals and for society. *Discourse and Society, 19*, 765–781.

Winter, E. (2007). Neither 'America' nor 'Quebec': Constructing the Canadian multicultural nation. *Nations and Nationalism, 13*, 481–503.

Wirtz, K. (2007). Making sense of unintelligible messages in divine communication. *Text and Talk, 27*, 435–462.

Witteborn, S. (2007). The expression of Palestinian identity in narratives about personal experiences: Implications for the study of narrative, identity and social interaction. *Research on Language and Social Interaction, 40*, 145–170.

Wodak, R. (2001a). What CDA is about –a summary of its history, important concepts and development. In R. Wodak and M. Meyer (Eds.), *Methods of Critical Discourse Analysis.* (pp. 1–13). London: Sage.

Wodak, R. (2001b). The discourse-historical approach. In R. Wodak and M. Meyer (Eds.), *Methods of Critical Discourse Analysis* (pp. 63–94). London: Sage.

Wodak, R. (2007). Discourses in European Union organizations: Aspects of access, participation and exclusion. *Text and Talk, 27*, 655–680.

Wodak, R. and de Cillia, R. (2007). Commemorating the past: the discursive construction of official narratives about the 'Rebirth of the Second Austrian Republic'. *Discourse and Communication, 1*, 337–363.

Wood, C. and Finlay, W. M. L. (2008). British National Party representations of Muslims in the month after the London bombings: Homogeneity, threat and the conspiracy tradition. *British Journal of Social Psychology, 47*, 707–726.

Wowk, M. T. (2007). Kitzinger's feminist conversation analysis: Critical observations. *Human Studies, 30*, 131–155.

Yamaguchi, T. (2007). Controversy over genetically modified crops in India: Discursive strategies and social identities of farmers. *Discourse Studies, 9*, 87–107.

Zubair, S. (2007). Silent birds: Metaphorical constructions of literacy and gender identity in women's talk. *Discourse Studies, 9*, 766–783.

Author Index

Identities in Context: Individuals and Discourse in Action, First Edition. Andrew McKinlay
and Chris McVittie.
© 2011 Andrew McKinlay and Chris McVittie. Published 2011 by Blackwell Publishing Ltd.

Subject Index

Abuse, 127, 130–131, 183
Accountability, 67
Acculturation, 61
Action orientation, 8, 10, 12
Affiliation, 185
Afghanistan, 57, 128
Age, 127, 169–70, 188, 195
Agency, 88, 130
Alcohol, 110
Ambiguity, 59, 92
Americans, 54, 57
Analogy, 144
Anxiety, 101, 189, 193
Apartheid, 31
Appearance, 49
Arbitration, 88
Asians, 54
Asylum seekers, 38, 40
Audience, 27, 36, 54, 59, 63, 67, 124–5, 127, 144, 153, 178, 182
Australia, 40, 51, 113, 134
Austria, 26
Authenticity, 51, 187, 189, 192, 197
Authoritative discourse, 67
Authority, 57, 80–81, 104–5, 115, 118, 129, 140
Avatar, 177

Banal nationalism, 13, 25
Bangladesh, 71
Being single, 77–8
Belonging, 23, 25, 31
Biology, 76
Black, 31, 71, 90
Blog, 47, 182
Bosnia and Herzegovina, 22
Boundaries, 23, 25–7, 32, 48–50
Brazil, 22

Canada, 36, 88
Cancer, 85, 98, 100, 105
Caregiver, 89, 108, 115–16, 154, 161
Case notes, 108
Castes, 50
Categorization, 13
Category contrasts, 128
Catholic, 28
Childhood, 36, 50, 76, 78–81, 88–90, 126, 130–131, 161, 166
Chile, 28
Chronic fatigue syndrome (CFS), 99
Citizenship, 66
Code-switching, 52, 56
Common knowledge, 89